SYMPHONIC PORTRAITS

SYMPHONIC PORTRAITS

A · CLASSICAL · PORTFOLIO

PHOTOGRAPHS BY
RAMON SCAVELLI

TEXT BY
THEODORE LIBBEY

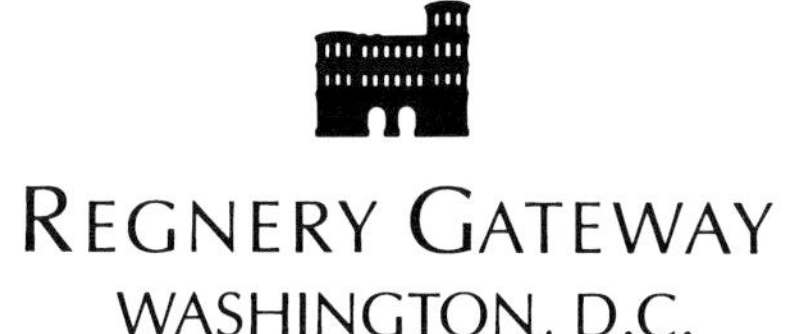

REGNERY GATEWAY
WASHINGTON, D.C.

LIBRARY OF CONGRESS CATALOGING-IN-PUBLICATION DATA

Scavelli, Ramon, 1934–
    Symphonic portraits.

    1. Musicians—Portraits.   I. Libbey, Theodore,
1951–   .   II. Title.
ML87.S28   1988   779′.2′0924   88-26546
ISBN 0-89526-557-5

Published by Regnery Gateway
1130 17th Street, NW, Washington, DC 20036

Distributed to the trade by Kampmann & Company, Inc.
9 E 40th Street, New York, NY 10016

Laser scan duotones by M E Aslett

Manufactured in the United States of America by
Horowitz/Rae, Fairfield, NJ

Designed by Libra Graphics/Christine Swirnoff

DEDICATION

This book is lovingly dedicated to my wife, Joan.
Your courage is my strength.

ACKNOWLEDGMENTS

This book could not have been produced without the recognition and help of Alfred S. Regnery to whom I am deeply grateful.

This section would not be complete without mentioning the Kennedy Center Concert Hall Stage Crew: Robert L. Lewis, Donald E. Tillett, Paul Farabee, Jr., and James S. Lucas, Jr., who were invaluable in their help concerning stage and house lights.

To the National Symphony Orchestra Management, my appreciation, especially Lois Howard for her cooperation in allowing me access to those great NSO files for my photographic research.

Also, to my colleagues of the National Symphony, past and present, my thanks for their support and cooperation all these years.

On a more personal note, I would like to acknowledge my late teacher, Gordon Kahn, violist of the Philadelphia Orchestra, who developed me, not only as a musician, but as a person, and whose tenacity opened new worlds for me.

Lastly, I wish to thank my parents, Ann and Joseph Scavelli, for life-long confidence in my abilities; they would have been so proud had they lived to see the accomplishment of this book.

Claudio Abbado	Aaron Copland
Maurice Abravanel	Clifford Curzon
Salvatore Accardo	Rafael Frühbeck De Burgos
Stephen Albert	Alicia De Larrocha
Gerd Albrecht	Gaetano Delogu
David Amram	James De Preist
Enrique-Garcia Asensio	Antal Dorati
Moshe Atzmon	Jacob Druckman
Christian Badea	Douglas Fairbanks, Jr.
Leonard Bernstein	Arthur Fiedler
Theodore Bikel	Leon Fleisher
Ray Bolger	Malcolm Frager
Victor Borge	Zino Francescatti
Willi Boskovsky	Claude Frank
Antonia Brico	James Galway
Sid Caesar	Nicolai Gedda
Pablo Casals	Bruno-Leonard Gelber
Van Cliburn	Michael Gielen
James Conlon	Emil Gilels

Morton Gould

Sol Greitzer

Leopold Hager

Marvin Hamlisch

Frans Helmerson

Günther Herbig

Christopher Hogwood

Eugene Istomin

Neeme Jarvi

Danny Kaye

Aram Khachaturian

Ralph Kirkpatrick

Toshiko Kohno

Erich Leinsdorf

Raymond Leppard

Reilly Lewis

Cecile Licad

George London

Yo-Yo Ma and
  Murray Perahia

Lorin Maazel

Neville Marriner

John Martin

Jean Martinon

Mesru Mehmedov

Zubin Mehta

Yehudi Menuhin

Olivier Messiaen

Nathan Milstein

Howard Mitchell

Anne-Sophie Mutter

David Oistrakh

Elmar Oliveira

Eugene Ormandy

Seiji Ozawa

Carlos Paita

Paul Paray	Doc Severinsen
Jon Kimura Parker	Dmitri Shostakovich
Richard Parnas	Maxim Shostakovich
Krzysztof Penderecki	Murry Sidlin
Ruggero Raimondi	Giuseppe Sinopoli
Jean-Pierre Rampal	Stanislaw Skrowaczewski
Kurt Roger	William Steck
Leonard Rose	Isaac Stern
Mstislav Rostropovich	Leopold Stokowski
Artur Rubinstein	Henryk Szeryng
Julius Rudel	Edouard van Remoortel
Max Rudolf	Galina Vishnevskaya
Kurt Sanderling	Ilse von Alpenheim
Hermann Scherchen	Alfred Wallenstein
Gunther Schuller	André Watts
Norman Scribner	Hugh Wolff
Andres Segovia	Nicanor Zabaleta
Peter Serkin	Pinchas Zukerman

*Ramon Scavelli's photographic portraits of musicians possess a very special quality—
musicality. Different artists were captured in the moment of musical creation.
Therefore, when I see my colleagues with their bows I not only view a face,
but can hear each distinctly personal sound—that which belongs to them alone.
It is a special talent of a photographer-musician, to be able to capture
those moments most characteristic of each individual artist.*

MSTISLAV ROSTROPOVICH

SYMPHONIC PORTRAITS

CLAUDIO ABBADO

At home on the concert stage and in the pit, Claudio Abbado has established himself as one of
the top conductors in the world today. Born in 1933, he attracted attention early in his career
by winning the Koussevitzky conducting prize at Tanglewood in 1958 and the Mitropoulos
Competition in 1963. Engagements with the world's leading orchestras quickly followed. By his
mid-30s he had proved to be one of the most exciting conductors in circulation; he has mellowed
considerably since then, while retaining his natural command of podium technique and
developing an increasingly refined approach to the classics. When all the elements are in place, his
interpretations of the symphonic repertory can be masterpieces of nuance, pacing, and drama.
His opera performances are notable for their musical integrity and potent theatricality. In 1986, he
was named music director of the Vienna State Opera.

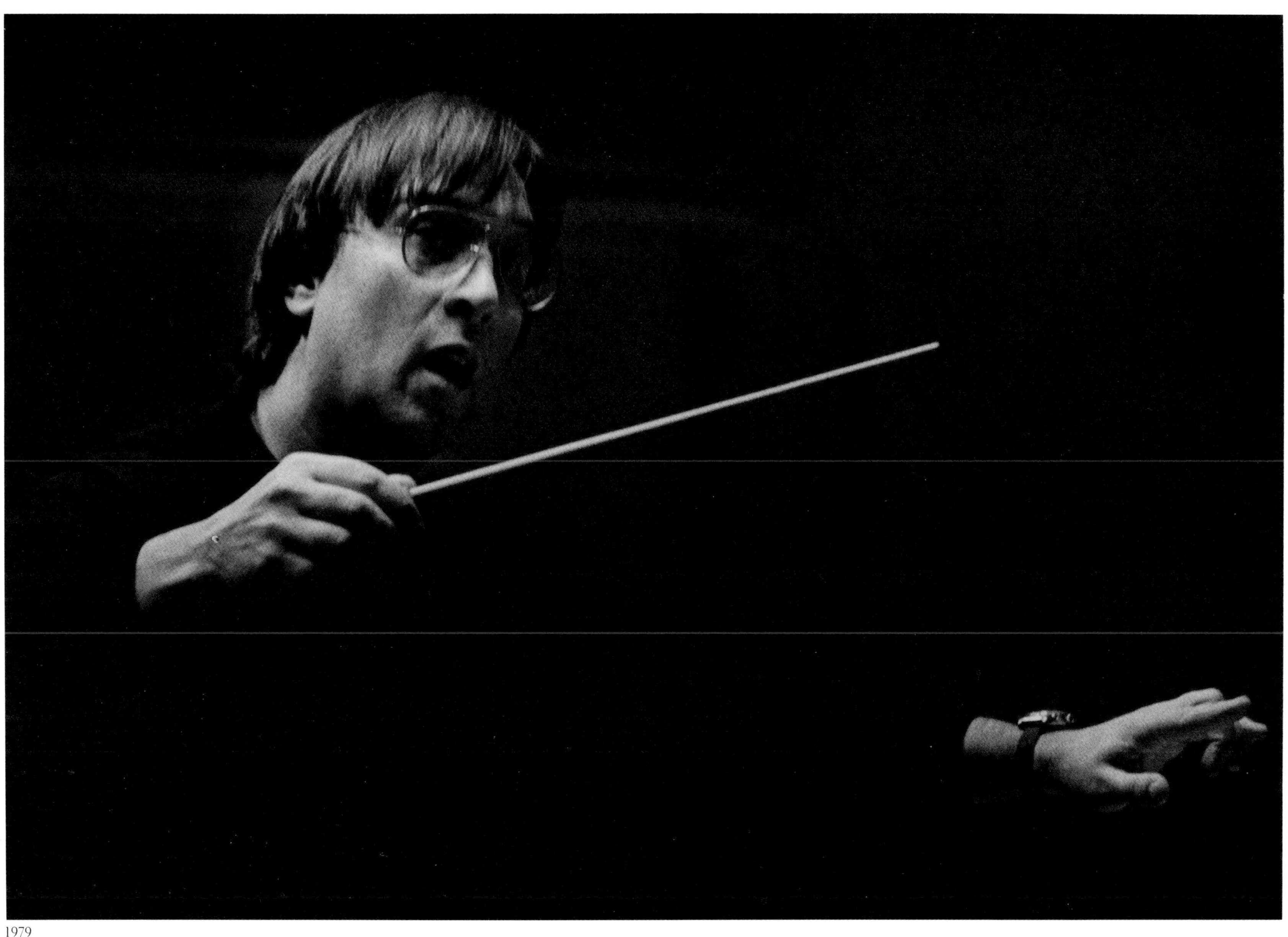

1979

MAURICE ABRAVANEL

Gentle and scholarly-looking, he has within him a dynamic, can-do personality that has triumphed over much adversity. Born in Greece, raised in Switzerland, educated in Germany—where he studied with and became a disciple of Kurt Weill—he was forced to flee Europe in the 1930s. He made his Metropolitan Opera debut in 1936, but was unable to find a secure artistic base until 1947, when he became music director of the Utah Symphony. In his 30-year tenure there, he established it as one of the country's major orchestras, conducting and recording repertory that no one else would touch, all the while raising standards and supporting American music and composers. He did further service to American music as a member of the National Council on the Arts, having come to be regarded as one of his adopted country's senior musical statesmen.

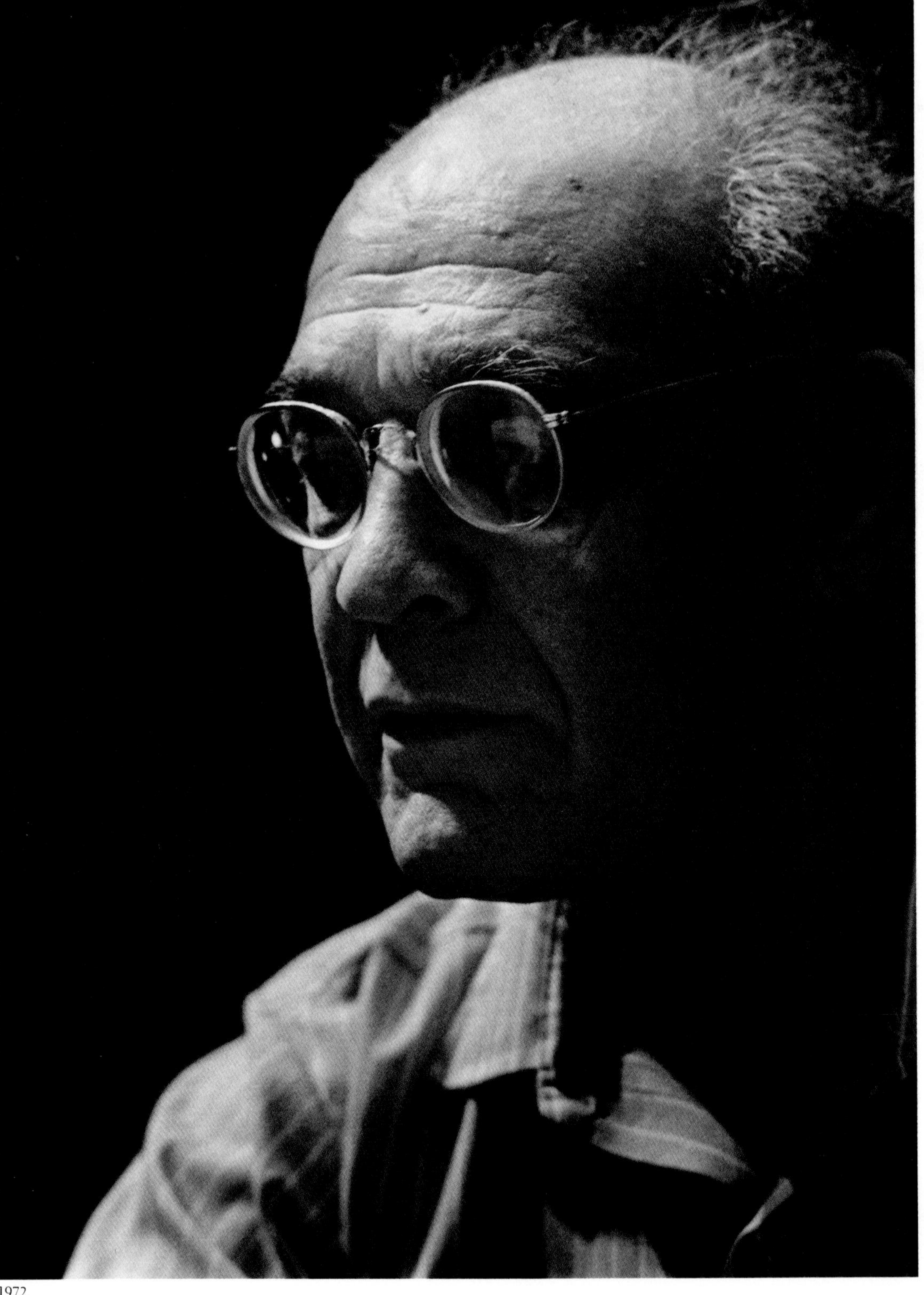

1972

SALVATORE ACCARDO

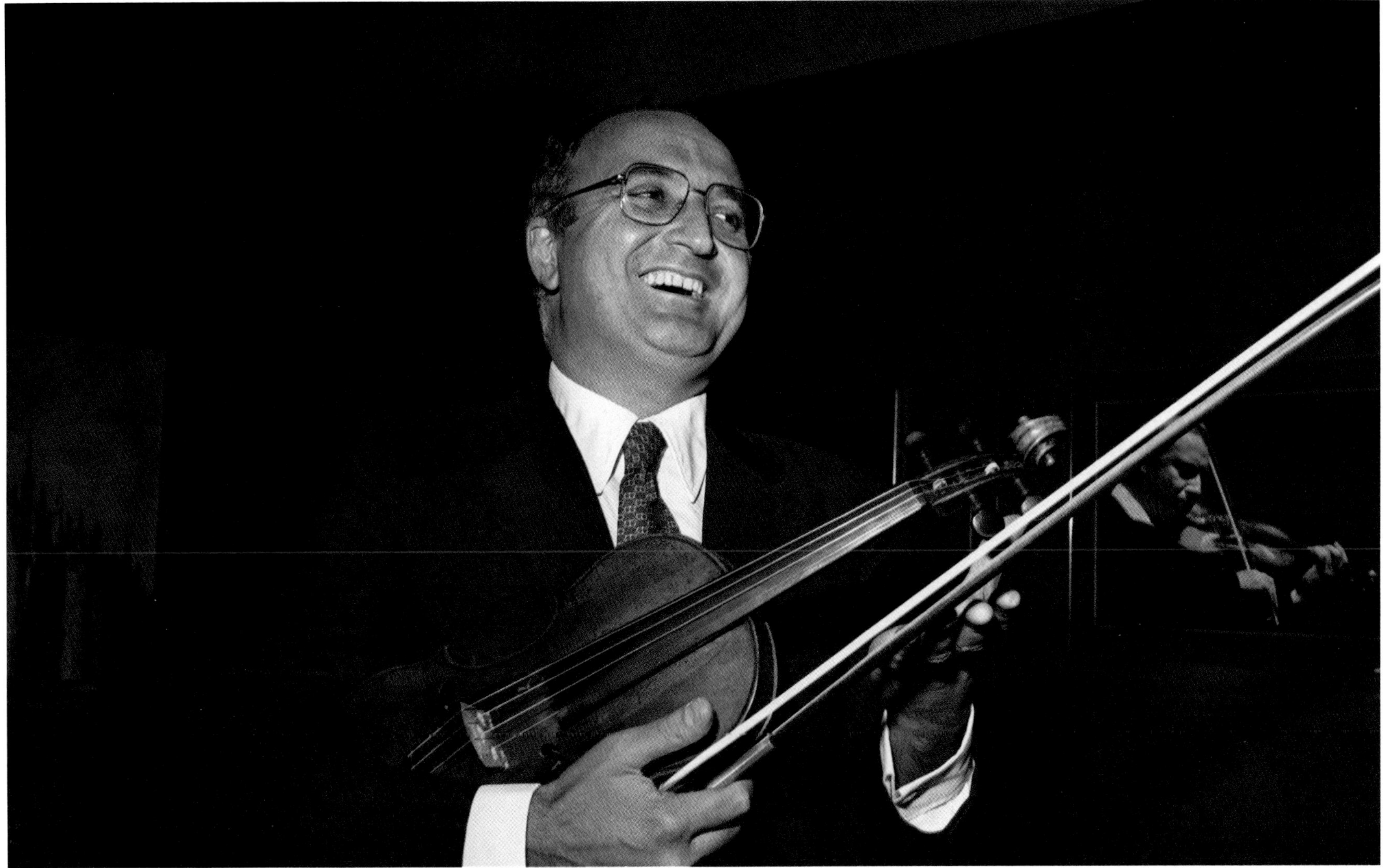

1983

A delightful man and a delightful musician, with an infectious sense of humor and a warm, sensitive nature. For all his ebullience, however, he exhibits a mature, thoughtful manner and thorough self-control in his playing. He is at his best in the poetic, delicate, most lyrical pages in the repertory, though he has a virtuosic sureness in display passages that few can rival. He is an exceptionally fine chamber musician, and has a command of style that enables him to render the major works of the 18th-century literature as capably as he does those of the 19th and 20th, to say nothing of contemporary music, of which he is a highly respected and convincing exponent.

STEPHEN ALBERT

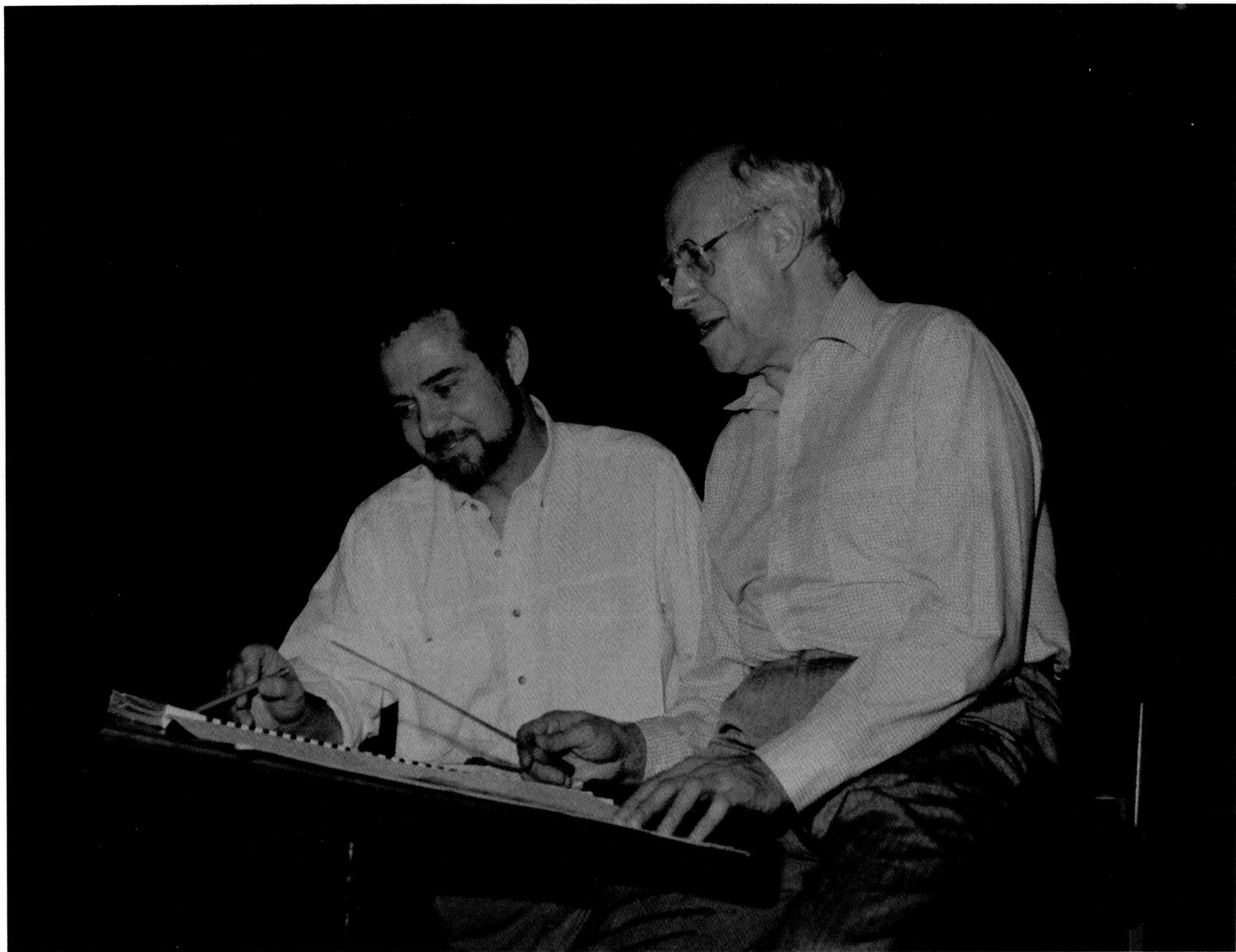

1987

Winner of the 1985 Pulitzer Prize in music for his first symphony, entitled *RiverRun*, he has developed a broadly expressive, eclectic, tonal idiom that stems in part from studies with such divergent figures as Bernard Rogers, Karl-Birger Blomdahl, Roy Harris, and George Rochberg. Most of his production has been in the realm of vocal and chamber music, and much of it has involved unusual instrumental groupings.

GERD ALBRECHT

After studies at the universities of Kiel and Hamburg, he worked in the opera houses of several West German cities before being named chief conductor of the Deutsche Oper Berlin, a post he held from 1972 to 1979. In 1975, he became the conductor of the Tonhalle Orchestra of Zurich.

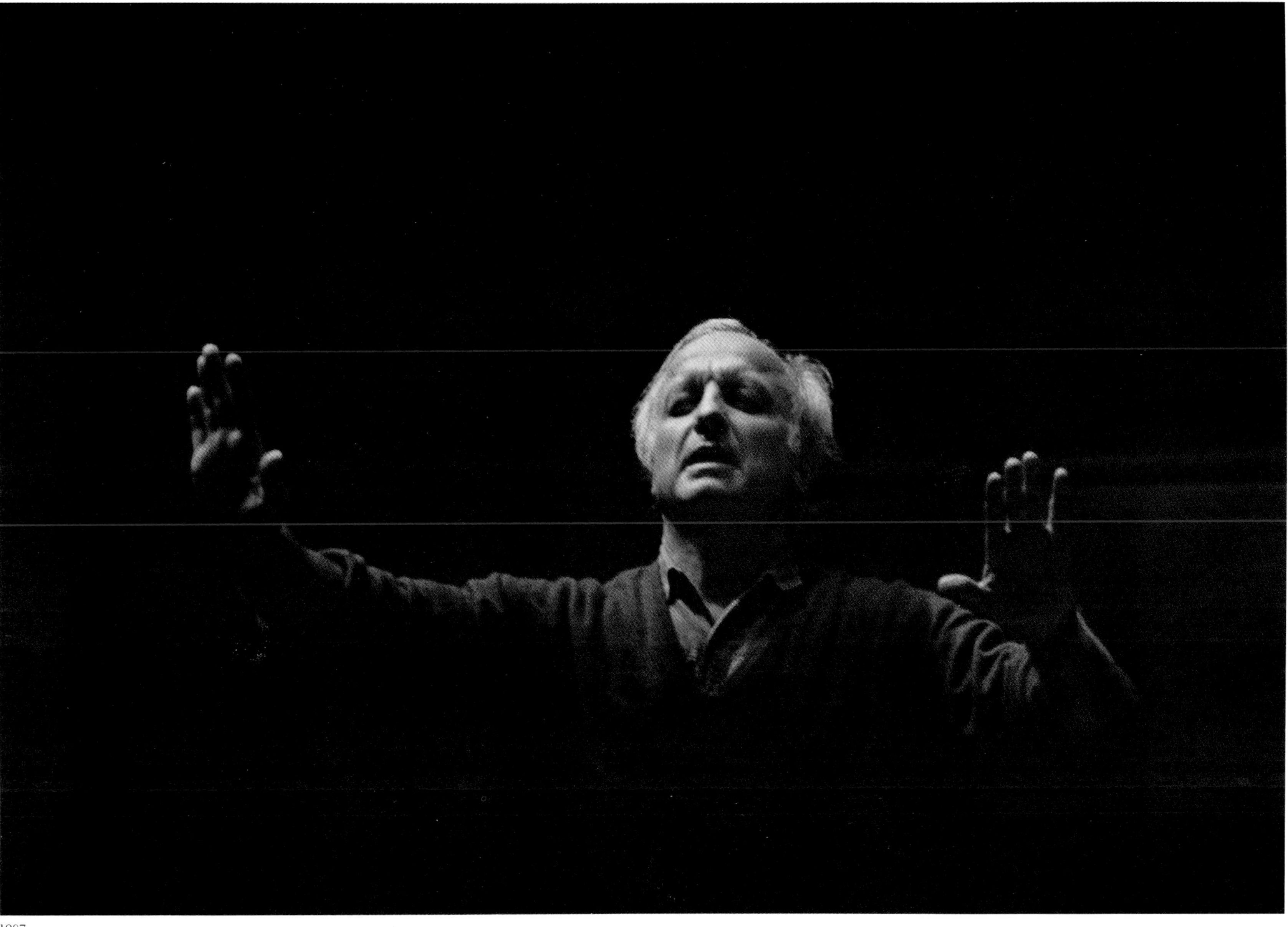

1987

DAVID AMRAM

A native of Philadelphia who grew up in Washington, D.C., he played the horn professionally before embarking on a career in composition. He achieved his first successes in the late 1950s and early 1960s writing music for several dozen off-Broadway productions and scoring such films as *Splendor in the Grass* and the long-suppressed thriller *The Manchurian Candidate*. His wide-ranging talent has led him to explore a variety of styles, including jazz and Latin American and other ethnic musics, and to compose for all manner of occasions. He is even a skilled performer on his own cranium, which he calls the "skullophone." He is pictured here with Kenneth Pasmanick, principal bassoonist of the NSO.

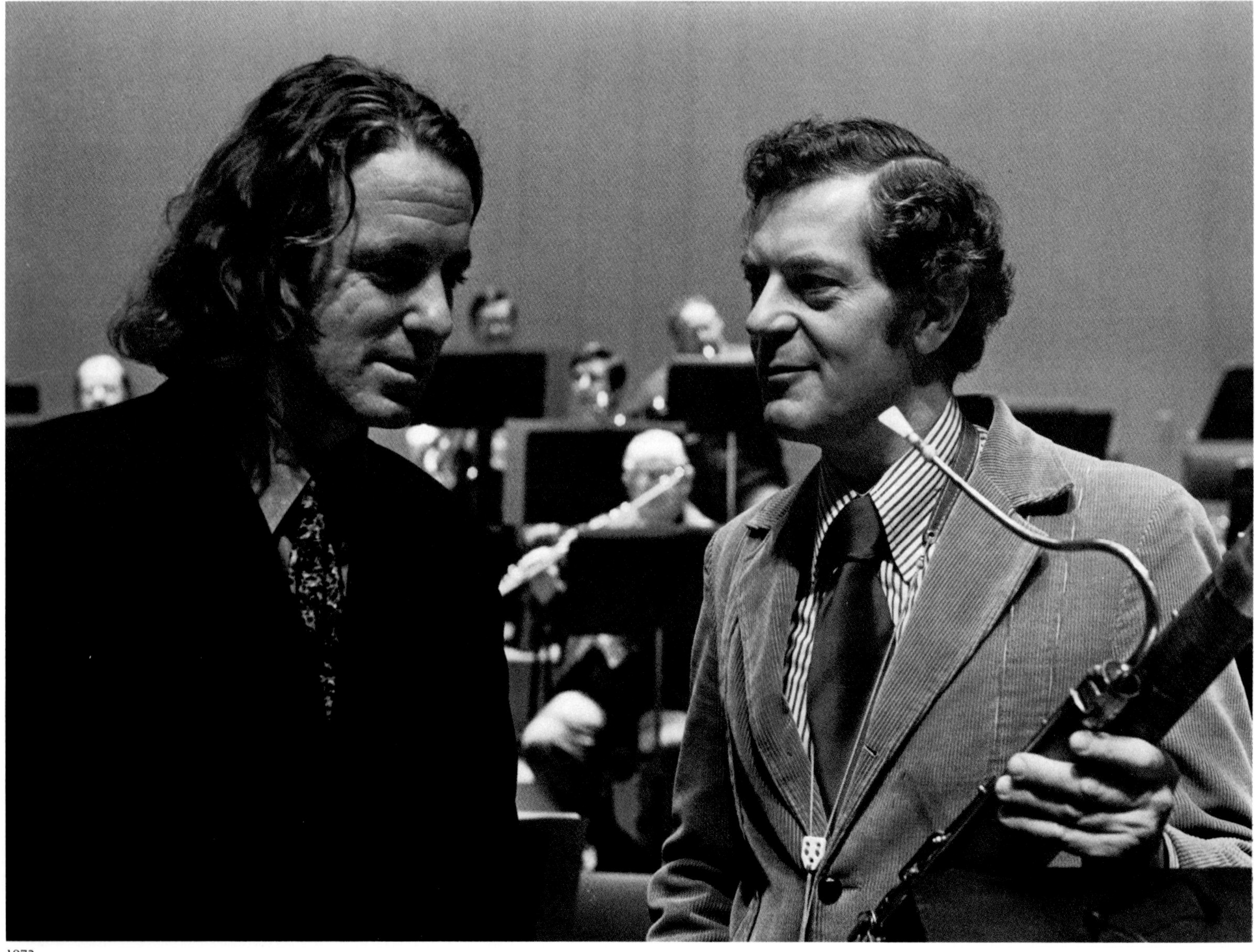

1972

ENRIQUE-GARCIA ASENSIO

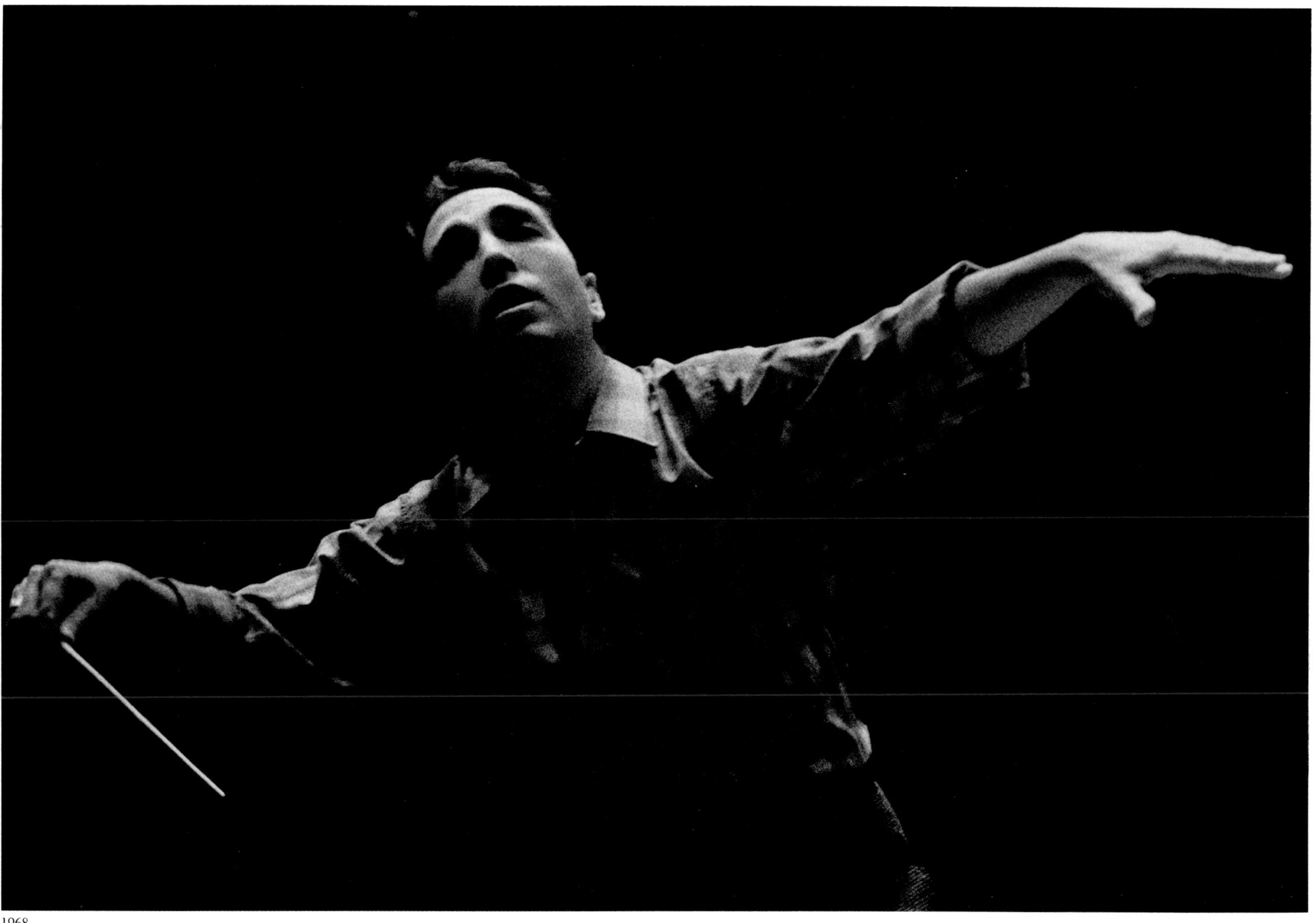

1968

Enrique-Garcia Asensio was born in Valencia and attended the Royal Conservatory of Music in Madrid, later studying conducting with the elusive Sergiu Celibidache. He became chief conductor of the Spanish Radio and Television Orchestra of Madrid in 1966, also serving as the assistant conductor of the National Symphony Orchestra during the 1967–68 season.

MOSHE ATZMON

Born in Hungary in 1931, Moshe Atzmon was educated at the Tel-Aviv Conservatory and the Tel-Aviv Academy of Music. He began his career leading orchestras in England, going to the Sydney Symphony Orchestra as chief conductor in 1969. In 1972, he became conductor of both the North German Radio Orchestra in Hamburg and the Basel Symphony Orchestra. He made his first appearance with the National Symphony Orchestra in 1973.

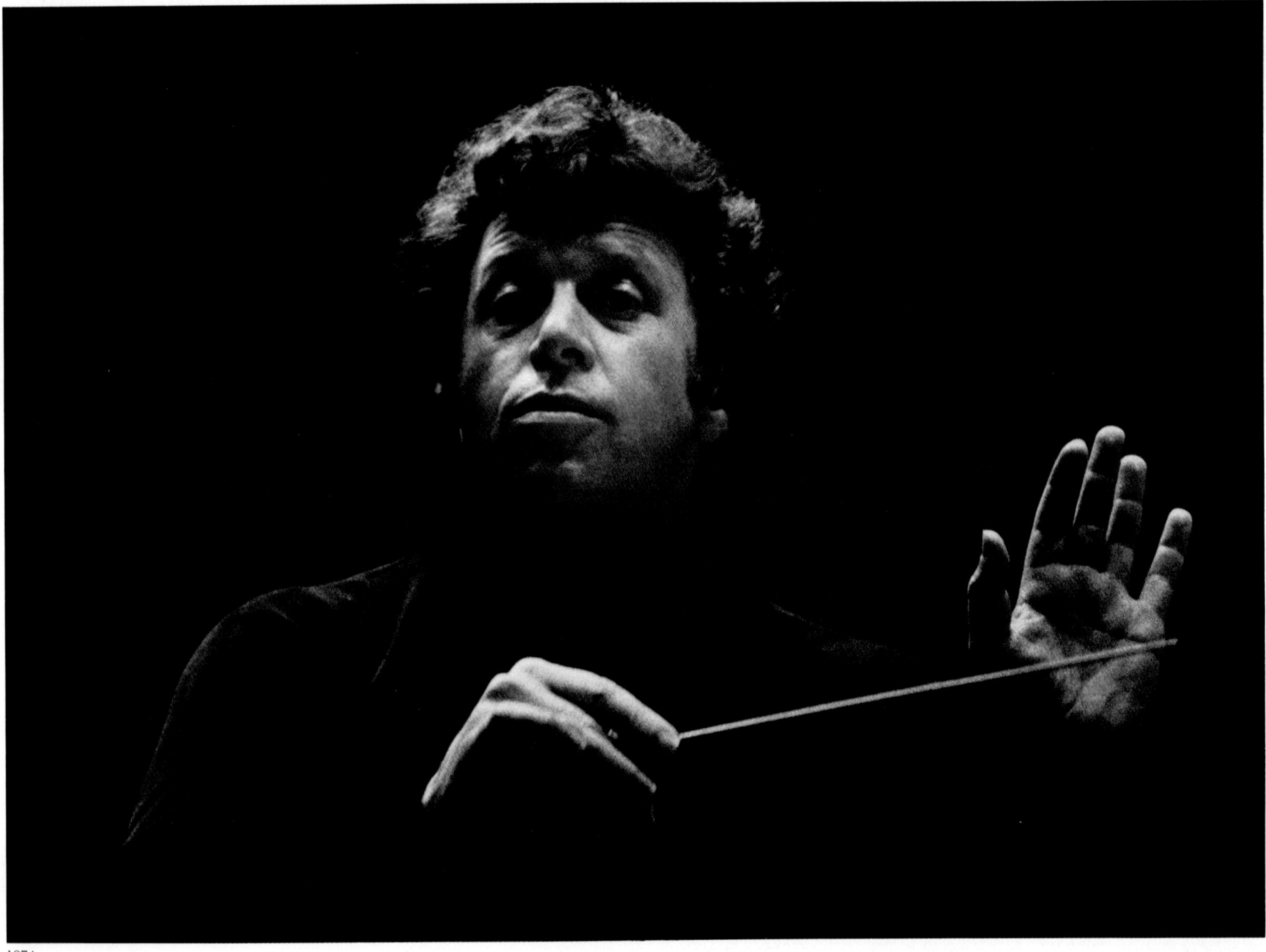

1974

Christian Badea

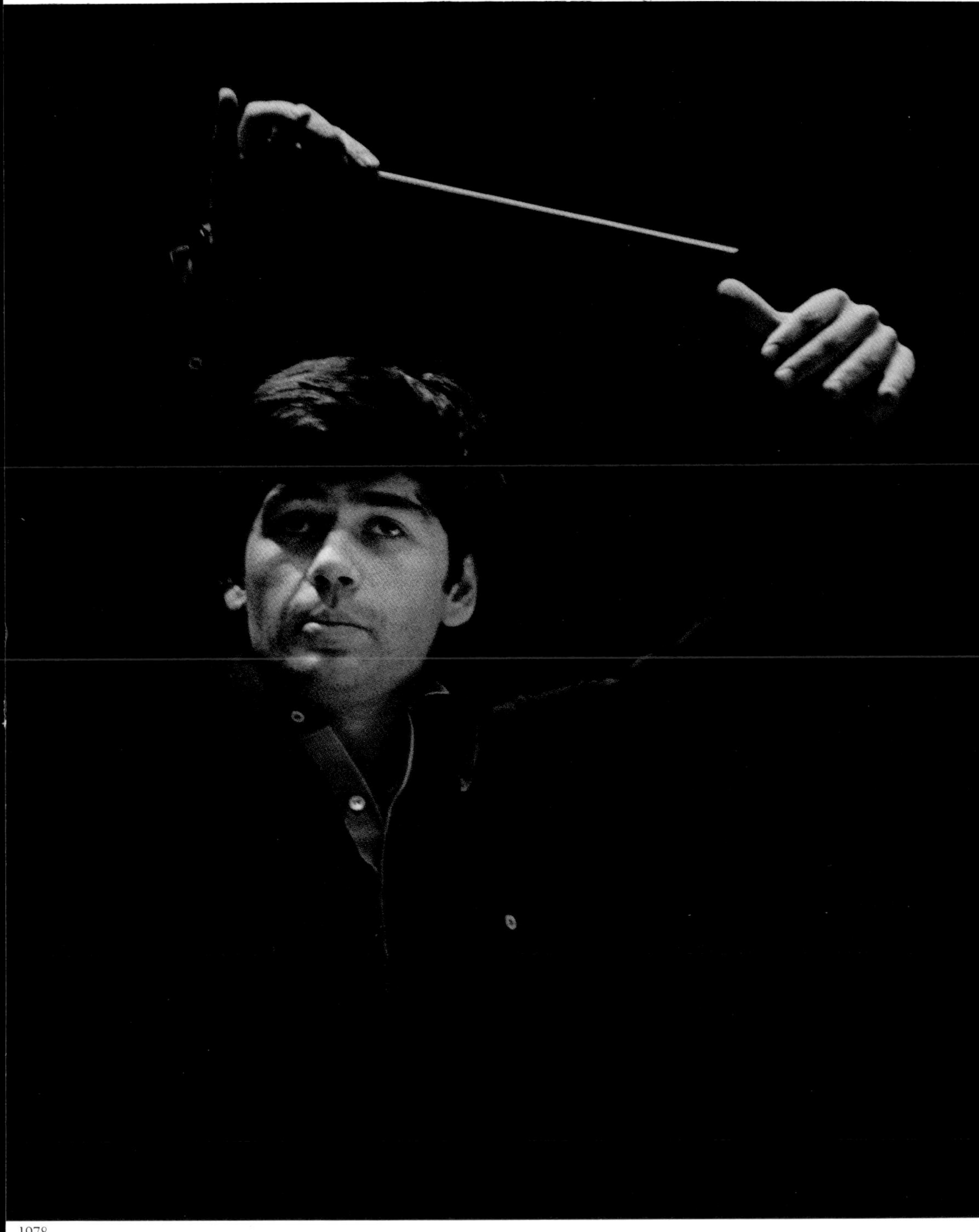

Currently music director of the Columbus (Ohio) Symphony Orchestra, this former assistant conductor of the National Symphony is capable of producing what one seasoned observer called "an electric arc of tension" whenever he stands on the podium.

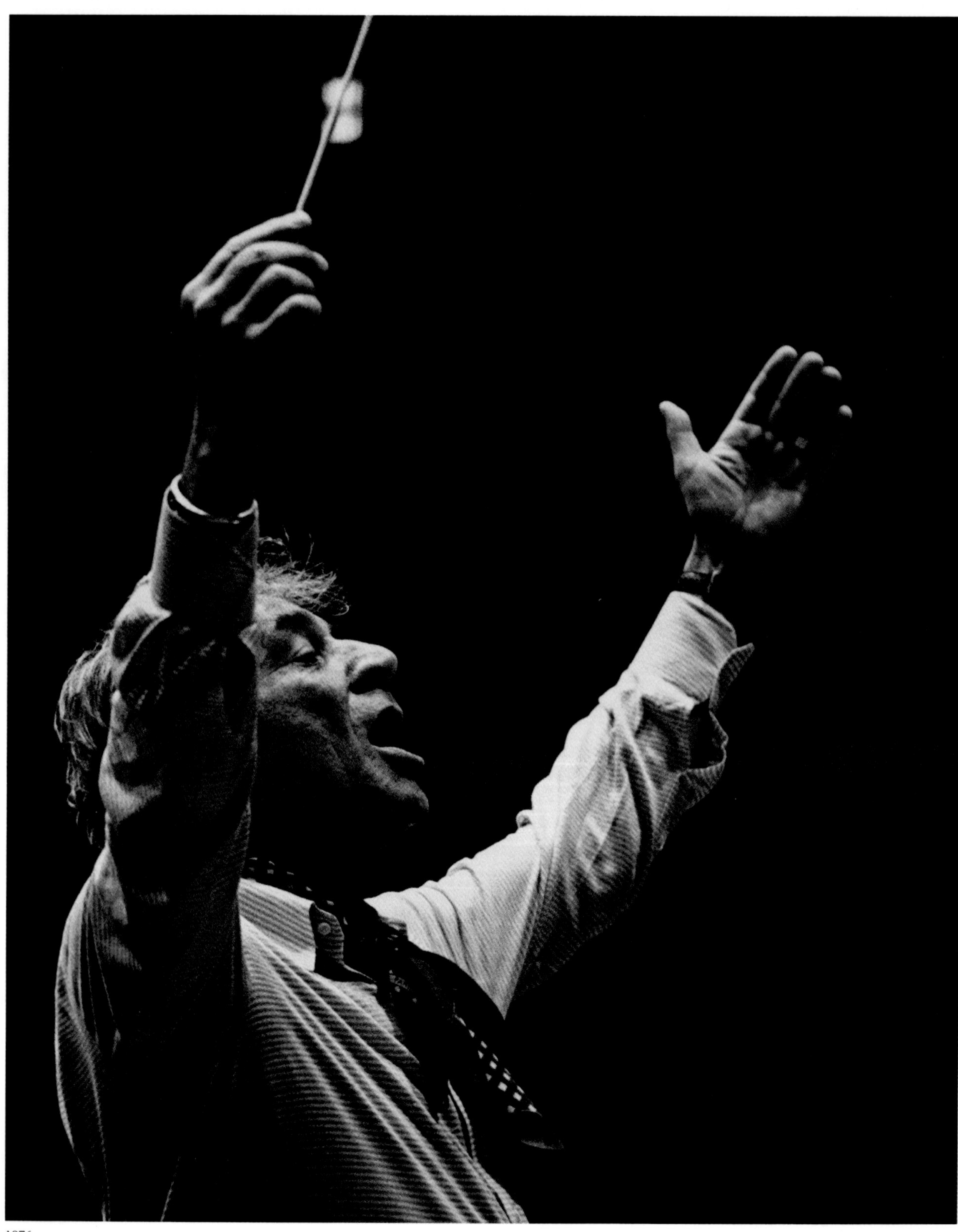

1976

The volatile, flamboyant *wunderkind* who was the first American-born and American-trained musician to be appointed music director of America's oldest orchestra, the New York Philharmonic, Leonard Bernstein has become *the* magisterial figure in American music. Now seventy, he is still a seeker, still an enthusiastic explorer in quest of artistic verity. His achievements as an instructor, pianist, conductor, and composer—of symphonies and of works for the stage— remain prodigious and unparalleled, and continue to astonish us all with their vitality. His *West Side Story* is one of the masterpieces of American musical theater. His *Mass* was written for the opening of the Kennedy Center and was the first work by an American composer ever produced at the Vienna State Opera.

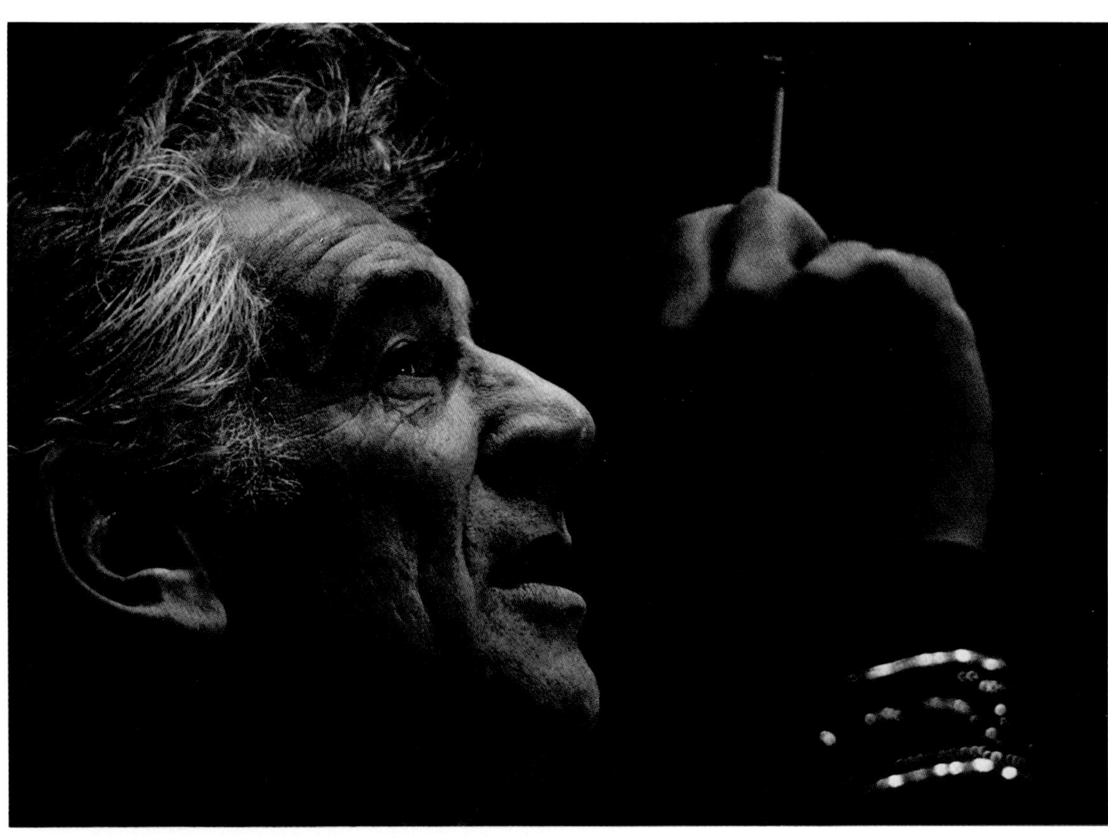

1976

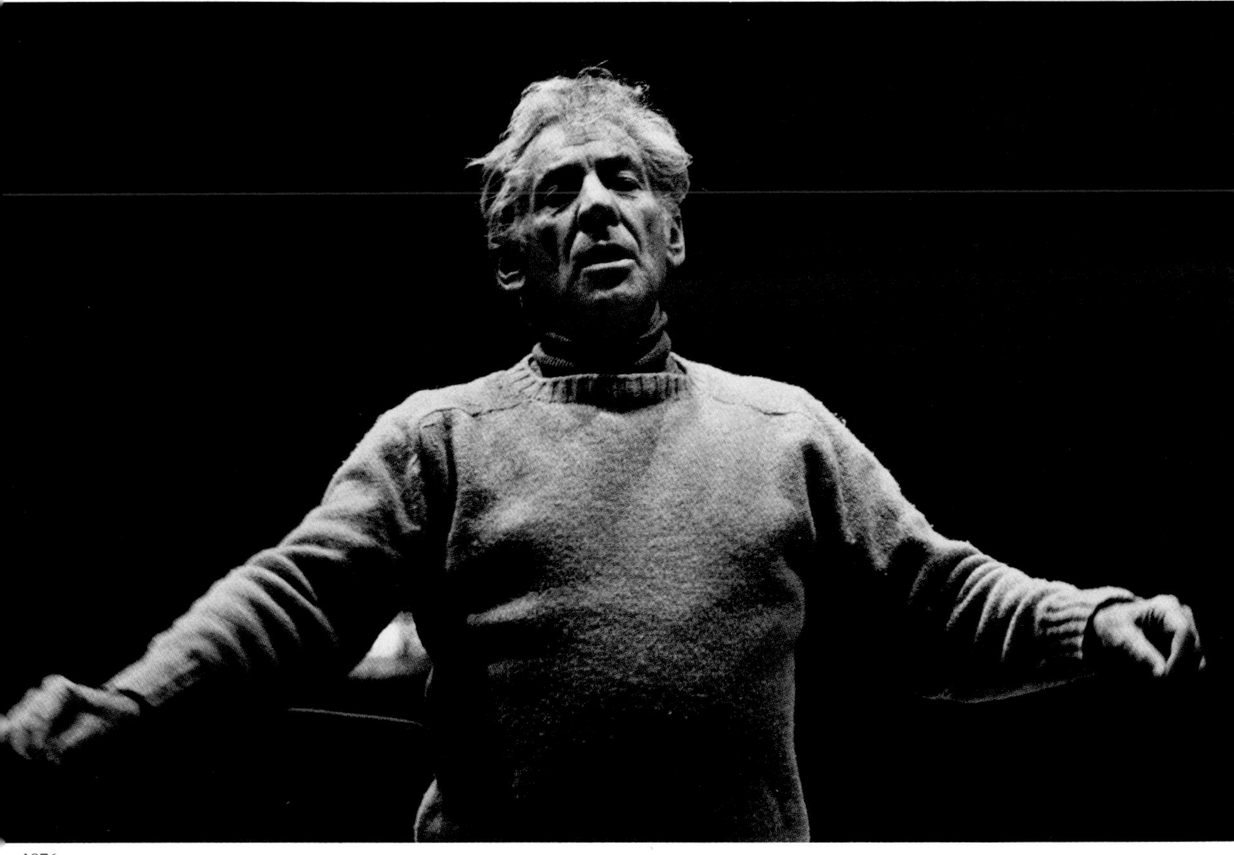

THEODORE BIKEL

Born in Vienna, Theodore Bikel was 13 when he and his parents left that city for Palestine. He began his acting career there in 1943, progressing from the Habimah Theatre to the Israel Chamber Theatre, which he helped found, before moving on to London's Royal Academy of Dramatic Art. Important roles on stage and screen followed during the 1950s and 1960s. Best known for his portrayal of Tevye in the national company performances of *Fiddler on the Roof,* he has also starred in numerous television dramas and has appeared in concert on many occasions as a balladeer and folk singer.

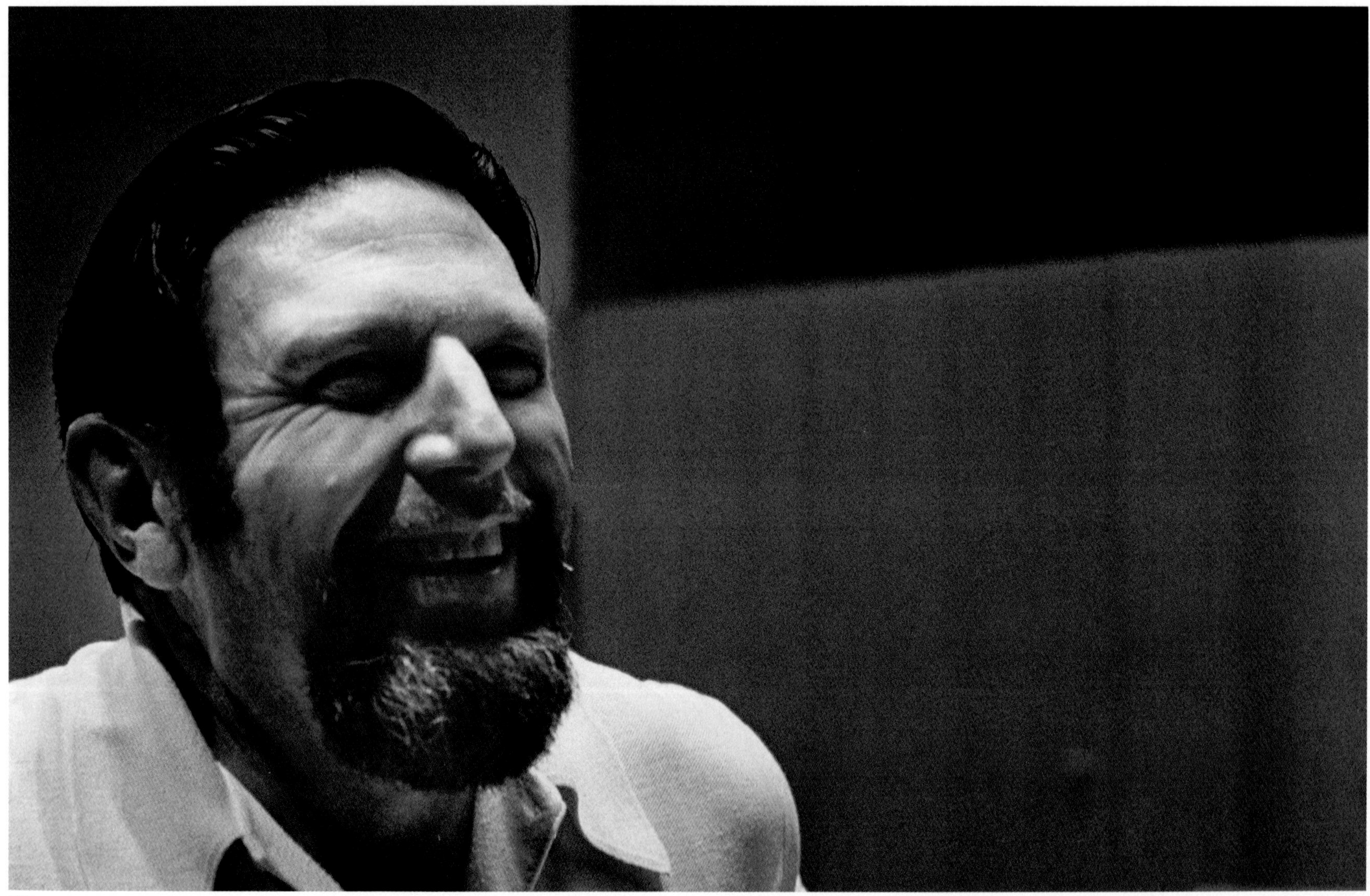

1974

RAY BOLGER

A top Broadway performer (he was in the original casts of *On Your Toes* and *Where's Charley?*), it was in film that Ray Bolger achieved immortality as the brainless scarecrow in *The Wizard of Oz*. One of America's most durable and beloved entertainers, he was the song-and-dance man *par excellence*.

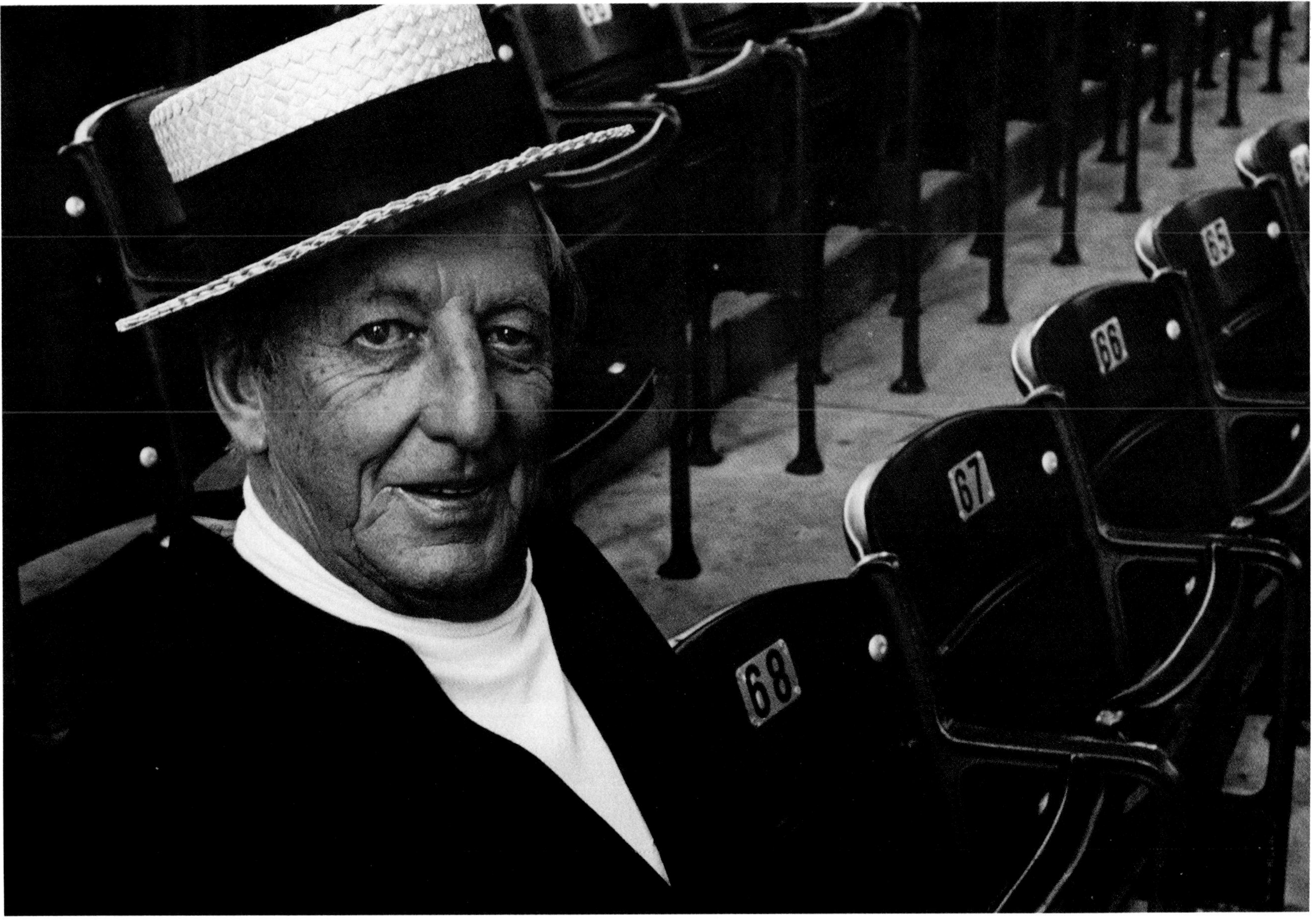

1976

VICTOR BORGE

His exceptionally creative approach to
comedy has endeared him to millions, most
of whom laugh without realizing how much
of what he does is possible only because he is
a fine serious musician. His wonderful
sendups of the classics are based on an
assured pianistic technique (he studied piano
in his native Copenhagen and had become
quite popular there by the time the German
occupation forced him to flee). Similarly, his
clowning around with orchestras reveals a
thorough musicianship and very substantial
knowledge of, and feeling for, the repertory.
To really appreciate Victor Borge, you have to
know the music by heart and love it a lot—
just as he does.

1969

Willi Boskovsky

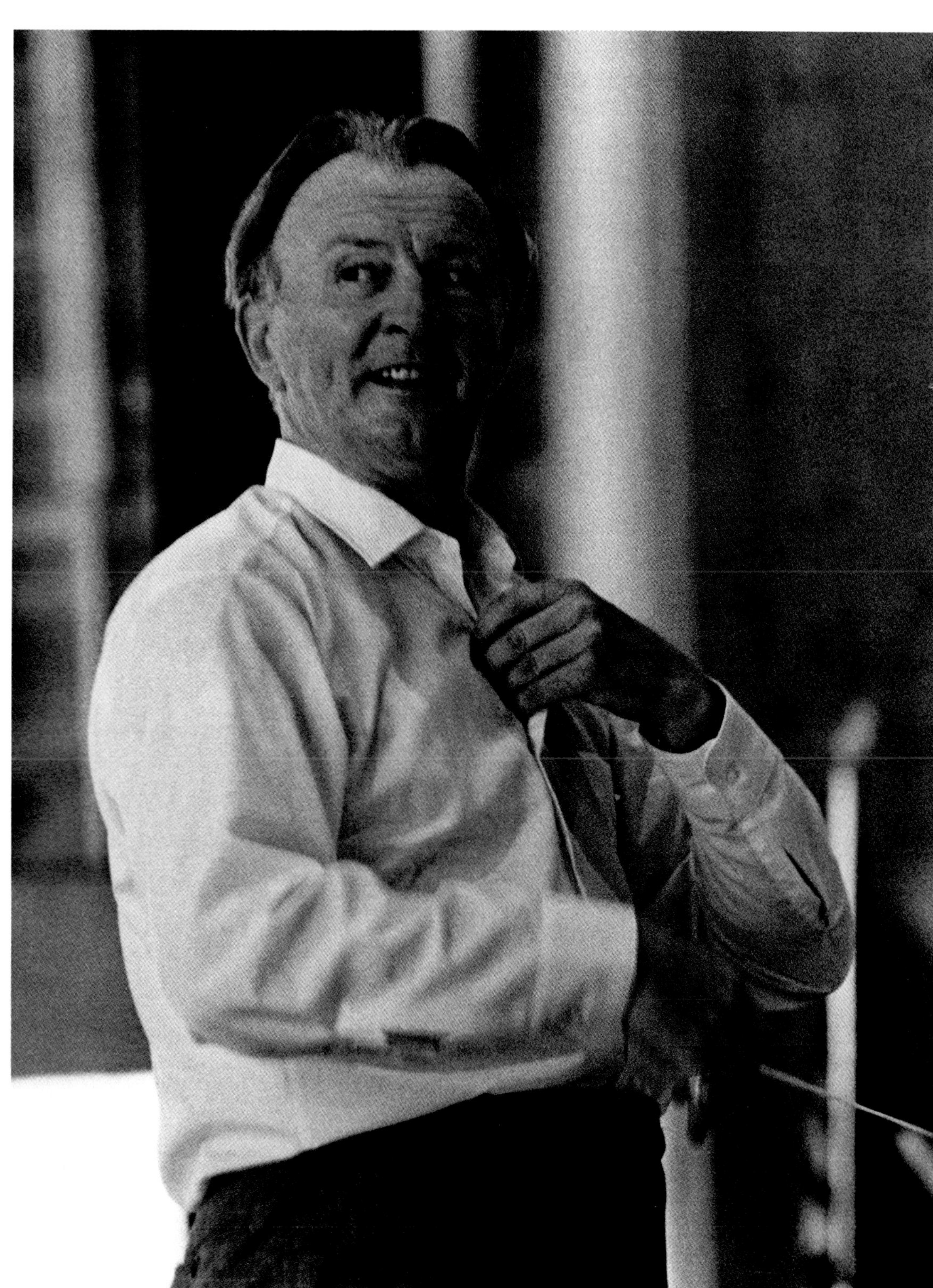

For many years the first concertmaster of the Vienna Philharmonic, he succeeded the venerable Clemens Krauss as conductor of the orchestra's gala New Year's concerts in 1955, becoming equally venerable in the years that followed. With the Philharmonic and other orchestras he recorded much of the music of the Strauss family, in beguiling interpretations that in many cases remain unchallenged.

1968

ANTONIA BRICO

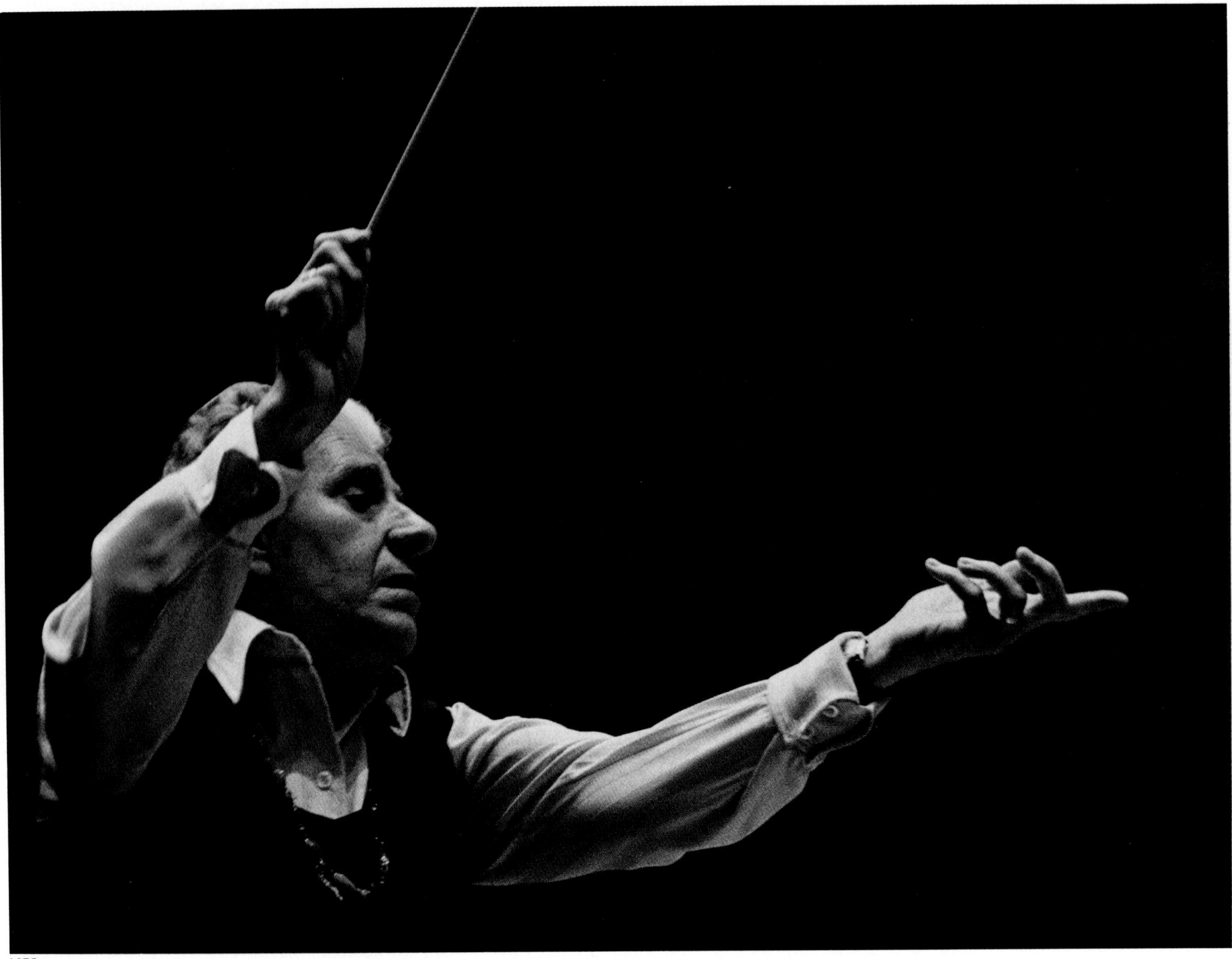

1975

A pianist and 1923 graduate of the University of California, she took conducting lessons from Karl Muck in Berlin, and in 1930 arranged to give a concert with the Berlin Philharmonic. She met with resistance in subsequent efforts to conduct major orchestras in America until, following the release in 1974 of the film *Antonia*, she received several engagements.

SID CAESAR

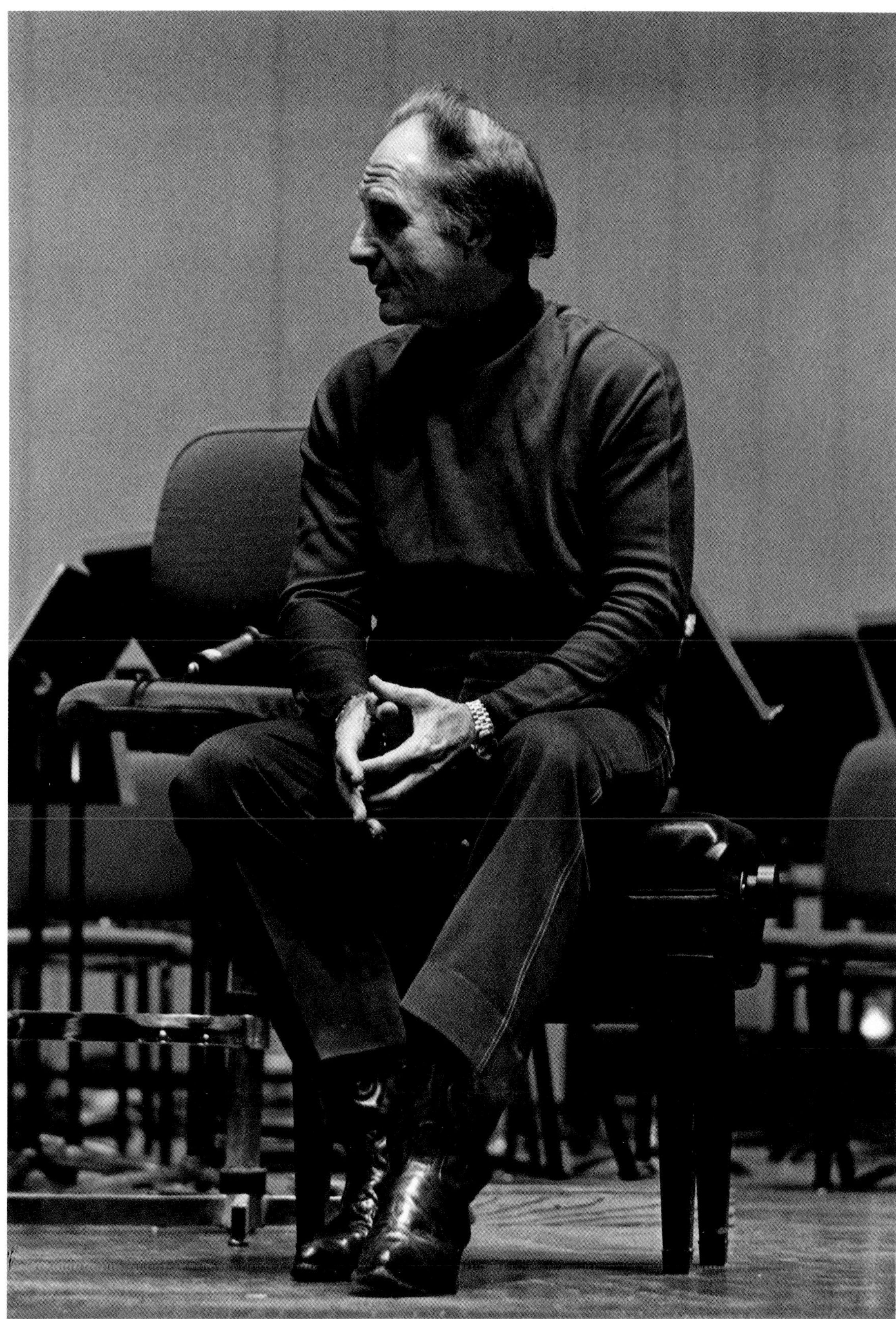

One of America's most resourceful and innovative comedians, he was among the first to develop a style geared for television. He has had a decisive influence on all his colleagues, and has helped bring along such talented performers as Mel Brooks and Woody Allen.

1987

PABLO CASALS

The first modern cellist and one of the last standard-bearers of the old order. A musician of legendary greatness and stature, he traveled and made music everywhere, and stood defiantly for art and freedom in the face of the destructive forces that drove him from his homeland and made him a virtual prisoner in occupied France during World War II. His interpretations of the solo, chamber, and symphonic repertory established him as one of the greatest musicians of all time and will remain among the benchmarks for future generations of performers. His inexhaustible energy and commitment to music served as a beacon to colleagues and music lovers everywhere in the world.

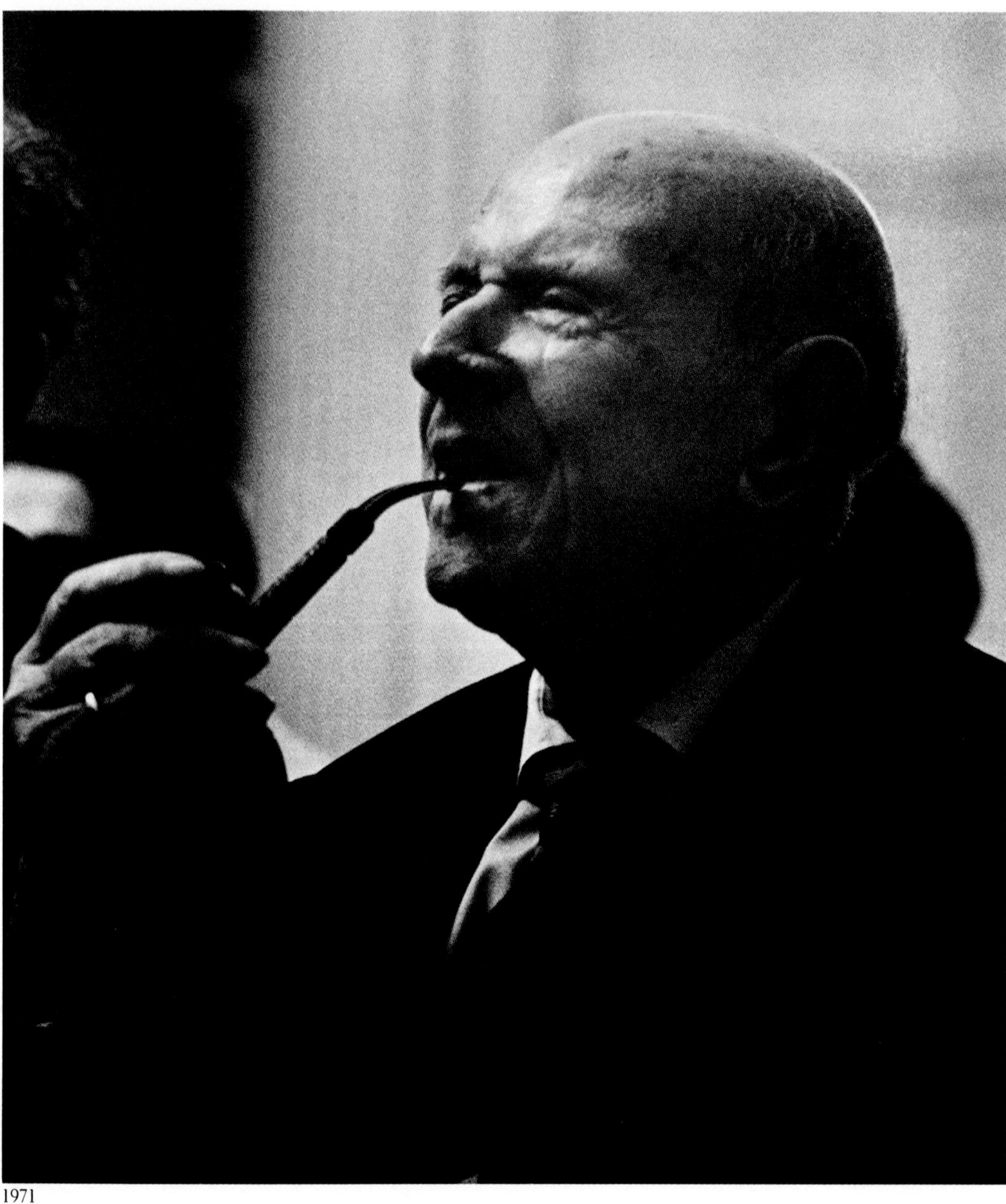

1971

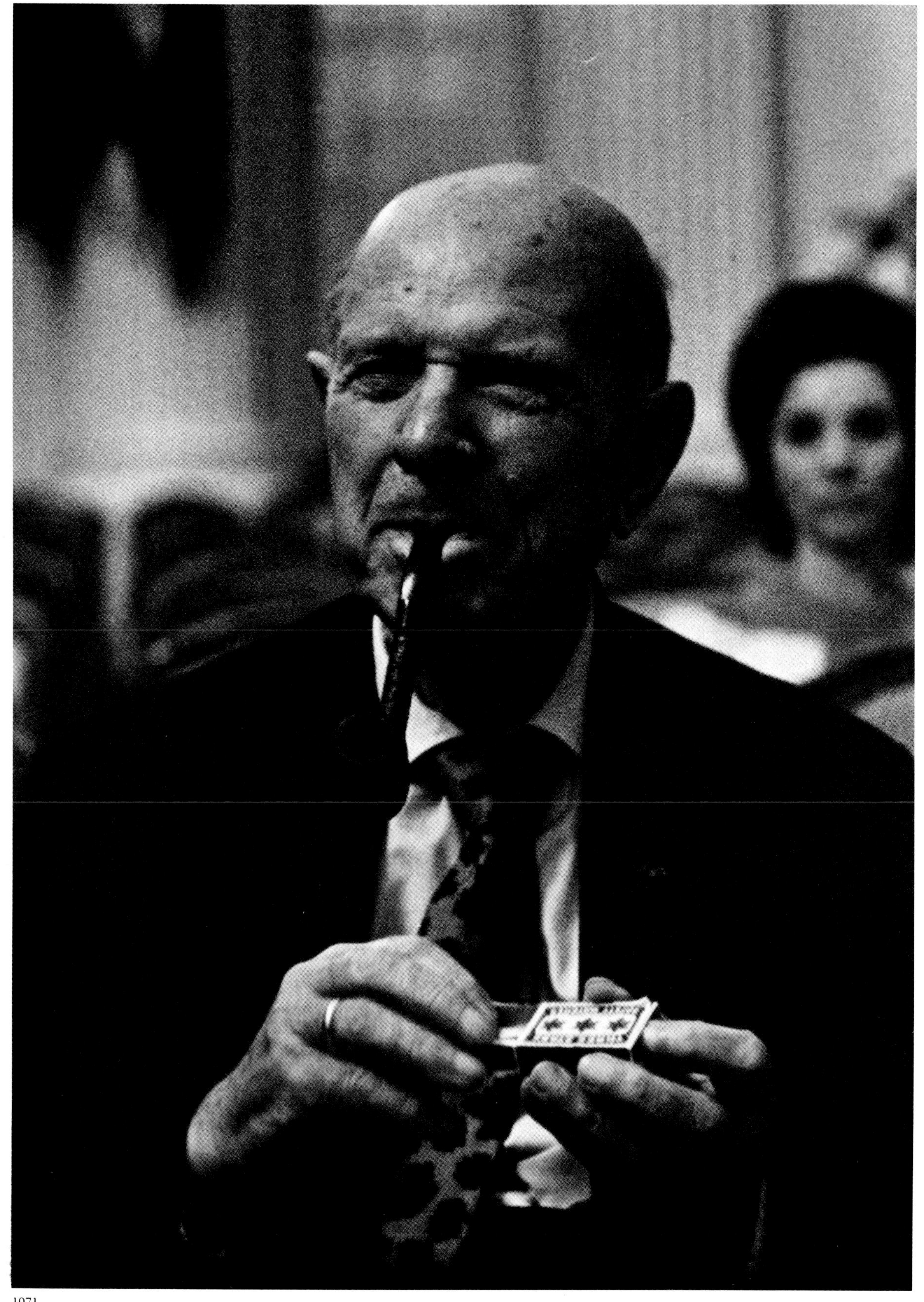

Van Cliburn

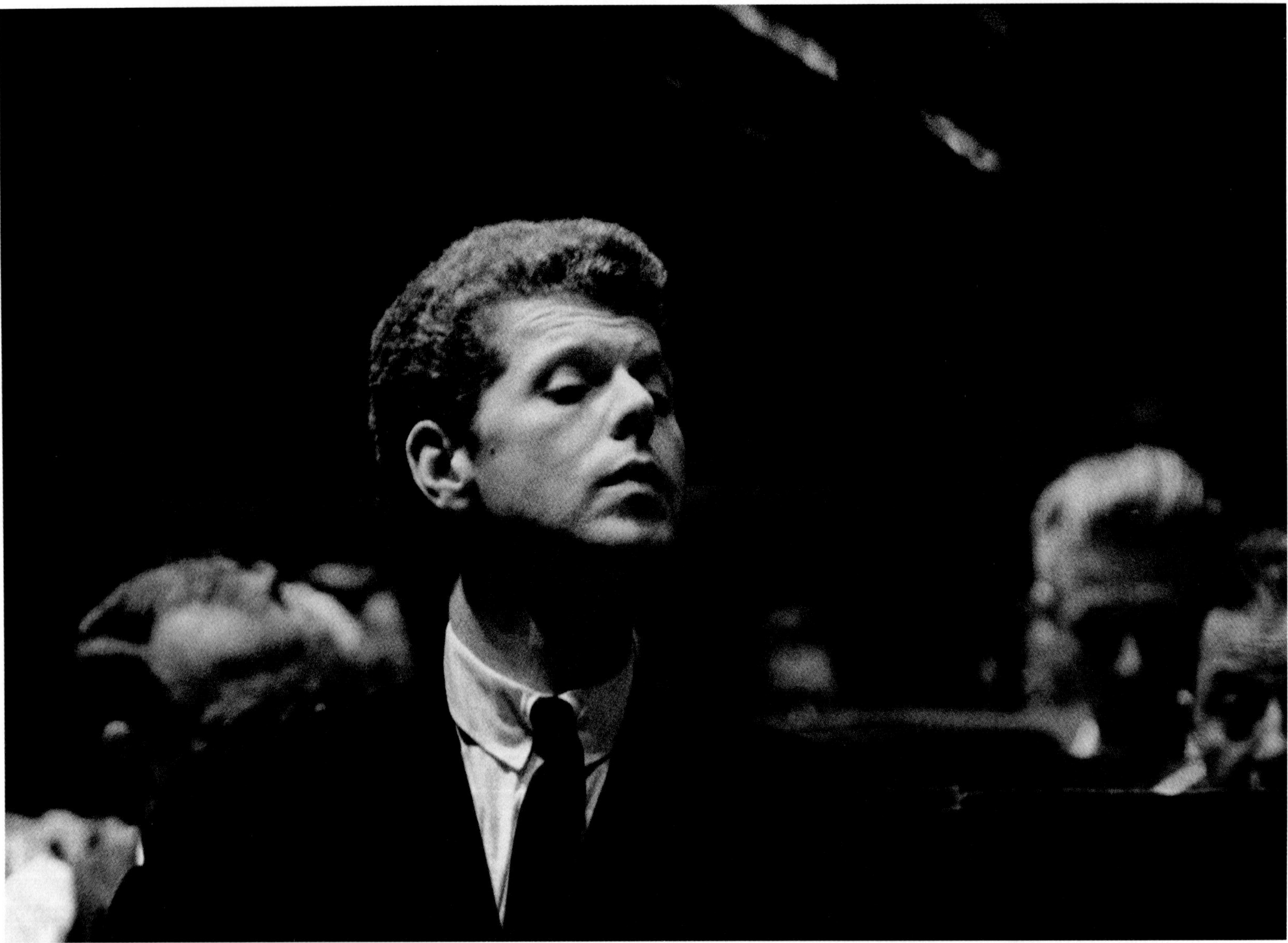

1968

One of the greatest pianists America has produced, Van Cliburn was catapulted to fame in 1958 by his victory in the first International Tchaikovsky Competition in Moscow. His playing combined technical brilliance, emotional warmth, power, sonority, sensitivity, and insight in a thoroughly unique fashion. But fame, wealth, notoriety, and the demands of family proved difficult for him to reconcile with his concertizing, and he retired from active performing in the mid-1970s. His recordings have sold in astronomical numbers, lasting reminders of his artistry, and he has helped to advance the careers of many other pianists through his support of the quadrennial competition in Fort Worth that bears his name.

JAMES CONLON

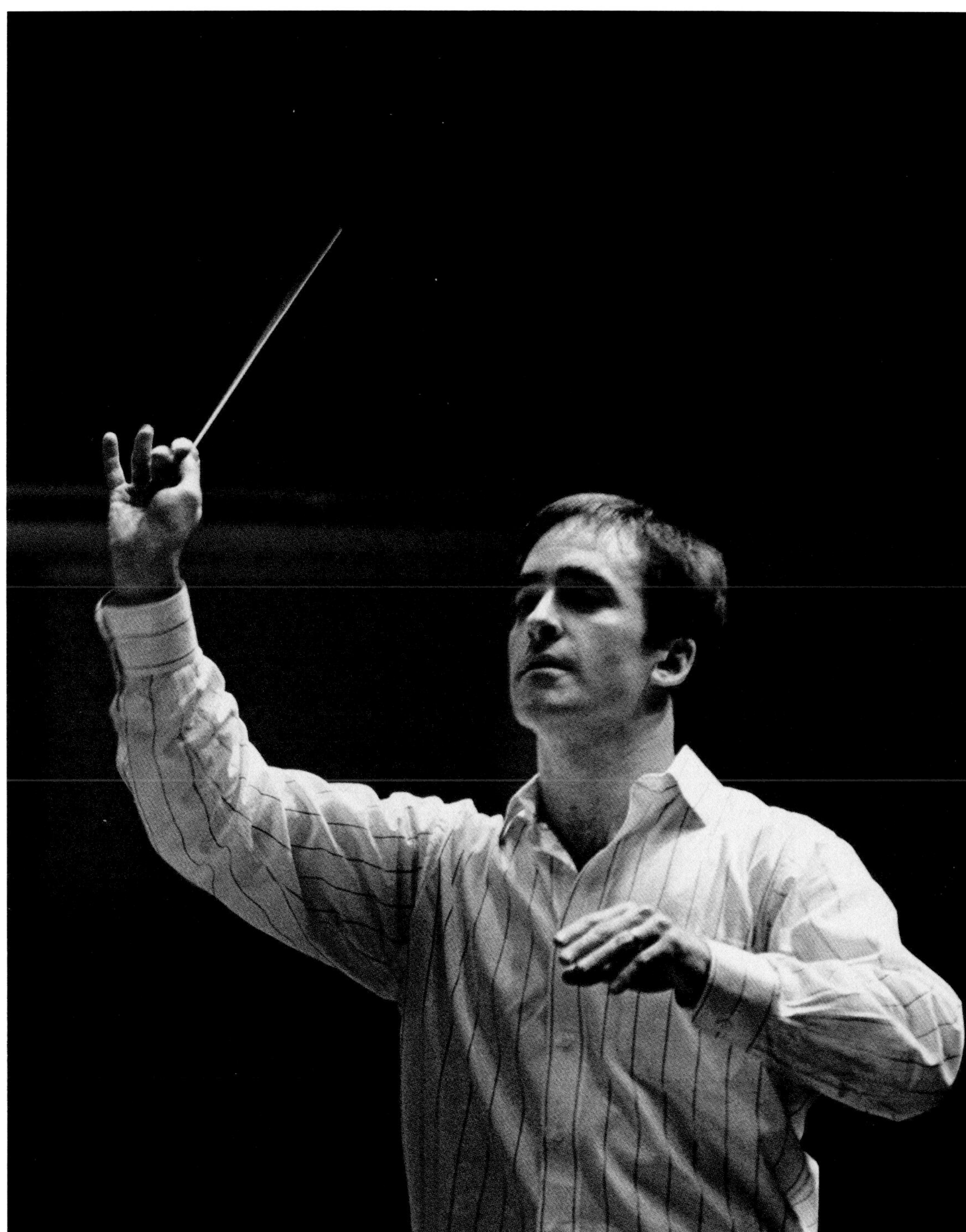

Prior to making a recording of Liszt's *Legend of St. Francis of Assisi*, he went to the hermitage where the saint had lived and the secluded grove where he had preached to the birds, to better interpret the music. Conlon rose quickly to the top of the musical world following the completion of his studies at Juilliard, becoming the youngest maestro ever invited to conduct a subscription concert of the New York Philharmonic. He had appeared in front of most major American orchestras, and had conducted often at the Met, well before he was 30. Today he heads the Rotterdam Philharmonic and guest conducts widely, ranging over much of the symphonic and operatic repertory.

1988

AARON COPLAND

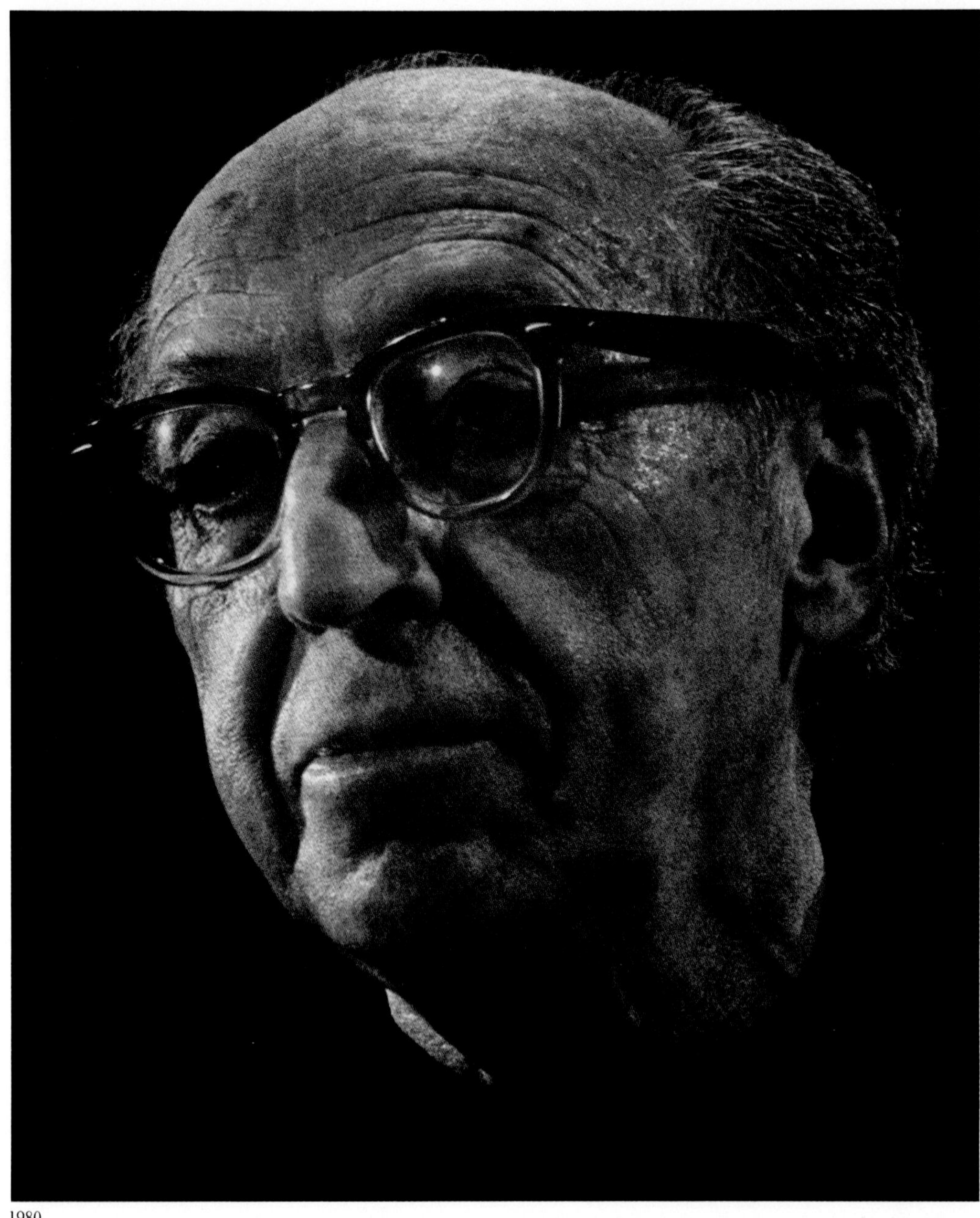

1980

Though Copland once said, "I don't compose—I assemble materials," he will surely be regarded as one of the greatest American composers. He has made an indelible mark on our culture through his remarkably original, vital, and quintessentially American scores. The accessible, tuneful style and nostalgic sentiment of such ballets as *Billy the Kid* and *Appalachian Spring*, the simple grandeur of *Fanfare for the Common Man*, the flavorful panache of *Rodeo* and *El Salon Mexico*, and the wistfulness of *Quiet City* have all been imitated, but Copland's music remains identifiably his, and will always be identifiably American.

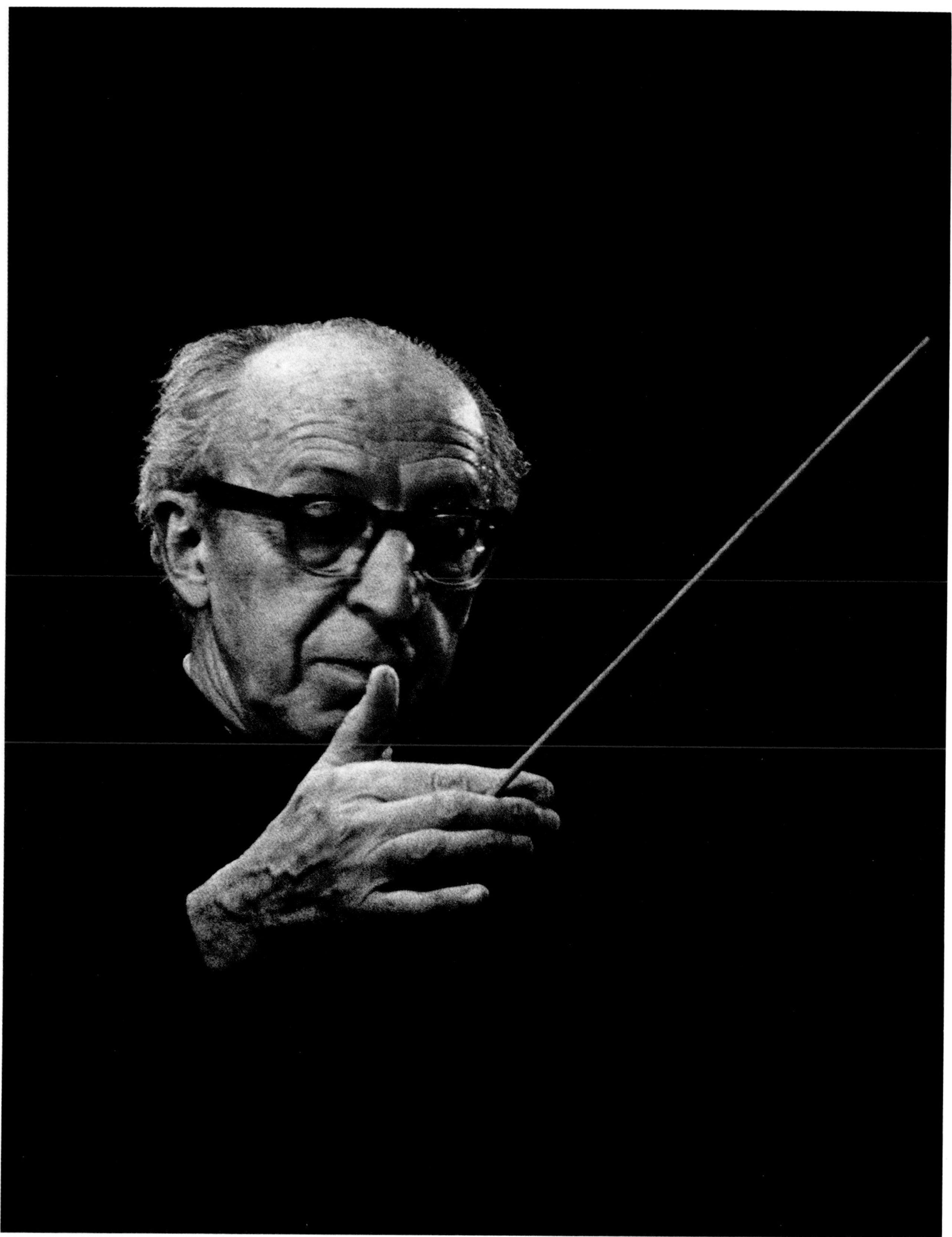

1980

Clifford Curzon

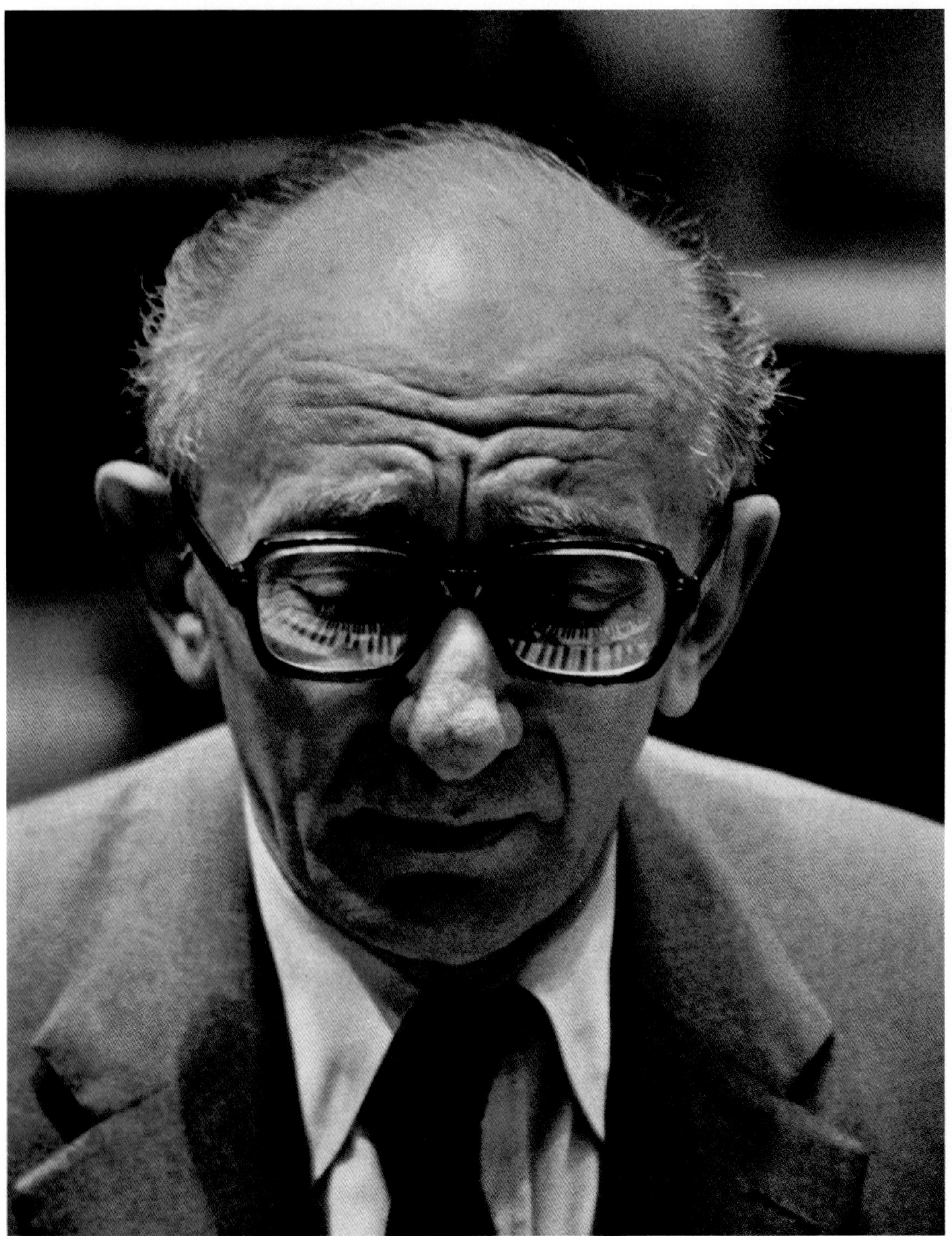

There was no better pianist in Mozart, and no finer chamber musician in any repertory, than this artist of patrician taste and flawless technique. A dignified and introverted figure, he was terrified of the microphone, and thus made comparatively few recordings. But in the few he did make one senses the depth of his musical and spiritual insights, and sees reflected, as clearly as in his concert performances, the extraordinary degree to which he thought about the works he played.

1975

Rafael Frühbeck de Burgos

Even though his name is German, he combines the aristocratic reserve of a true Spaniard with
the ardent emotion of . . . a true Spaniard. A master technician, and, when necessary,
an exacting disciplinarian, he has an extraordinary ear for sound and has made a specialty of the
atmospheric and coloristic repertory of the 20th century. Outside of Spanish music, which he
conducts superbly, he has distinguished himself in the works of Mahler, Strauss, Reger, and Orff,
and in Debussy, Stravinsky, and Ravel.

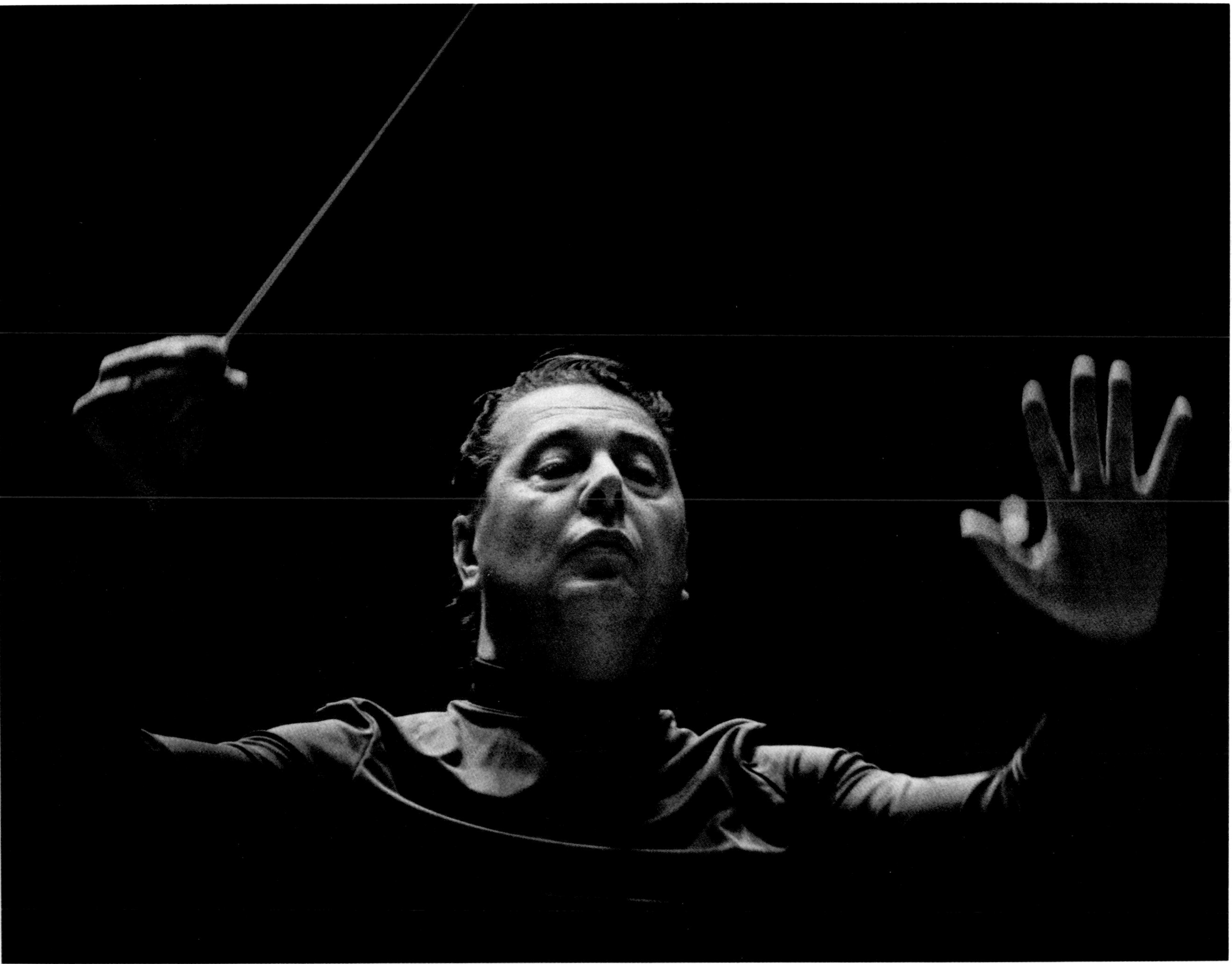

1984

ALICIA DE LARROCHA

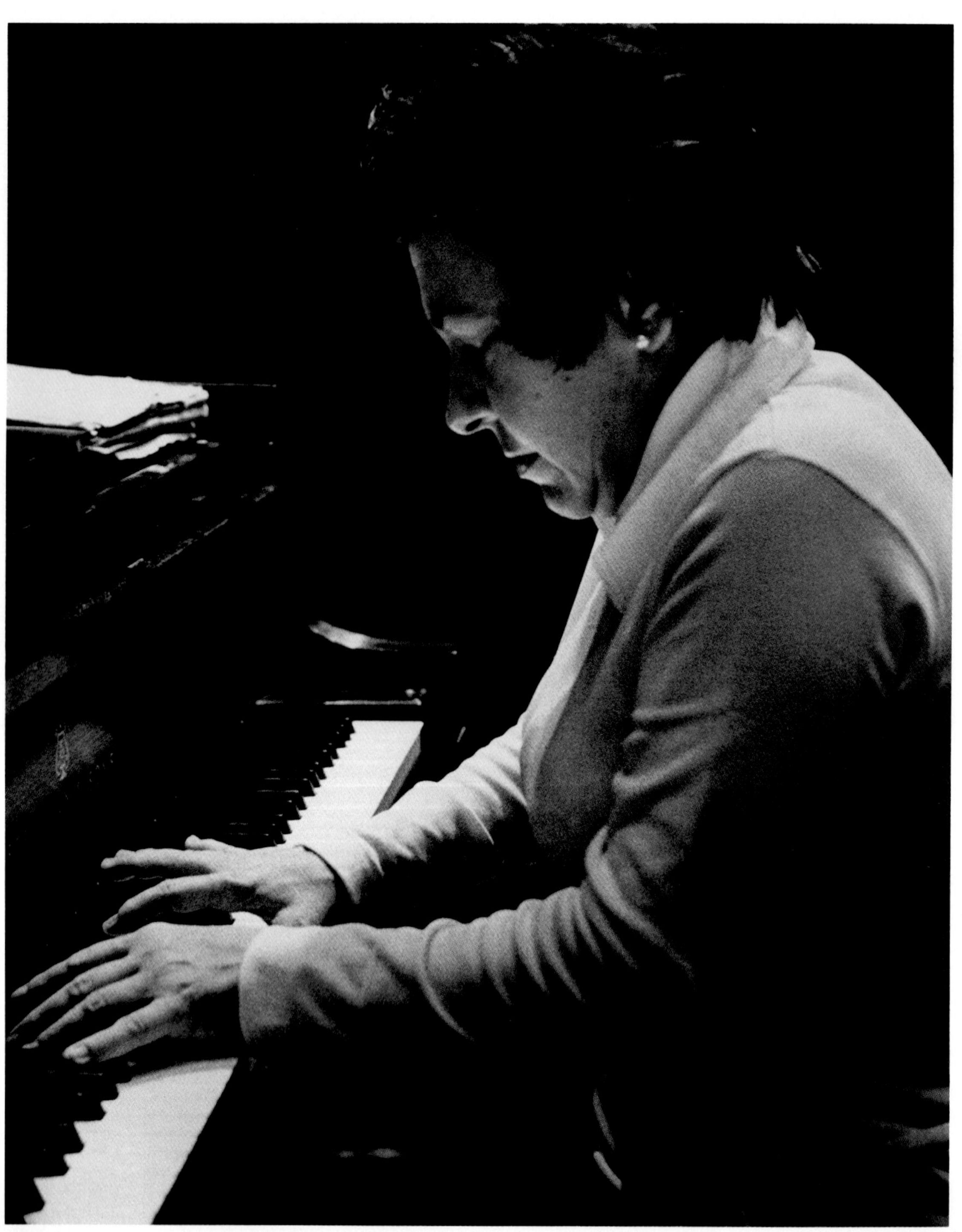

1976

A peerless performer of Spanish keyboard music, Alicia de Larrocha has built a large following through numerous recordings and concert performances all over the globe. Her spirited response to the music of Albéniz and Granados has won these composers many admirers among listeners who might otherwise never have encountered their works, while her often poetic accounts of standard items from the Classical and Romantic repertory, especially the sonatas of Mozart and the concertos of Beethoven, have ensured her reputation with the critics.

GAETANO DELOGU

The son of a professor of Spanish who was himself a superb amateur musician, Gaetano Delogu studied law and music, taking a degree in the former and winning honors in the latter. Born in Messina in 1934, Delogu learned to play the violin—still his first love—before he learned to write. His career as a conductor began when he won a competition in Florence, in 1964. He spent the next four years in front of Italy's major orchestras, winning the Mitropoulos Competition in 1968. The following season he worked with both the New York Philharmonic, as an assistant to Leonard Bernstein, and the National Symphony. He served as music director of the Denver Symphony Orchestra from 1979 to 1986.

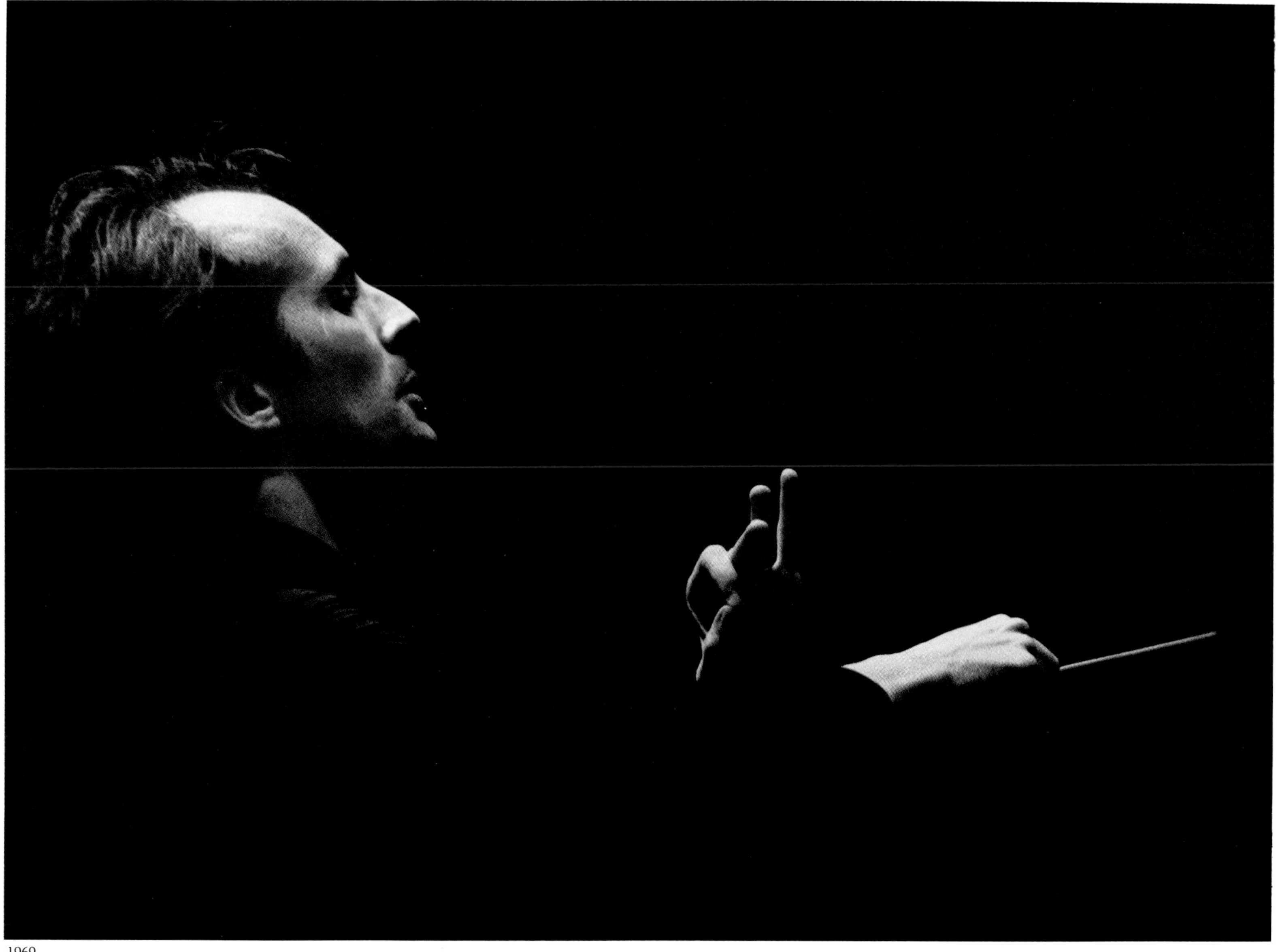

1969

JAMES DE PREIST

This black American conductor, the victim of polio contracted as an adult while he was on a State
Department assignment in southeast Asia, is a world-class musician whose work puts him in the
front rank of our country's orchestra leaders. Currently music director of the Oregon Symphony, he
served as associate conductor of the National Symphony from 1972 to 1975, and as music director
of the Quebec Symphony from 1976 to 1982. An impressive podium manner and solid command
of the symphonic literature have made him a valuable guest conductor, and a string of highly
successful recordings is helping to further his career. De Preist is a nephew of the great American
soprano Marion Anderson.

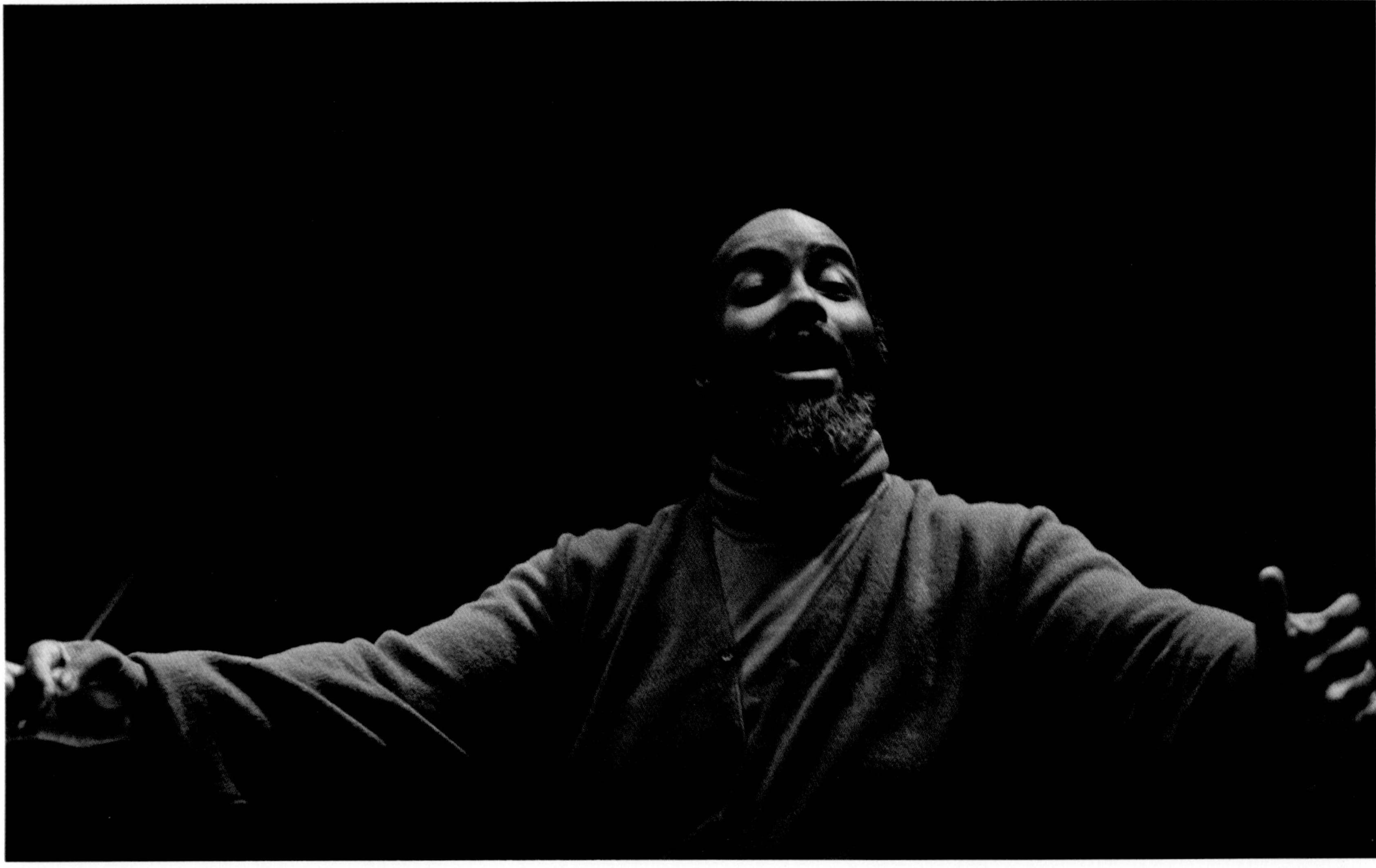

1976

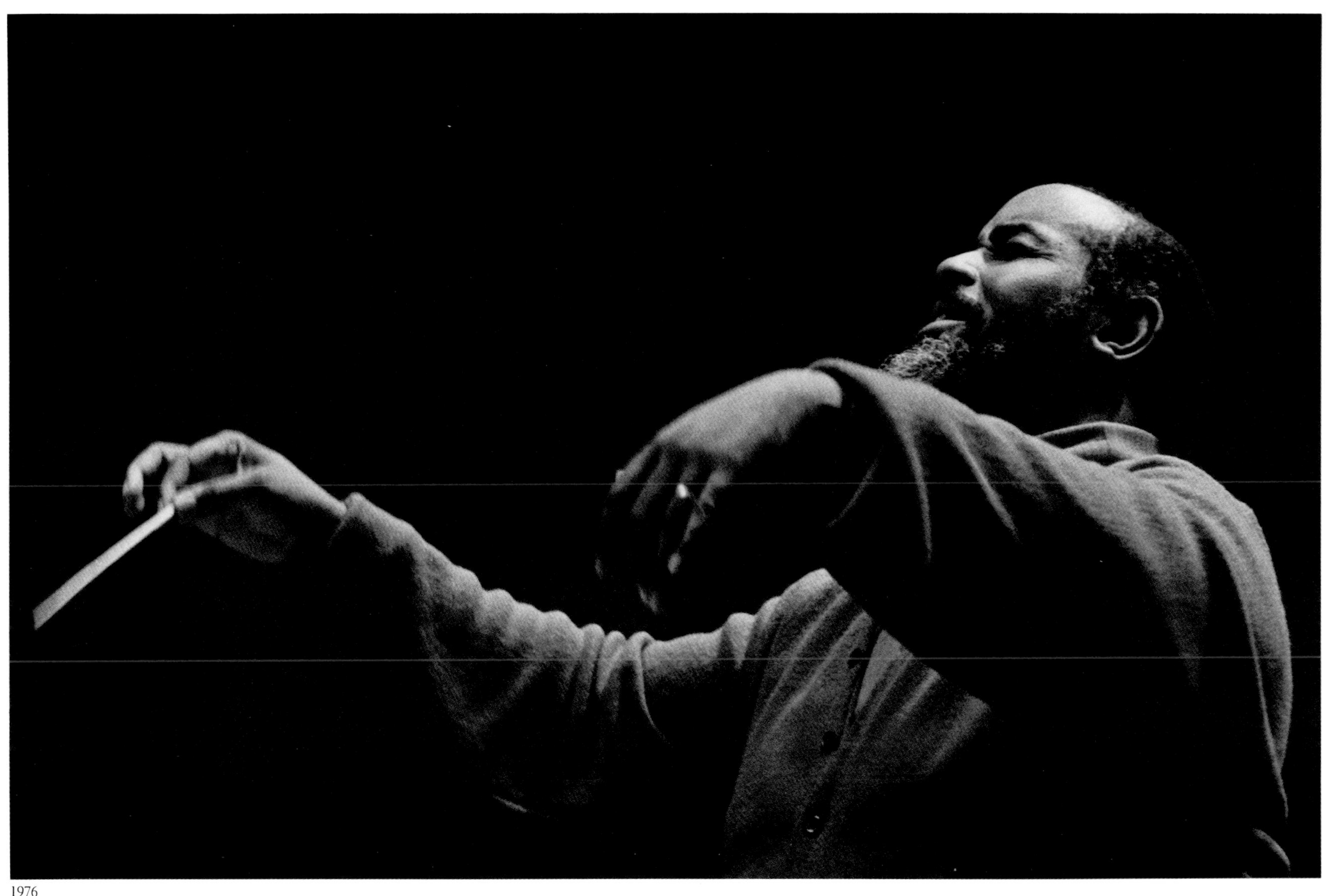

1976

ANTAL DORATI

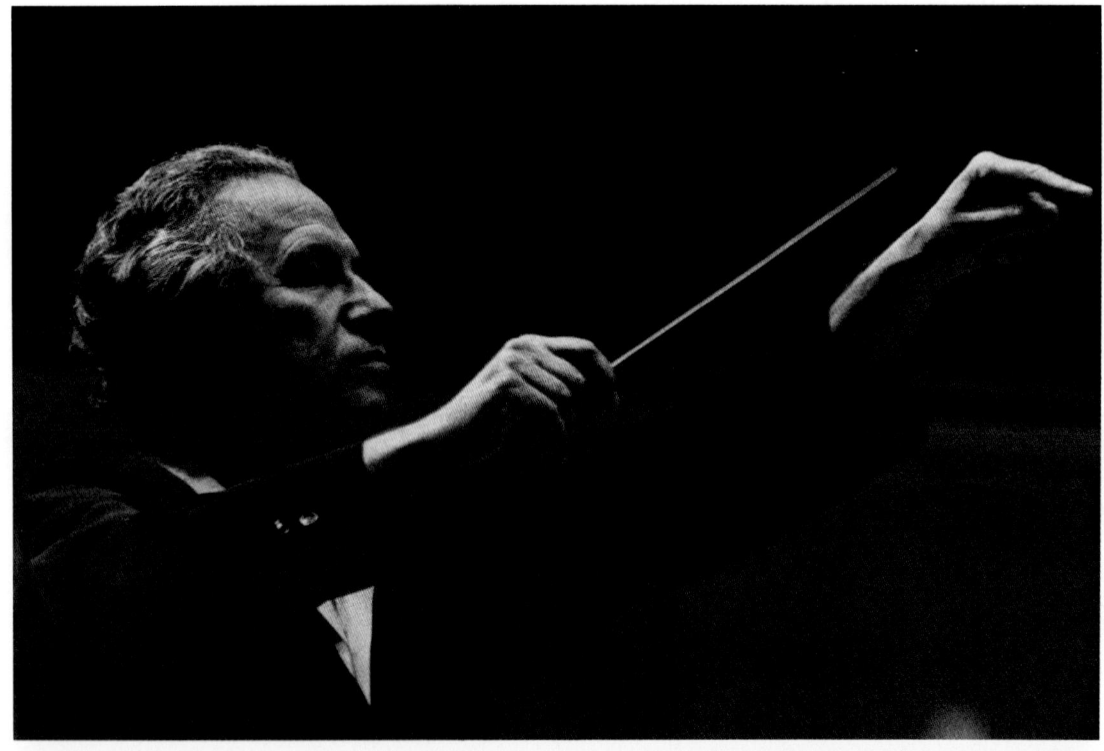

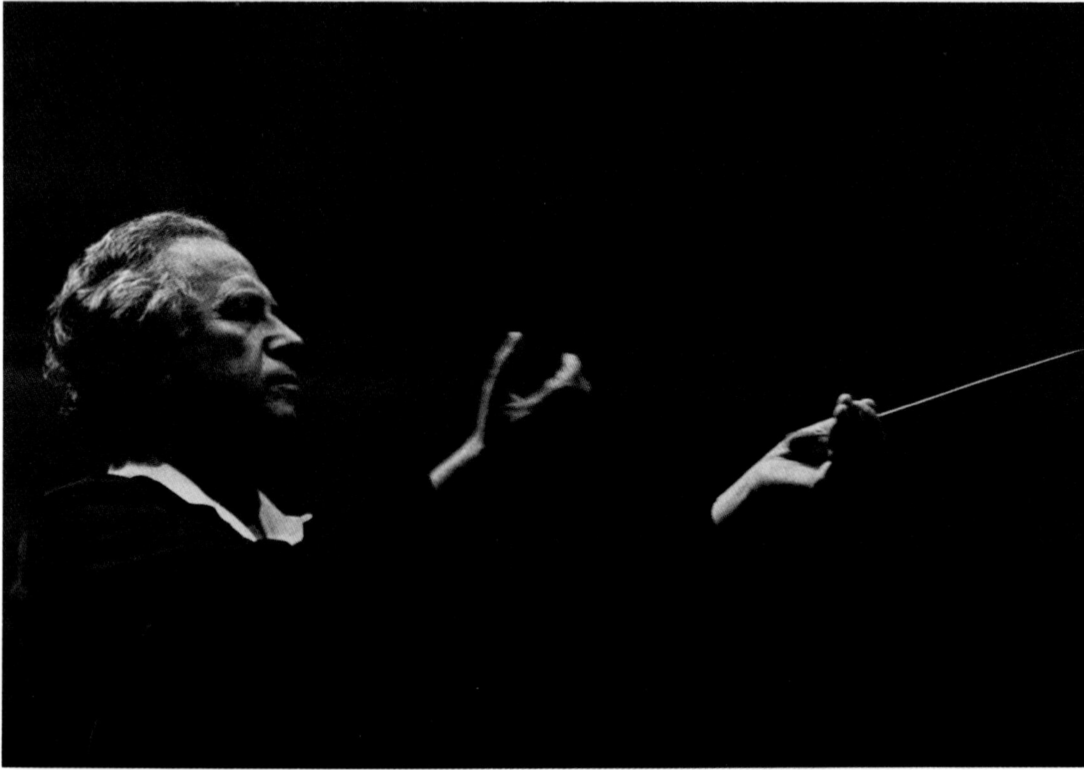

A musician's musician, a builder and maintainer of first-class orchestras, a composer-conductor who can, with equal sureness, write a brilliant solo work for oboe, lead a Haydn symphony from the harpsichord, or conduct from memory a massive choral-orchestral score, Antal Dorati brings together the best of the old school and the new. Born in Budapest and steeped in the musical tradition of pre-war Europe (his teachers included Weiner, Bartók, and Kodály), he was one of the first conductors to really take advantage of modern musicology and the phonographic medium (his landmark integral recording of the symphonies of Haydn stands as an early example of both tendencies). His recorded legacy is one of the largest in history, amounting to more than 500 discs, and he has to his credit a number of important recording and performance premieres. His repertory encompasses everything from Haydn to Dallapiccola, and is especially deep in ballet, owing to his vast experience in the pit. The cities of Dallas, Minneapolis, Washington, Stockholm, London, and Detroit all owe him an enormous debt for the work he has done to shape their orchestras.

1972

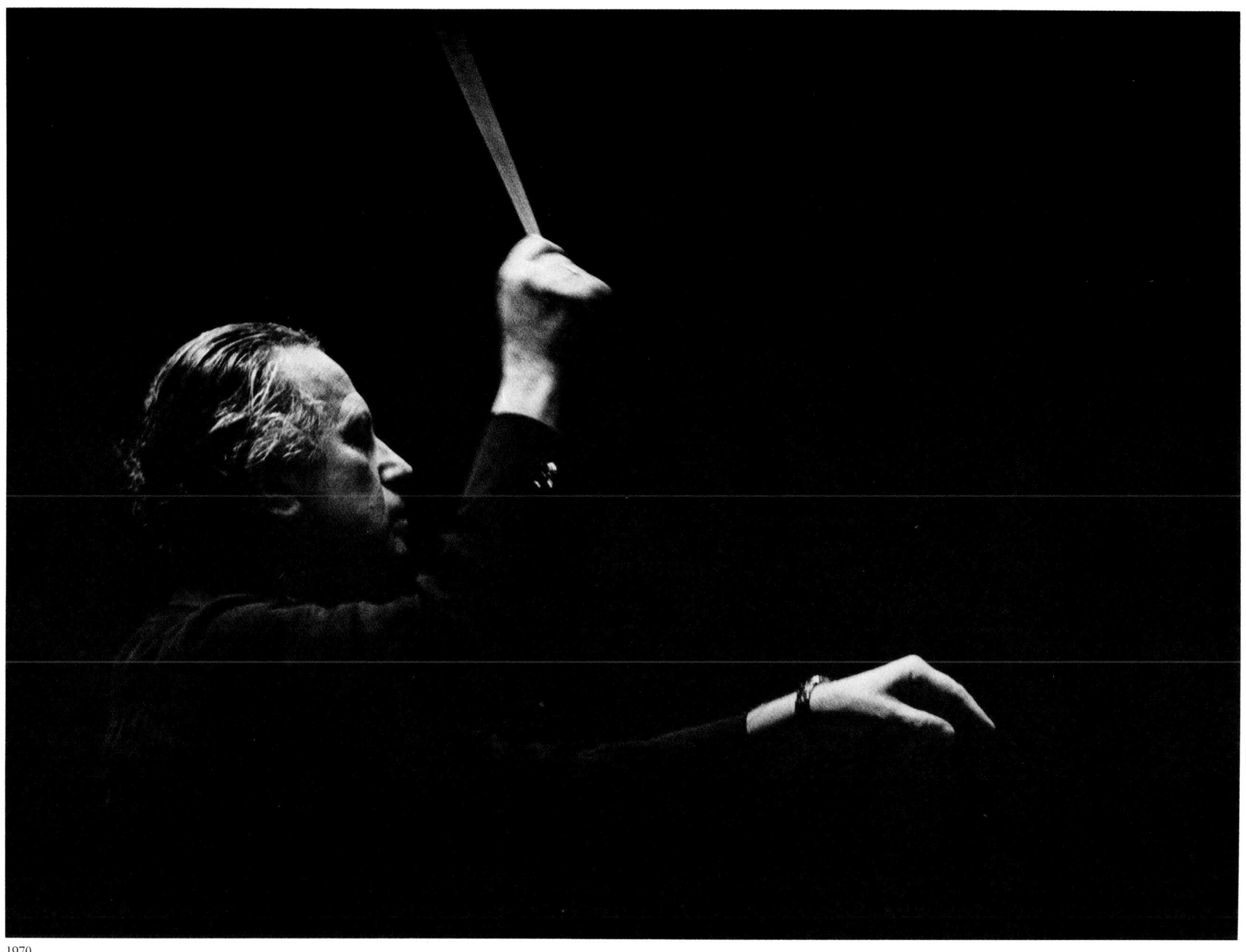

1970

JACOB DRUCKMAN

Winner of the 1972 Pulitzer prize in music for *Windows,* and composer of one of the most effective big-orchestra scores of recent years, *Aureole,* he is a leader in the movement away from system-based composition and toward a new directness of musical language. He is an influential teacher, and a generous champion of other composers' music.

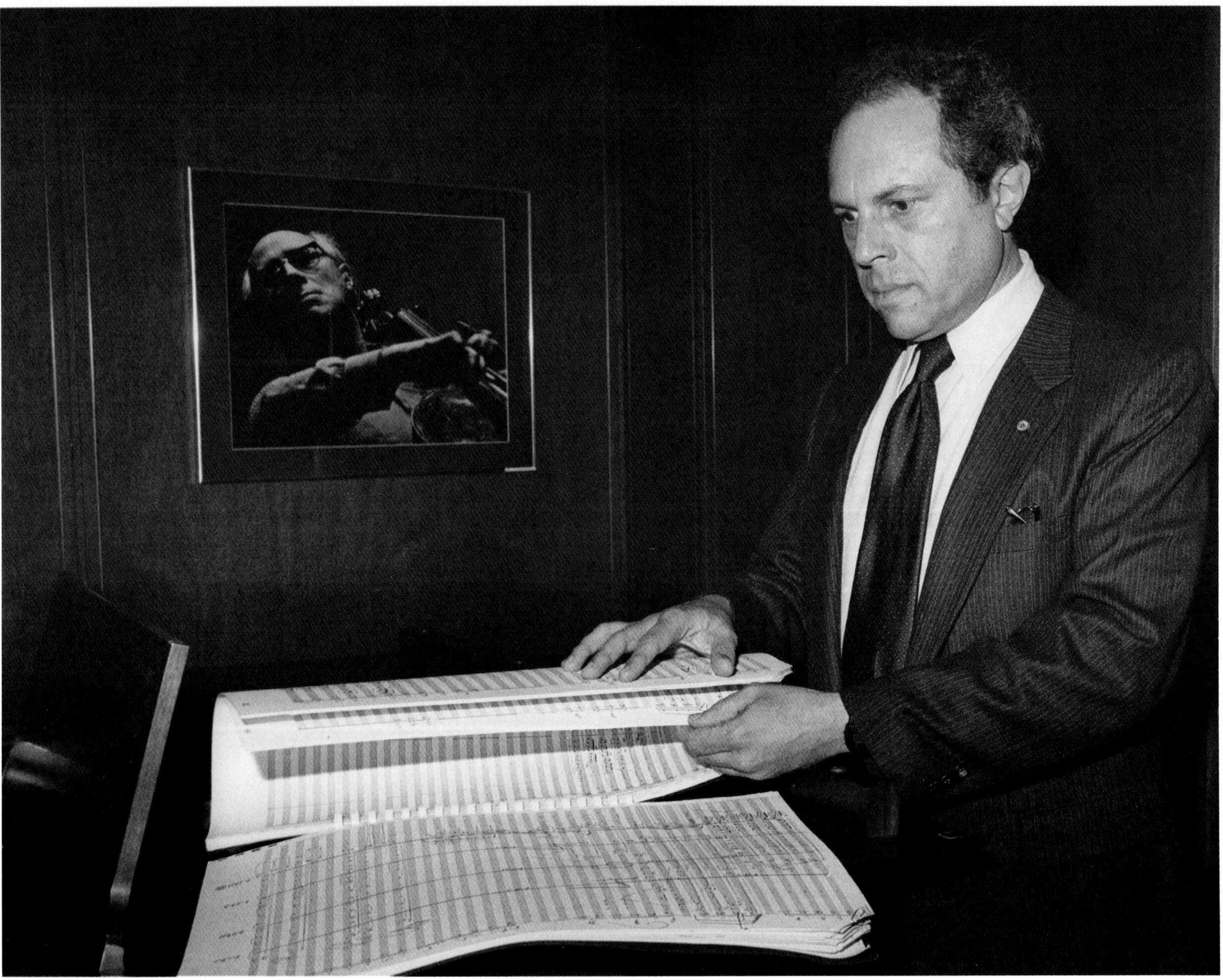

Douglas Fairbanks, Jr.

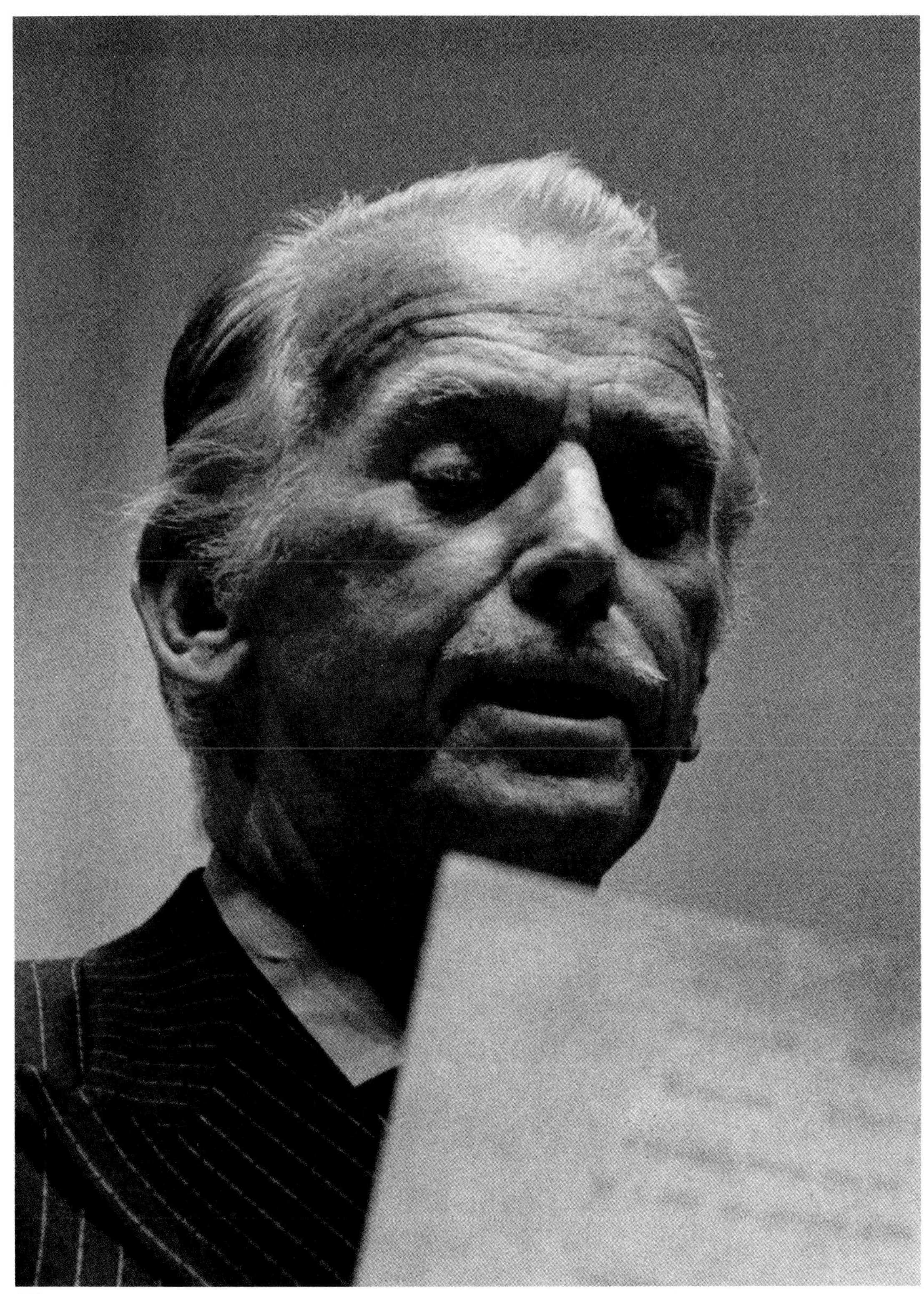

Douglas Fairbanks, Jr., made his film debut in 1923. Over a long and distinguished acting career he appeared in more than 75 films. He was active in radio and recording, and produced a series of 160 one-act plays for television, performing in more than 50 of them. Beginning in 1970, he appeared as a narrator with orchestra in such works as Stravinsky's *Oedipus Rex* and Copland's *Lincoln Portrait*. He narrated the world premiere of Alan Hovhaness's *The Rubaiyat of Omar Khayam*. Among the orchestras with which he has performed are the New York and London Philharmonics, and the National Symphony.

1978

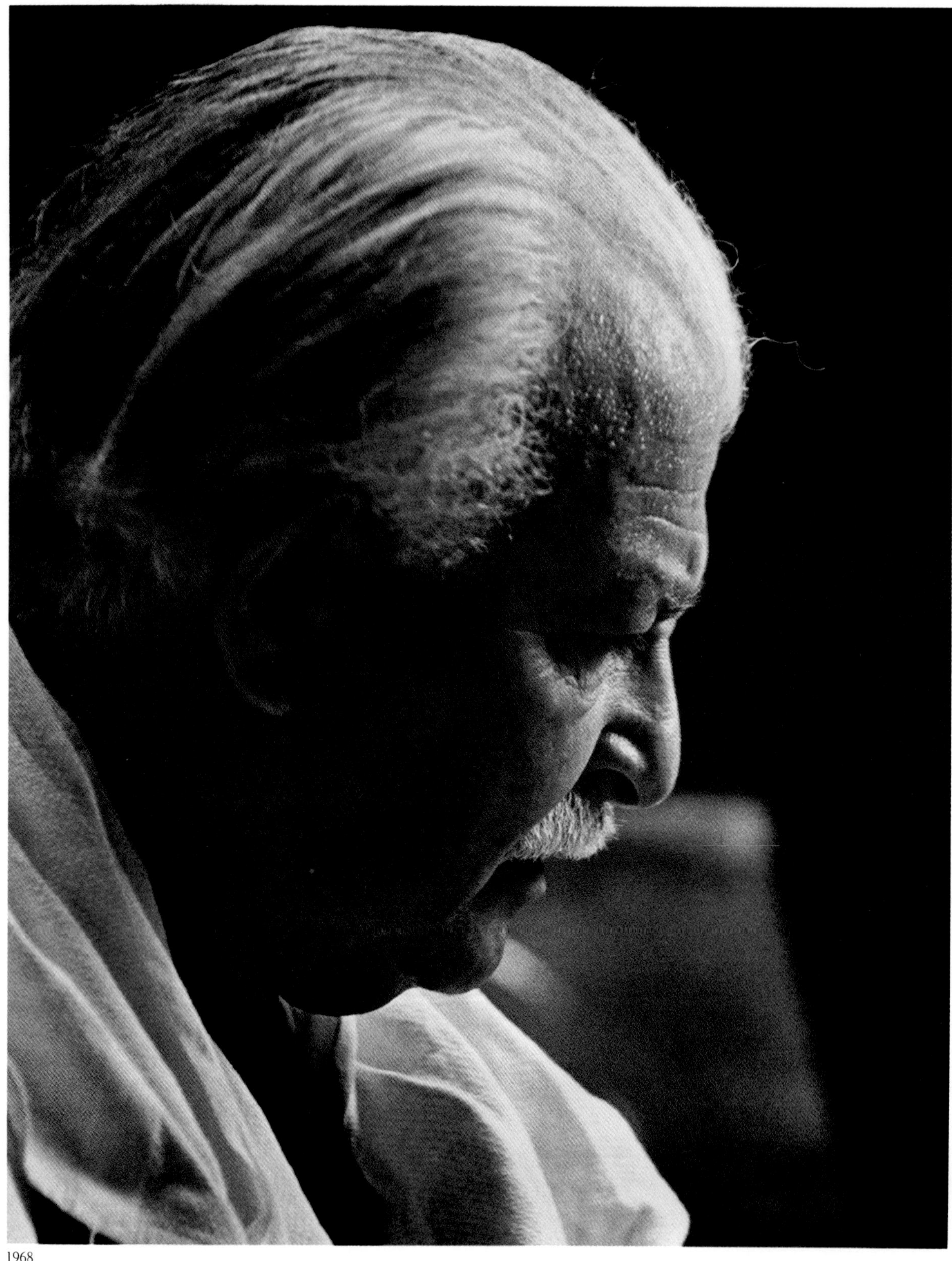

1968

Known affectionately as "Mr. Pops," (although he was nobody's Mr. Nice Guy) Arthur Fiedler became an American institution in spite of his limited conducting technique and rather stolid approach to the orchestral showpieces that figured so prominently in his repertory. His ability to mix popular favorites, light classics, and more serious fare in just the right proportions made him the right man for the job for nearly 50 years in Boston, whence spread his renown for his dapper image, remarkable natural showmanship, and love for fire engines.

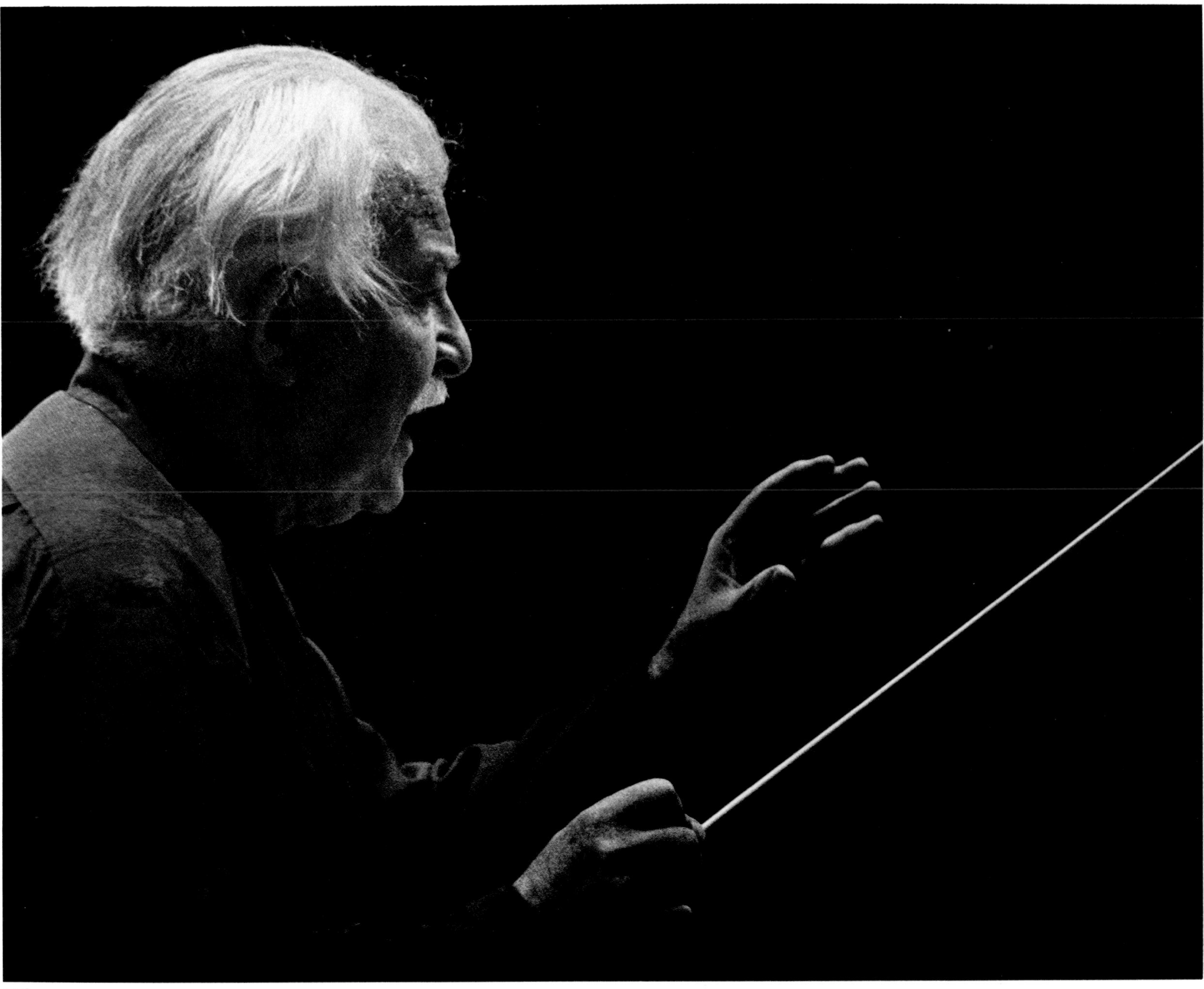

1968

LEON FLEISHER

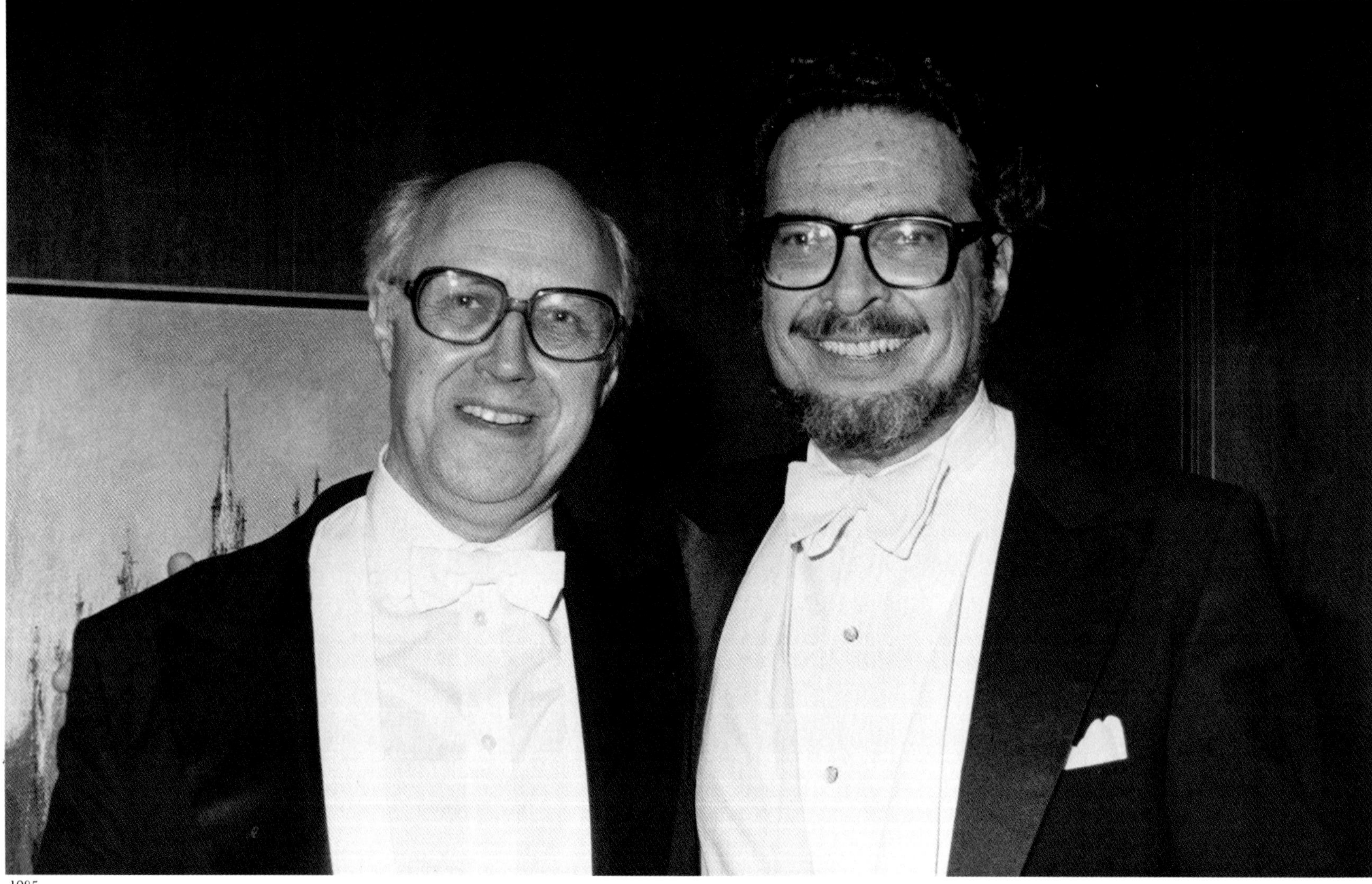

1985

America has given the world only a handful of great pianists, of which he is clearly one. His spectacular rise to prominence began with his victory in the Queen Elisabeth of Belgium International Competition in 1952, when he was 24. In the years that followed, he dazzled audiences with his technical brilliance and his exceptional intelligence and sensitivity. He left an indelible impression in recordings of numerous major works that, from an interpretive standpoint, have yet to be bettered. This phase of his career came to a precipitous end in the mid-1960s, when he developed carpal tunnel syndrome in his right hand and had to give up playing the standard repertory. He turned to the concerto repertory for the left hand and began a second career as a conductor and coach, serving as the artistic director of the Theater Chamber Players of the Kennedy Center, music director of the Annapolis Symphony, and associate conductor of the Baltimore Symphony.

Following surgery, he appeared as soloist at the gala opening of Baltimore's Meyerhof Symphony Hall in September 1982, playing Franck's *Symphonic Variations* and, as an encore, a nocturne by Chopin. It was the first time in 17 years that he had performed in public as a two-handed pianist, and it was a moving experience for all who witnessed it. He is shown here with Mstislav Rostropovich.

MALCOLM FRAGER

A genial *wunderkind* who majored in Russian at Columbia and had won the Leventritt Award and the Queen Elisabeth International Piano Competition in Brussels by the time he was 25, Frager combines the restless intellect of a scholar with the natural warmth of a storyteller. A masterful interpreter of Mozart, Beethoven, Schubert, Schumann, and Chopin, he is equally at home in the music of Bartók and Prokofiev. Over the years, he has indulged his musicological bent by painstakingly tracking down unknown variants and original versions of some of the better known works in the repertory, including the concertos of Schumann and Tchaikovsky.

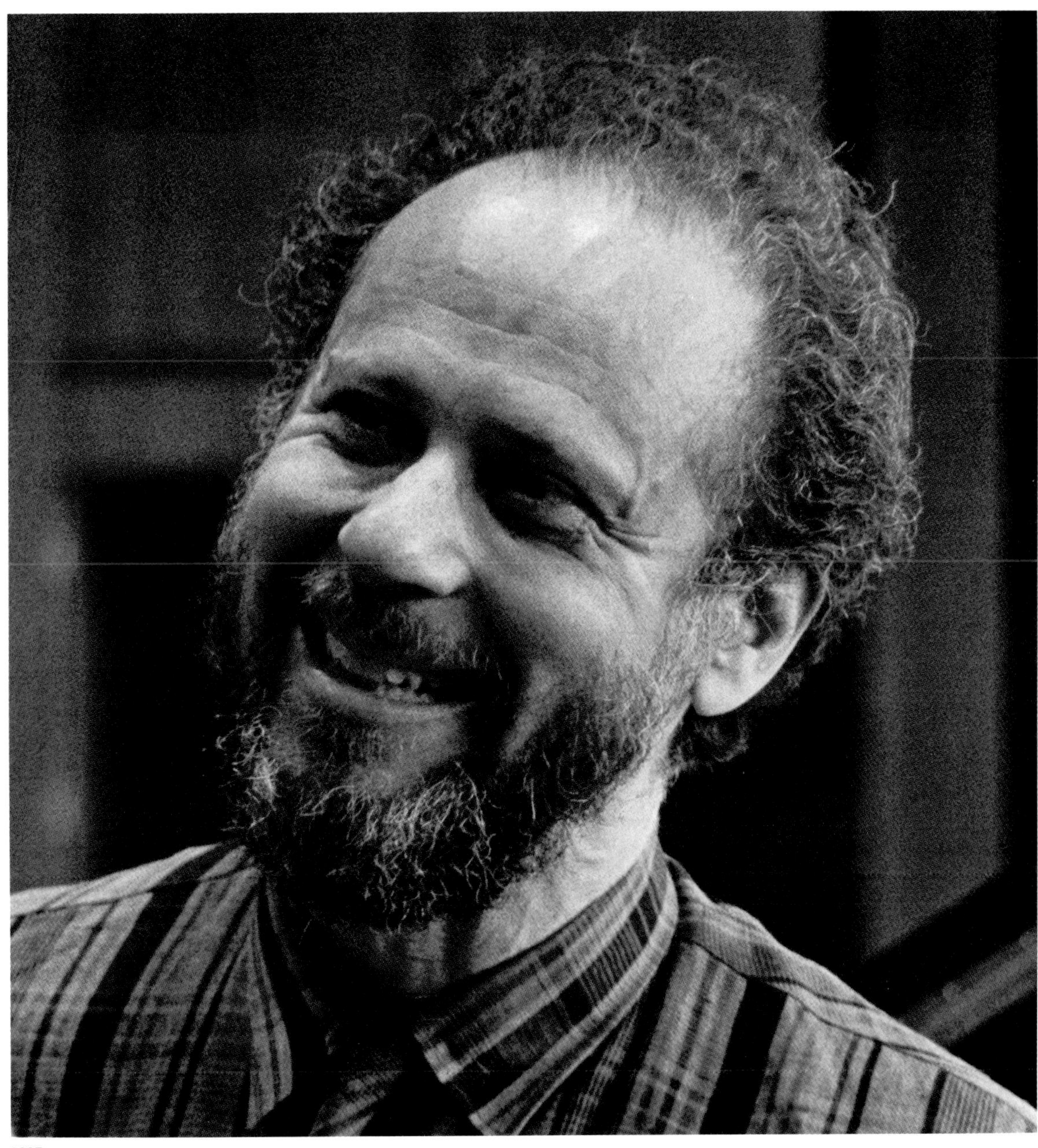

1987

ZINO FRANCESCATTI

This brilliant French violinist performed in his youth with Ravel, and later with such estimable collaborators as Bruno Walter and Robert Casadesus. A master of the classic repertory—including Paganini, which he played with an authority few could approach—he was particularly noted for his interpretations of French music. His American debut took place in 1939 with the New York Philharmonic; in that year, he also became a resident of the United States. After many years in this country, he returned to live in the south of France, where he was born. His instrument was the famous 1727 Stradivari, the "Hart."

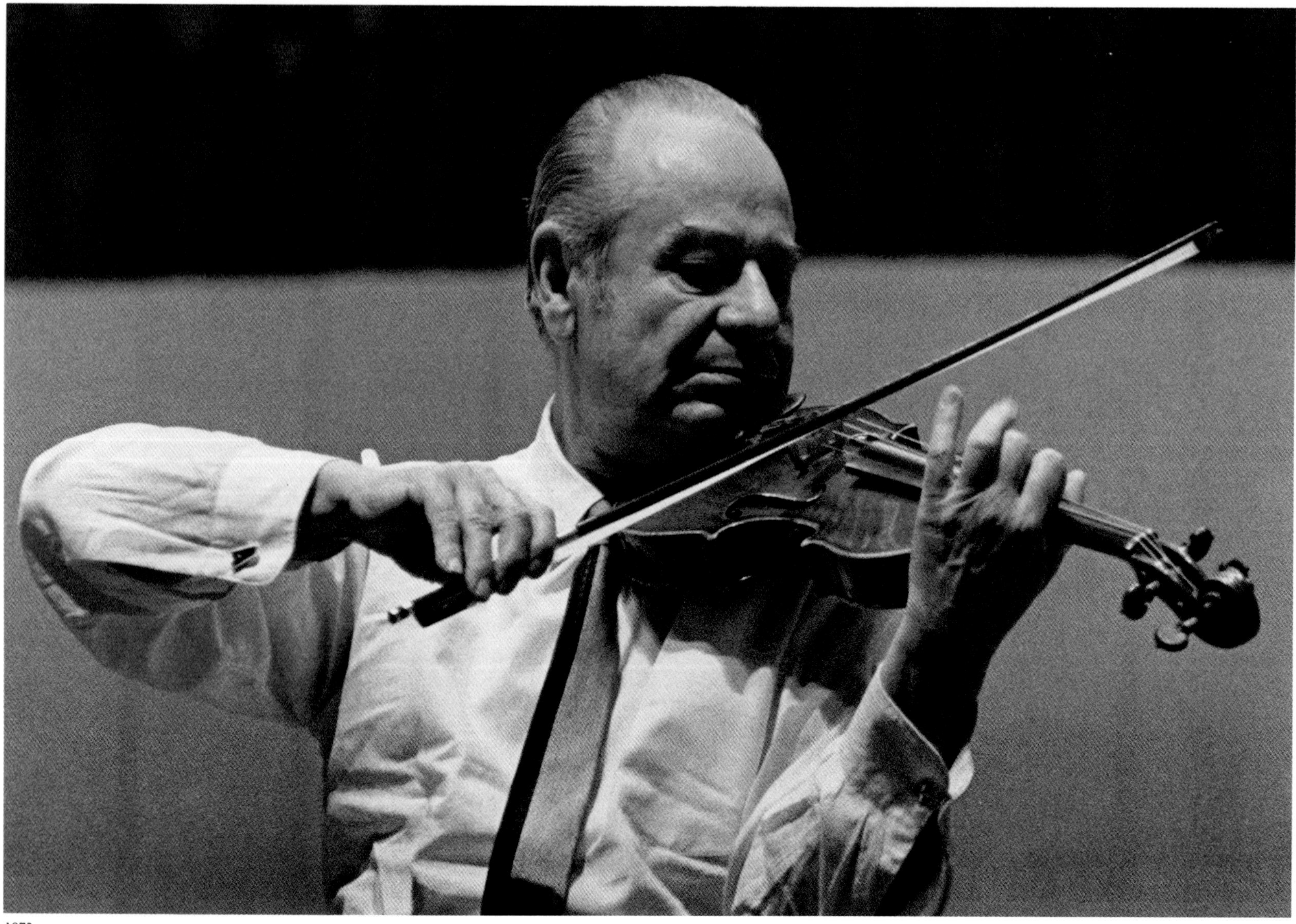

1973

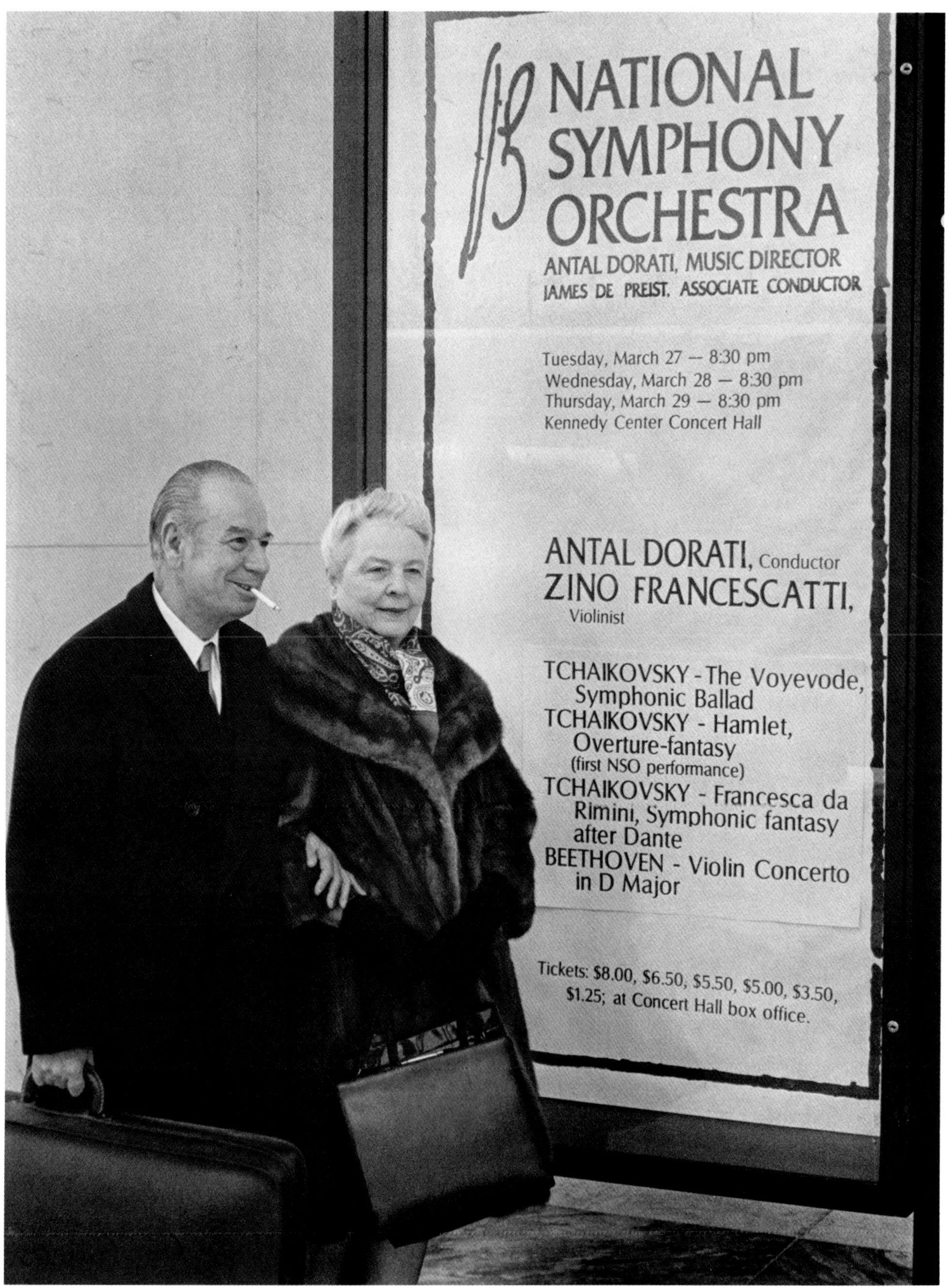
NATIONAL
SYMPHONY
ORCHESTRA
ANTAL DORATI, MUSIC DIRECTOR
JAMES DE PREIST, ASSOCIATE CONDUCTOR

Tuesday, March 27 — 8:30 pm
Wednesday, March 28 — 8:30 pm
Thursday, March 29 — 8:30 pm
Kennedy Center Concert Hall

ANTAL DORATI, Conductor
ZINO FRANCESCATTI,
Violinist

TCHAIKOVSKY - The Voyevode,
Symphonic Ballad
TCHAIKOVSKY - Hamlet,
Overture-fantasy
(first NSO performance)
TCHAIKOVSKY - Francesca da
Rimini, Symphonic fantasy
after Dante
BEETHOVEN - Violin Concerto
in D Major

Tickets: $8.00, $6.50, $5.50, $5.00, $3.50,
$1.25; at Concert Hall box office.

1973

CLAUDE FRANK

This distinguished American pianist of German birth became a student of Artur Schnabel upon moving to New York in 1940. Since 1948, he has been a leading teacher in his own right. He is highly regarded among connoisseurs for his command of the repertory and tasteful interpretive approach.

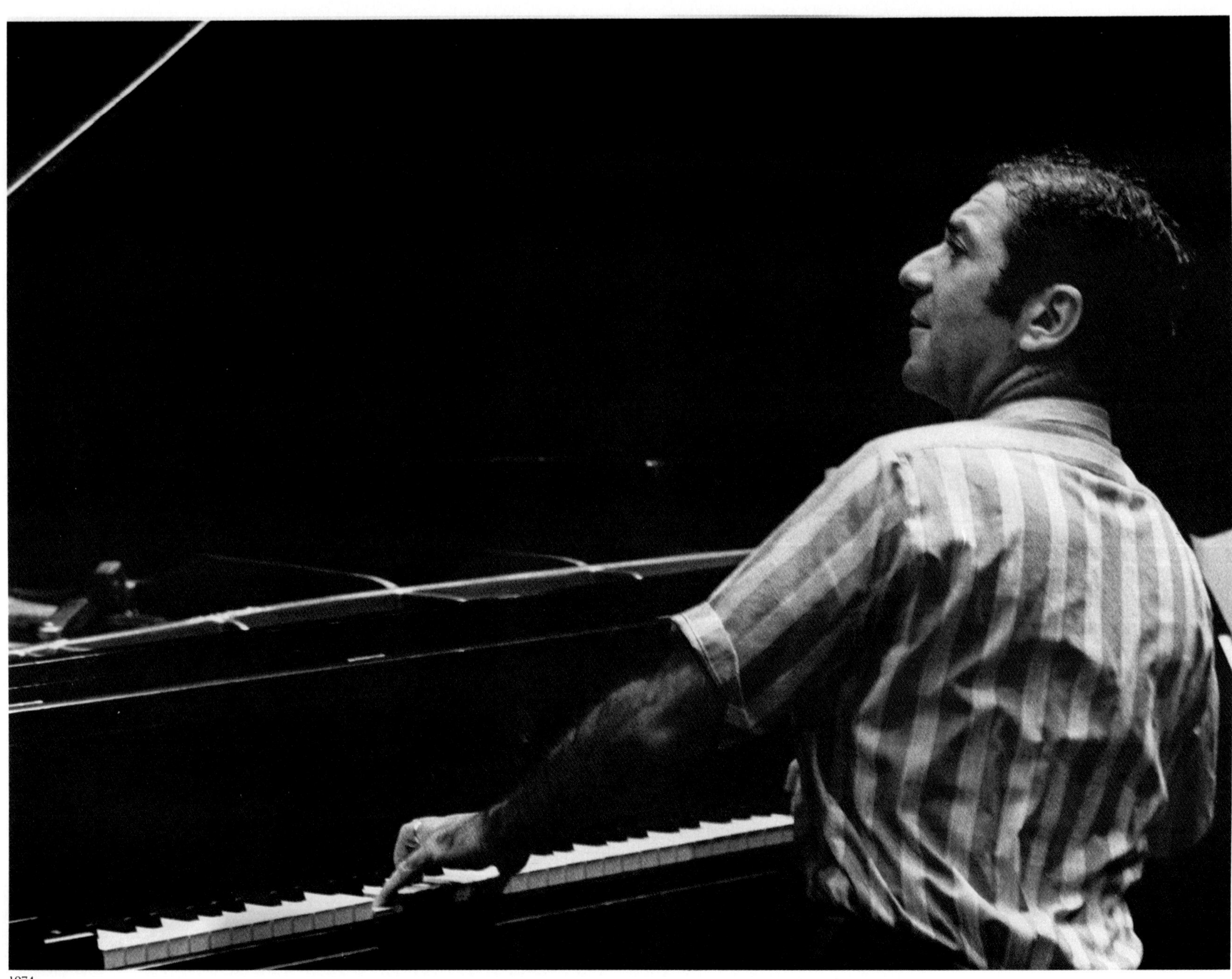

James Galway

The most gifted flutist of the day and one of the world's most sought after musical celebrities, James Galway has an inimitable performing style and roguish sense of humor that have charmed millions, disarmed even the meanest critics, and won countless converts to the instrument. Because of his popularity, some observers have tended to underestimate his formidable musicianship, but among performers—wind players in particular—he has long been regarded as a paragon. His bright, focused tone was shaped by experience in several English orchestras and six years as principal flute of the Berlin Philharmonic under von Karajan. His recordings and television specials have broadened the audience for the flute, just as his numerous commissions have served to broaden the instrument's repertory.

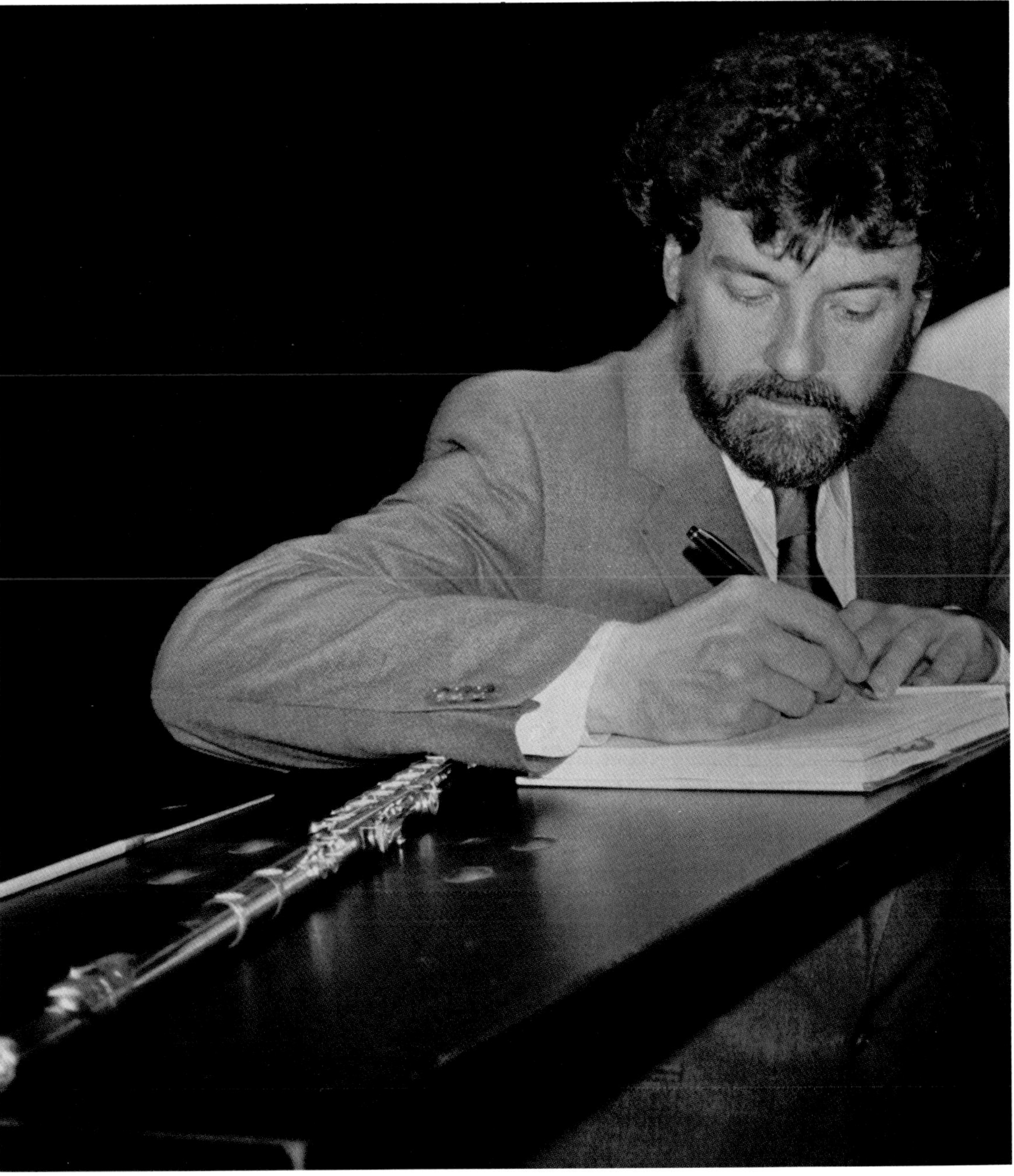

1980

NICOLAI GEDDA

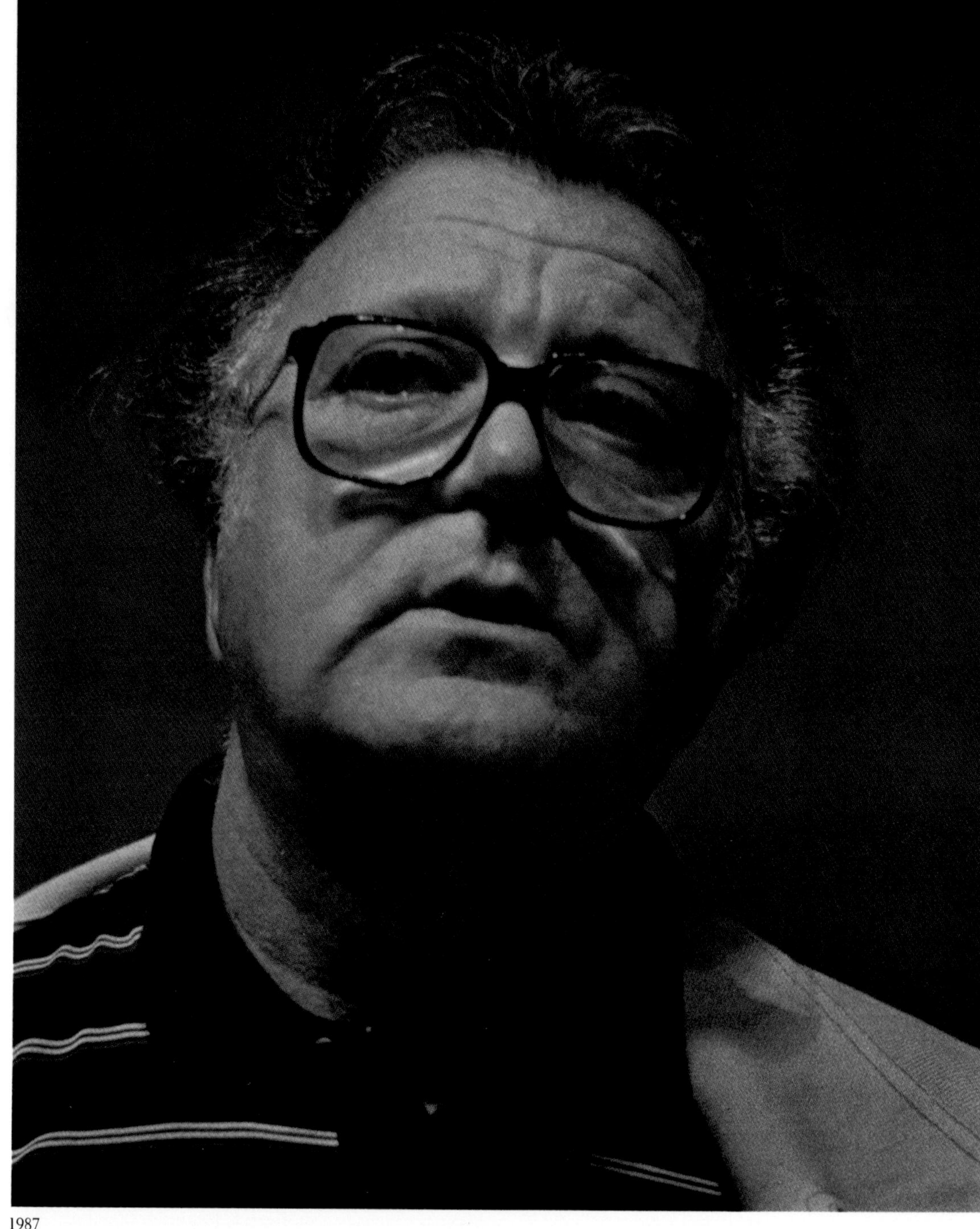

A greatly gifted natural artist, he has an unforgettable voice whose beauty and ringing tone have been well preserved through more than 30 years of singing on the top international level. The son of a White Russian immigrant to Sweden, Gedda has been the outstanding Lensky of modern times. His proficiency at language has made him equally adept in Russian, French, German, and Italian repertory. But his singing is more than the successful combination of words and music. He is one of the most insightful actors among today's leading tenors, whose understanding of character and culture enables him to inhabit the roles he takes on.

1987

Bruno-Leonardo Gelber

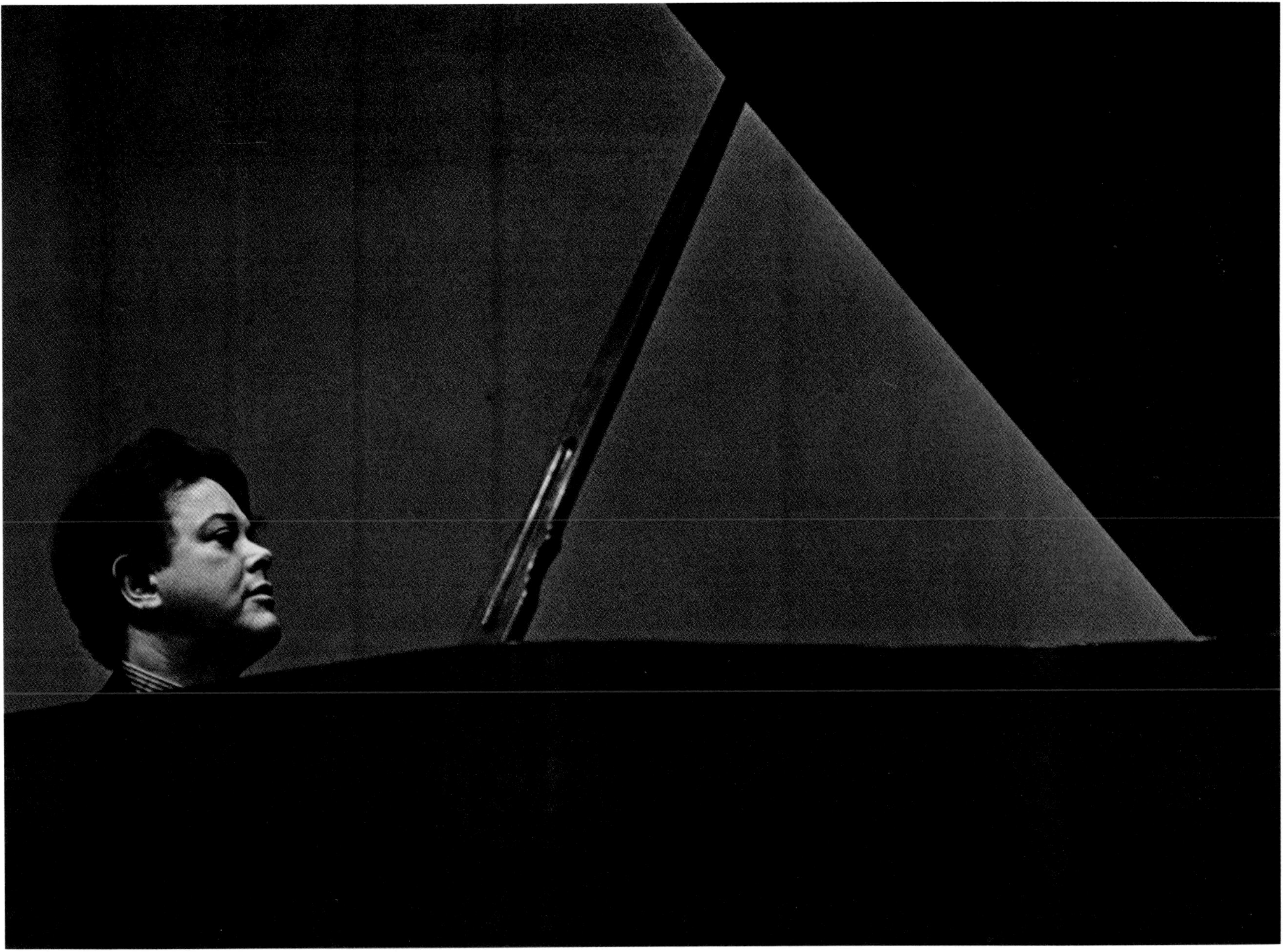

1987

Bruno-Leonardo Gelber was born in Buenos Aires into a musical family, and made rapid progress
as a young pianist. Afflicted by polio at the age of seven, he fought the disease for several years,
continuing to practice on a piano specially made so that his bed could slide under it. At the age
of nineteen he went to Paris to study with Marguerite Long, and after winning third prize in the
Long-Thibaud International Competition he began a busy career as a concert and recording artist.

Michael Gielen

Best known as a fearless champion of "difficult" 20th-century music, he is also a composer loyal to the intellectual tradition of the second Viennese school. His daring, sometimes defiant, programming got him into trouble in Cincinnati, where he served several seasons as music director of the Cincinnati Symphony. He is more at home in the world of opera, and more comfortable where the once *avant*, now *derrière*, *garde* is thoroughly entrenched. He has certain blind spots, but he conducts what he believes in with a conviction that is rare in today's concert whirl.

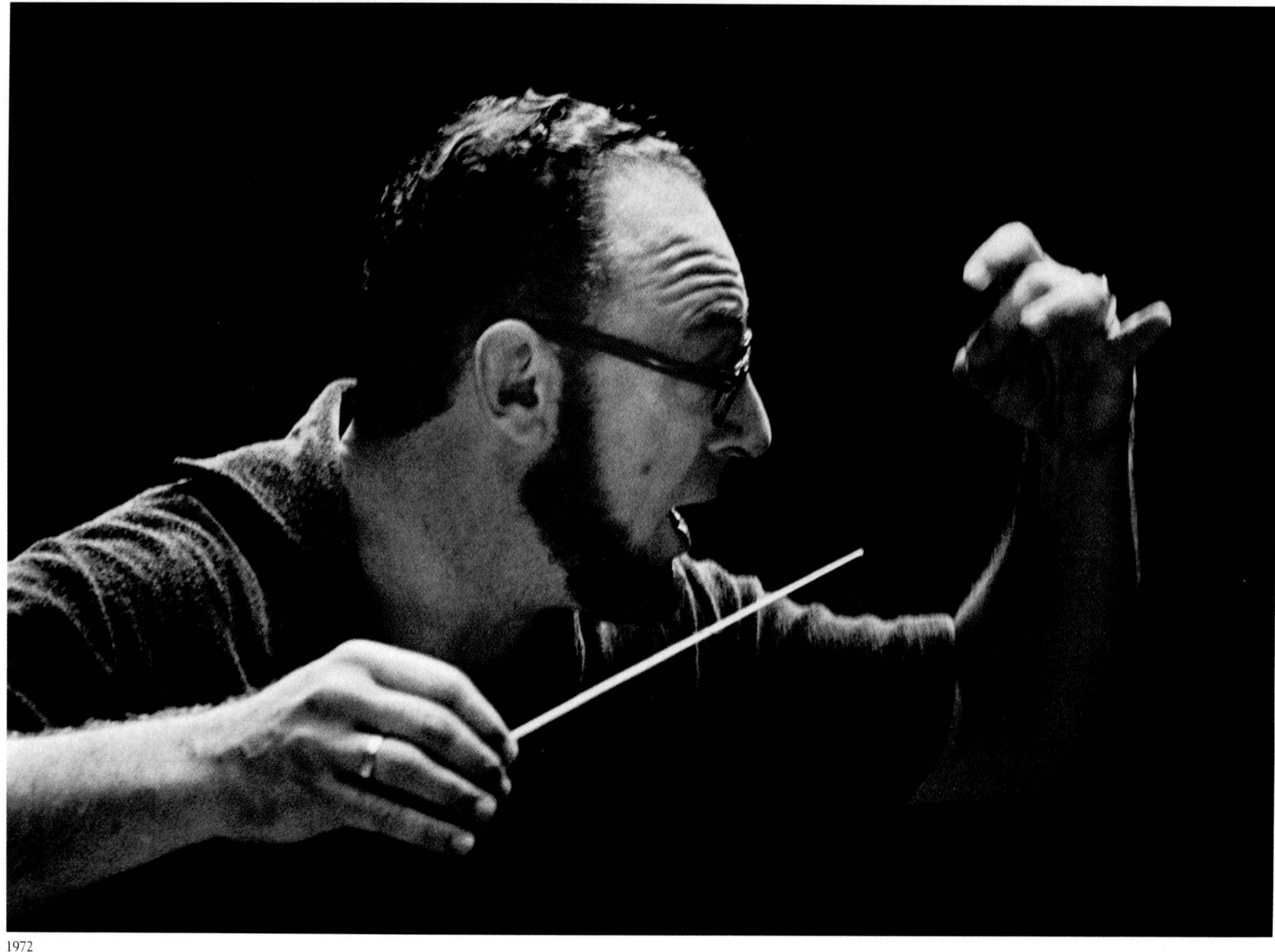

1972

EMIL GILELS

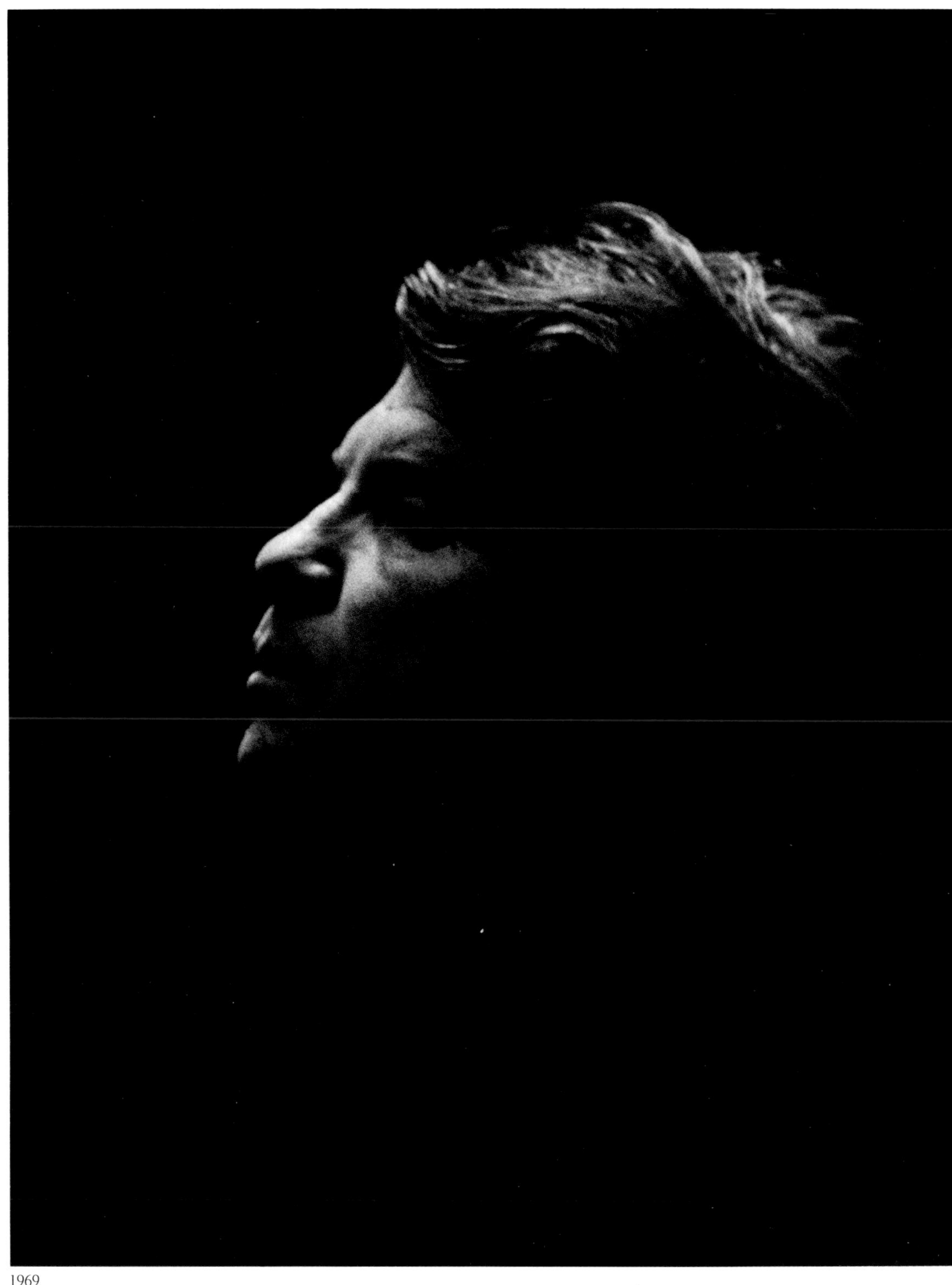

This great Soviet pianist, rivaled only by
Richter, was an extraordinary interpreter of
Beethoven, Brahms, and Tchaikovsky. A
dazzling performer who debuted in America
in 1955, he possessed enormous energy and
power, but always preferred the intellectual
to the elemental approach. His recordings,
especially of Beethoven, are landmarks in
interpretive history—bold, manly, articulate,
and technically brilliant.

1969

Morton Gould

Morton Gould has been a prolific creator of musicals, medleys, film scores, ballets, and concert and occasional pieces, most of which draw in one way or another on the rich heritage of American folk, ethnic, and popular music. He is a brilliant orchestrator and arranger, and unerringly delivers commissioned works that fill the bill. Currently the president of the American Society of Composers, Authors, and Publishers, he remains a tireless champion of our country's musical culture, and has proven a strong support to his colleagues.

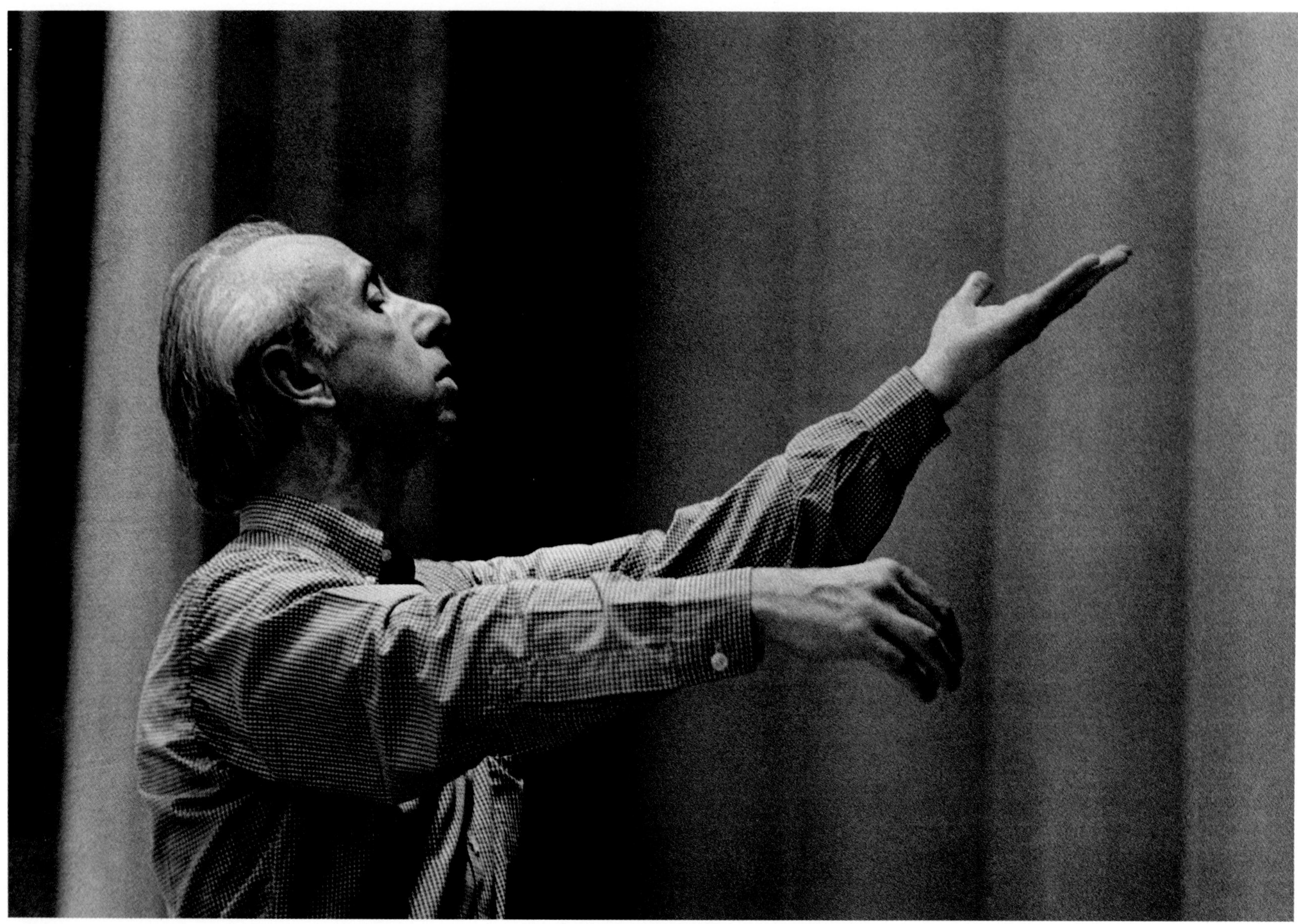

1967

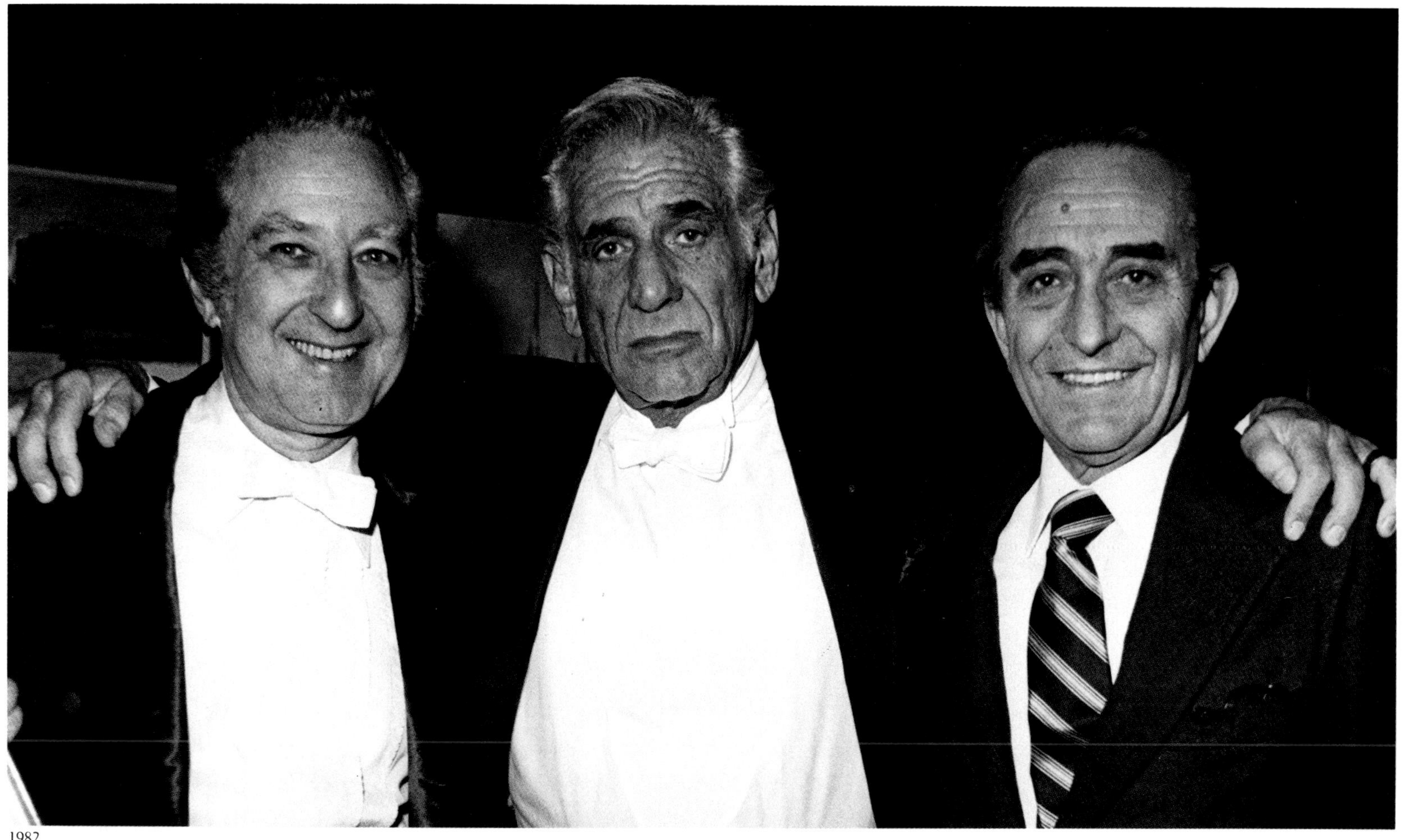

1982

Sol Greitzer (left), outstanding musician and teacher and the head of a very musical family, was for many years the principal violist of the New York Philharmonic. He is shown here with Leonard Bernstein and violin maker Sergio Peressun.

LEOPOLD HAGER

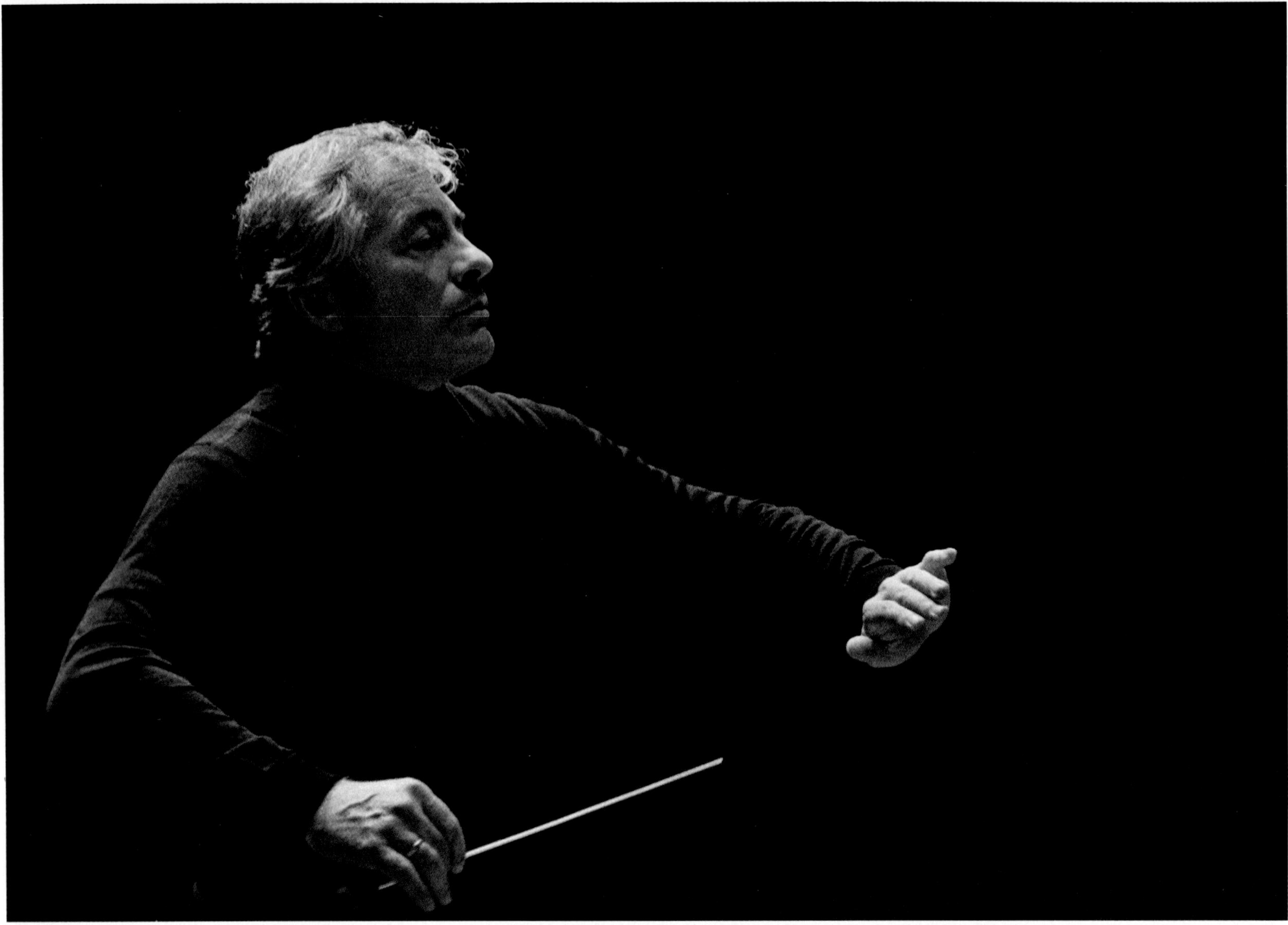

1988

As befits a conductor frequently associated with the works of Mozart, Leopold Hager is a deft
practitioner capable of drawing the sublest nuances from an ensemble and yet of making the most
complex works seem delightfully, and winningly, simple. Born in Salzburg in 1935, he studied
both at the Salzburg Music Academy and the Mozarteum. He was the music director of the
Mozarteum Orchestra from 1969 to 1981, and is a permanent guest conductor of both the Munich
State Opera and the Vienna State Opera. He has conducted at major opera houses and with
orchestras around the world and recorded all of Mozart's piano concertos.

MARVIN HAMLISCH

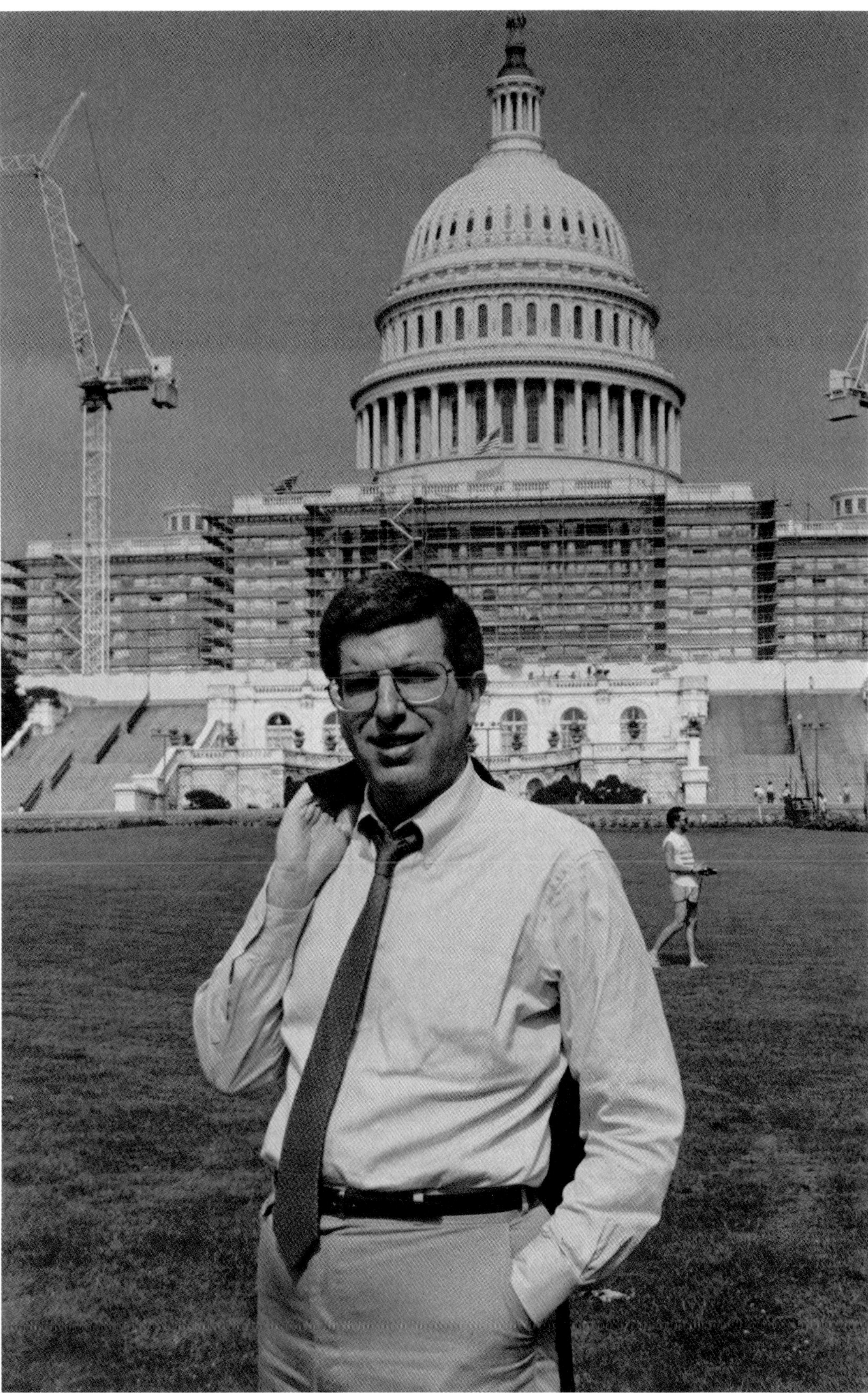

The composer of the musical *A Chorus Line*, which he completed when he was only 30, he stands as one of America's finest songwriters. Among the films he has scored are *Take the Money and Run* and *The Sting*, which won an Academy Award.

1987

Frans Helmerson

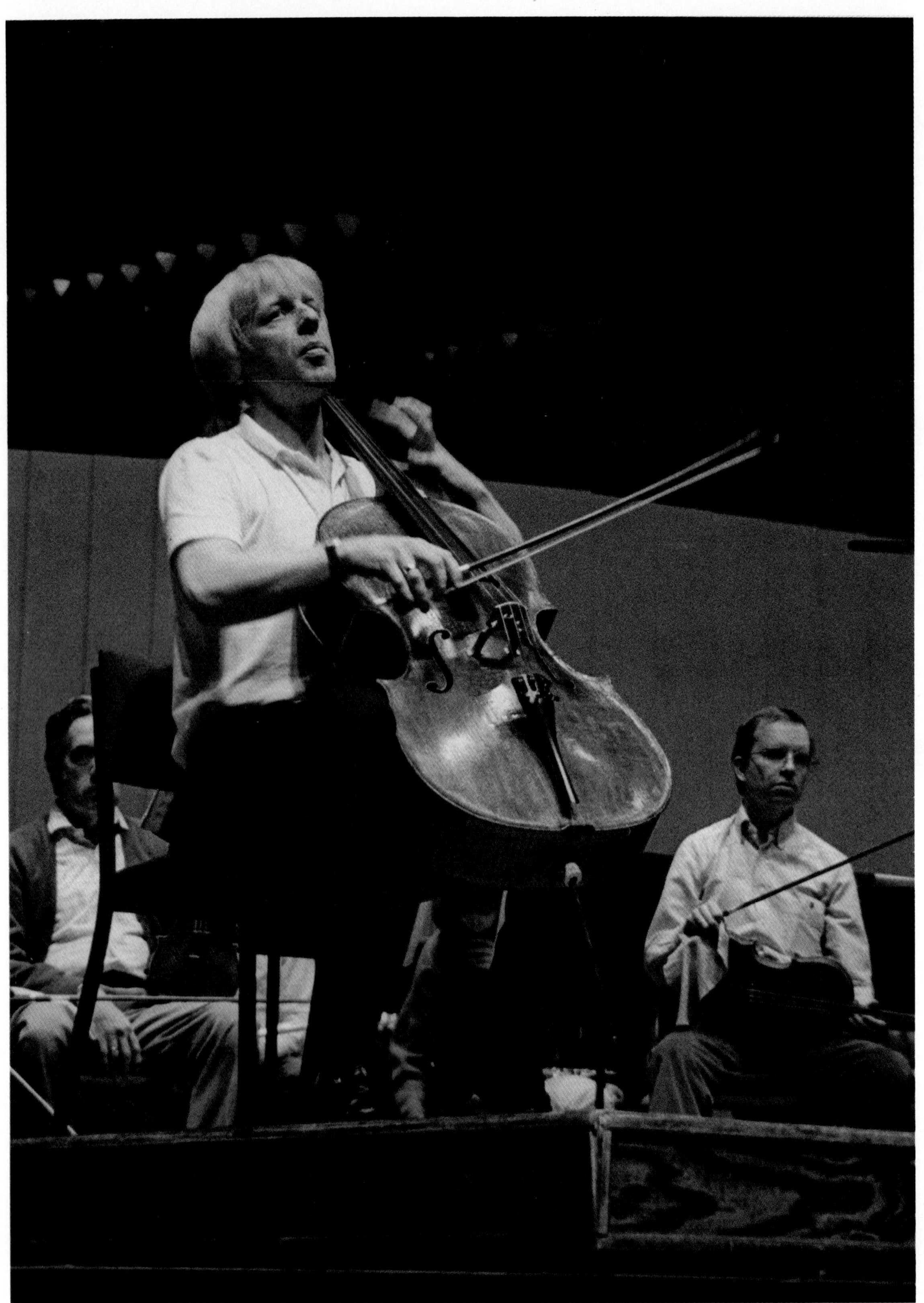

1987

A leading cellist of his generation, and one of Sweden's leading musicians, Helmerson has performed widely and made a number of outstanding recordings. A favorite of Rostropovich, who has been instrumental in furthering his career, he has a highly controlled, purposeful manner as a performer and a brilliant technique.

GÜNTHER HERBIG

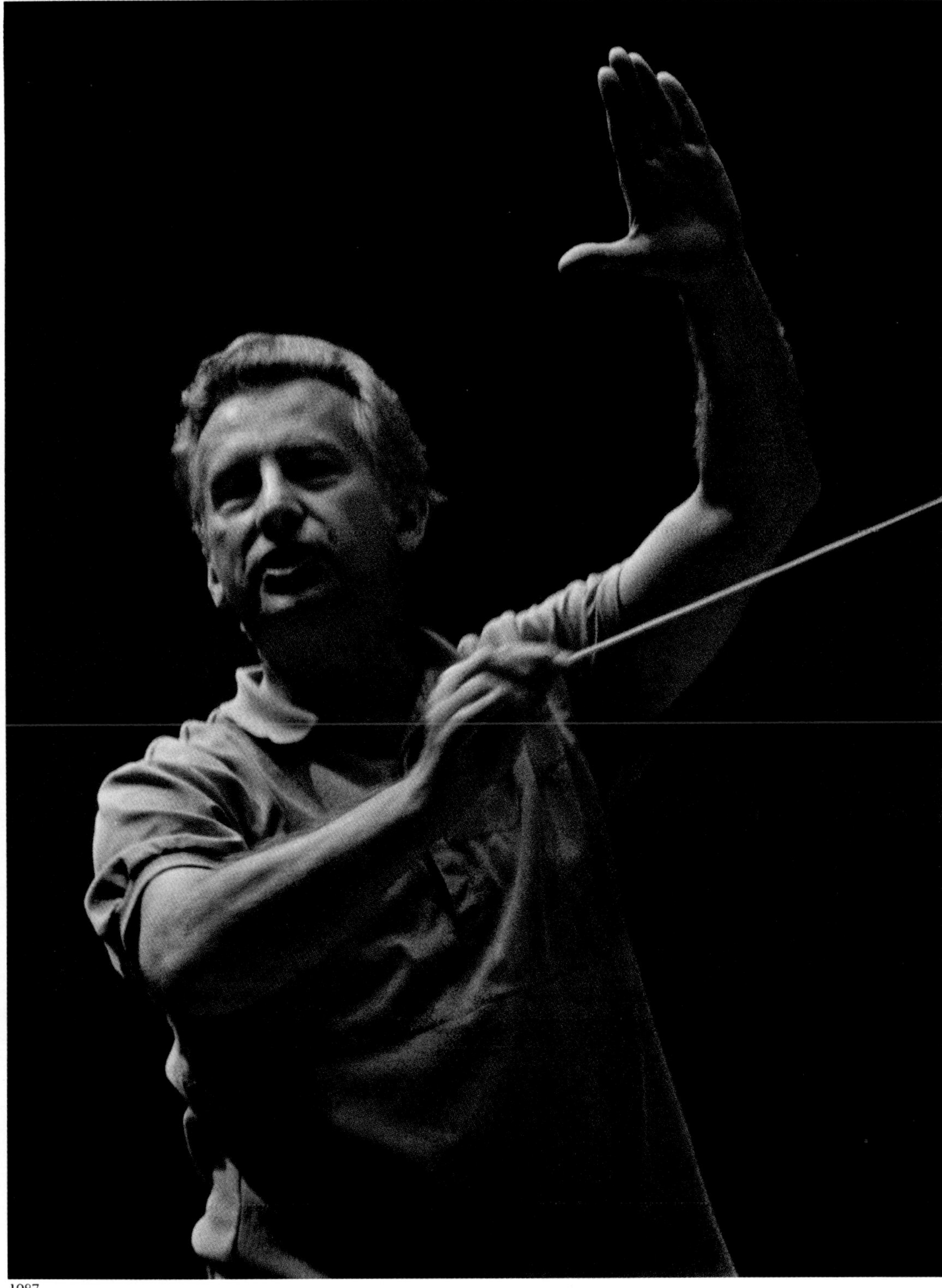

This highly regarded German conductor became the music director of the Detroit Symphony in 1984. Prior to that he had held similar positions with orchestras in Dresden and East Berlin. A maestro of the old school who studied with Abendroth and Scherchen, among others, he worked his way up in the municipal and regional opera houses of East Germany.

CHRISTOPHER HOGWOOD

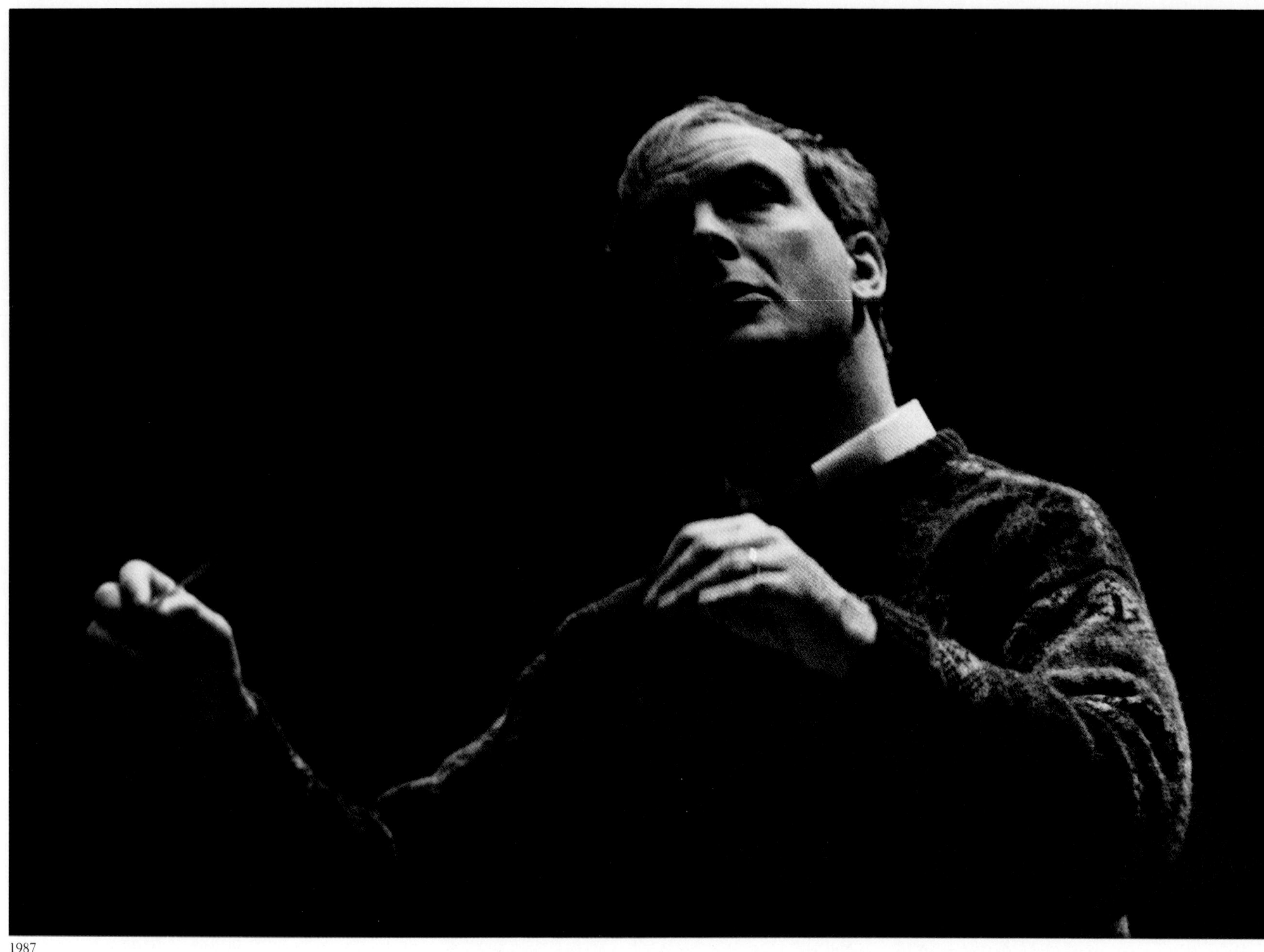

1987

Without him, it is doubtful that the early music movement could have achieved the widespread popularity it has enjoyed since the late 1970s. Educated at Cambridge, he had already begun to form his ideas about the performance of Baroque, Classical, and pre-Romantic music on original instruments during his years as a keyboard player with David Munrow's Early Music Consort of London. He formed the Academy of Ancient Music in 1973, and through his recordings with that ensemble—which include a landmark cycle of the Mozart symphonies—has done more than anyone to advance the cause of period performance practice of the orchestral repertory. He has an exceptionally acute mind, and has written a useful study of Handel, as well as a book entitled *Haydn's Visits to England*.

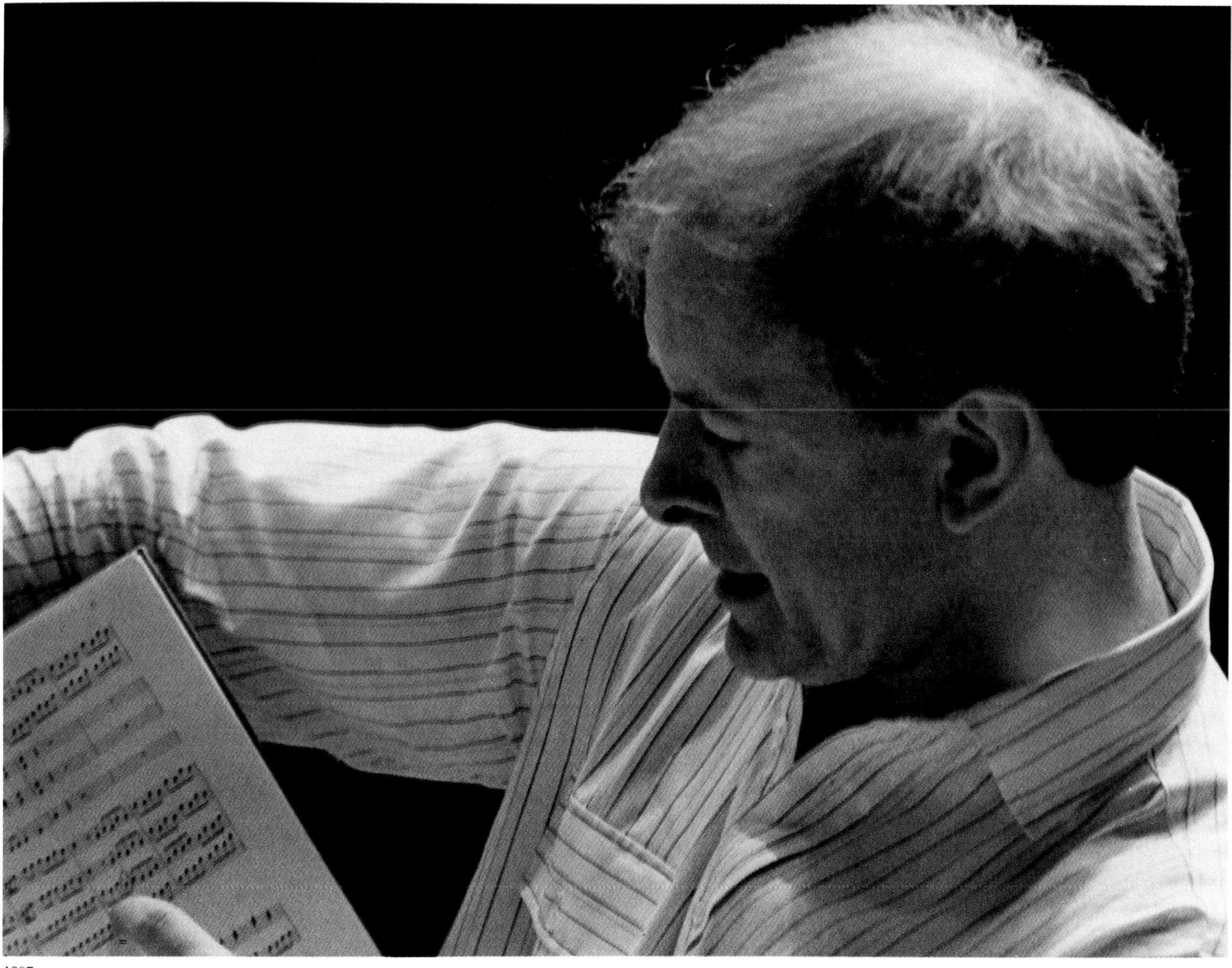

EUGENE ISTOMIN

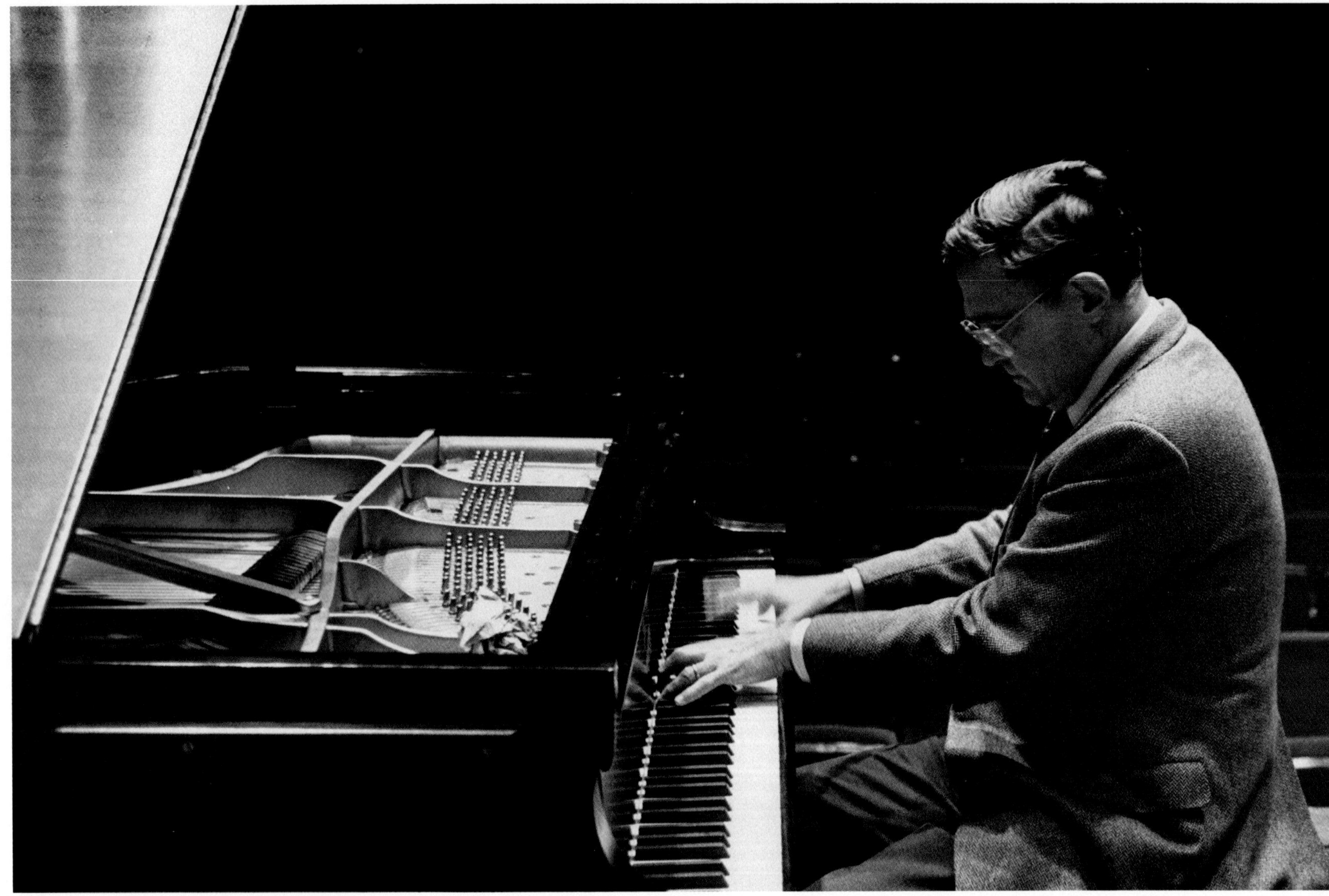

1988

Le Figaro has called him "one of the five greatest pianists of the world." Since his debut with the New York Philharmonic and Philadelphia Orchestra—at the age of seventeen—Eugene Istomin has gone from triumph to triumph, maintaining a schedule of appearances that keeps him traveling around the world, sometimes covering as much as 100,000 miles a year. Born in New York City of Russian parents—both of whom were singers—Istomin's career has spanned a half-century, but he has never lost the inspiration of youth nor frittered away the experience that has brought him depth and maturity.

NEEME JARVI

"Hemisemidemi" Neeme Jarvi, as certain idiosyncratic orchestral musicians have been known to call him, is one of the most interesting yet least publicized of today's orchestral conductors. The Estonian-born maestro studied in Leningrad under Evgeny Mravinsky, and before emigrating in 1980 had risen to the post of chief conductor of the Estonian State Symphony Orchestra. Since coming to the West he has built his reputation primarily on recordings of infrequently heard repertory, among which have been highly praised cycles devoted to the symphonies of Berwald, Martinu, and Prokofiev. A quick study, but also a fine craftsman, he was appointed music director of the Scottish National Orchestra in 1984.

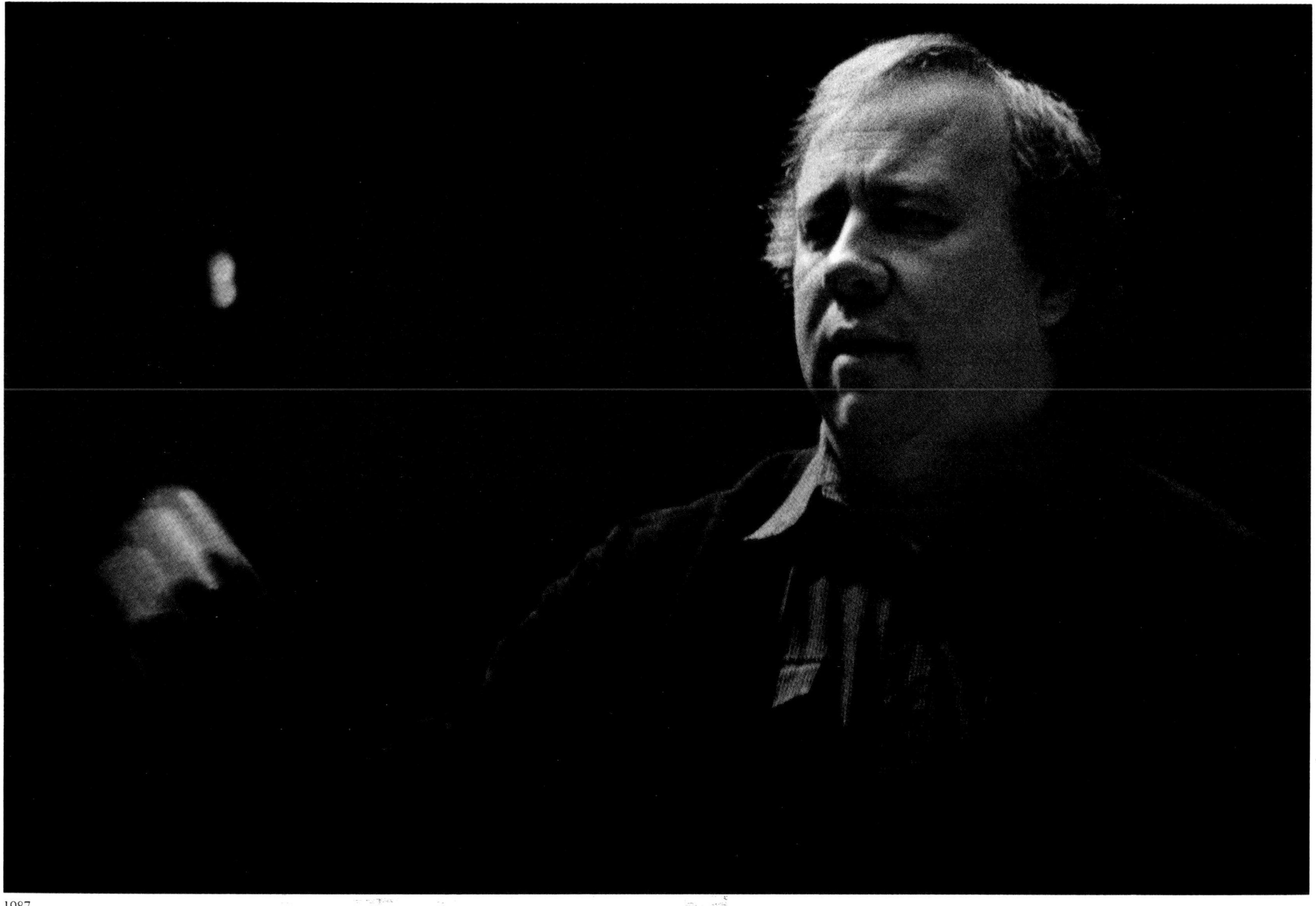

Danny Kaye

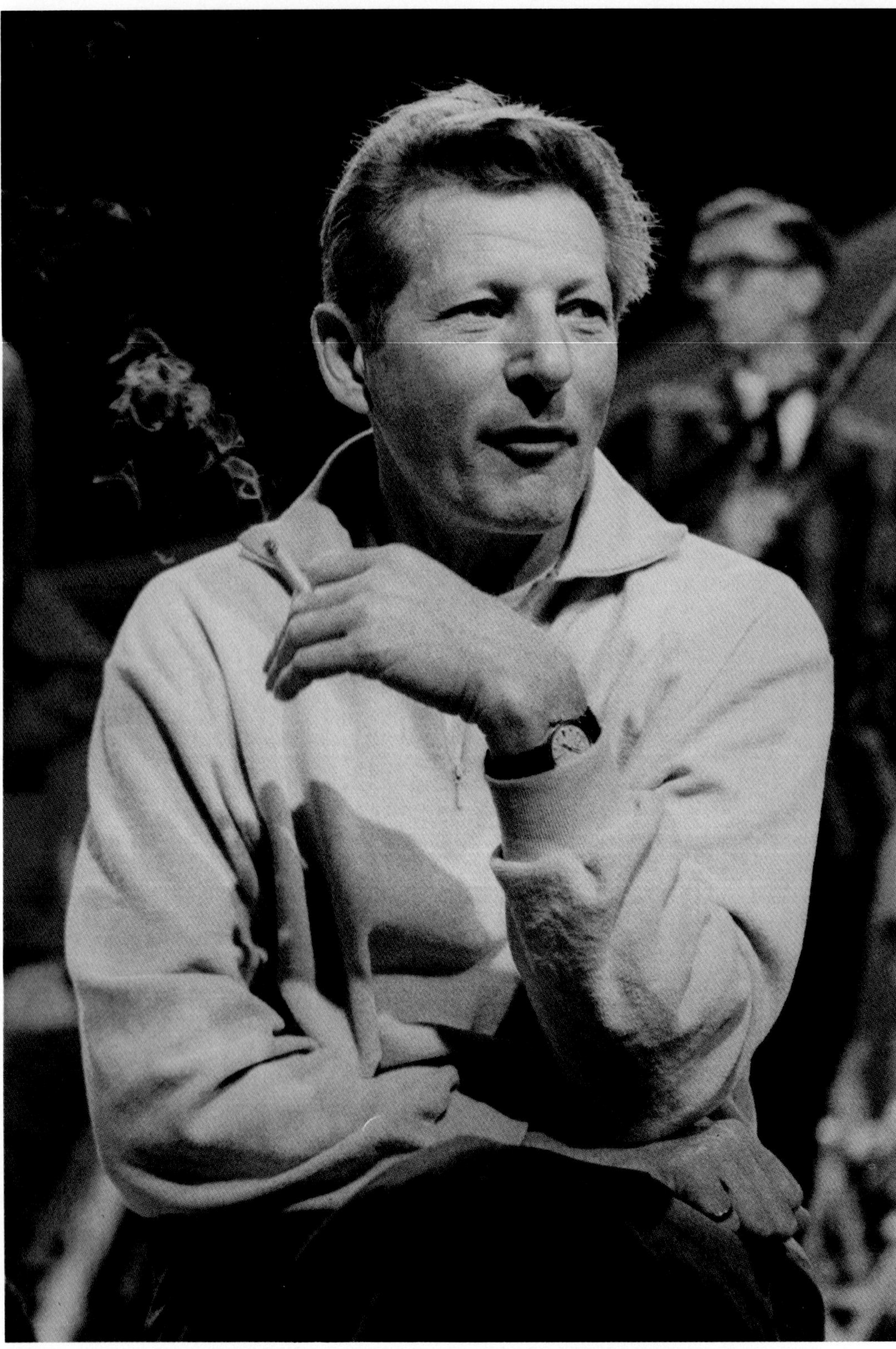

He was one of the most talented musical comedians we have known. During a rehearsal with the New York Philharmonic in the heyday of dictatorial conductors, he won the hearts of the musicians with a tough-talking preemptive strike against two notoriously difficult principal players—all in fun, of course. He brought his brilliant wit and phenomenal energy to whatever he did, whether it was singing, acting, or dancing.

Aram Khachaturian

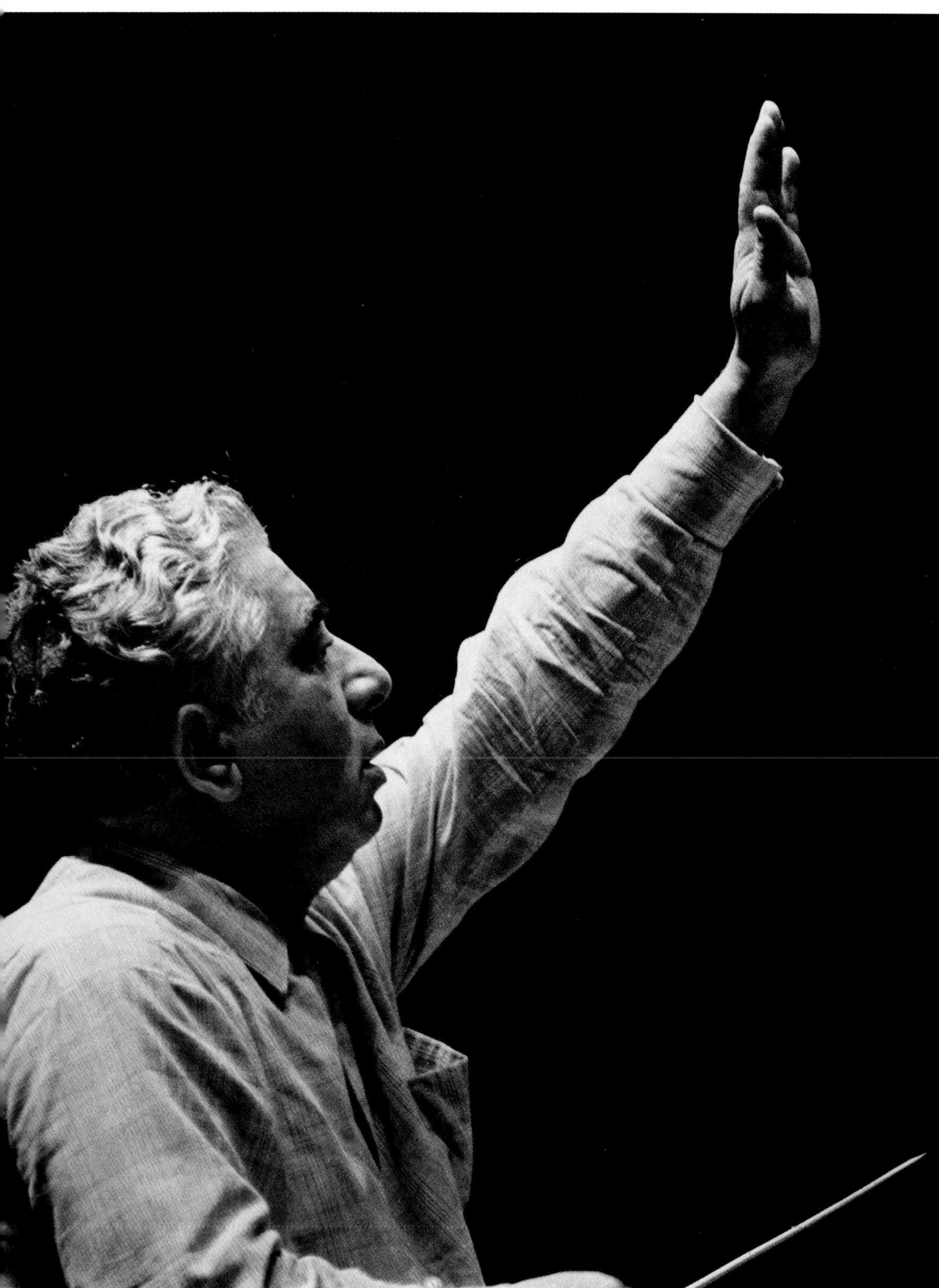

That most marvelous of rarities, a show-and-tell composer. The Armenian-born Khachaturian, photographed here at a rehearsal prior to his American conducting debut with the National Symphony Orchestra, became one of the most popular classical composers of the 20th century—yet he was still denounced by the Central Committee of the Communist Party in 1948 for "formalist tendencies." In his fiery, energetic, impulsive, and familiar music he spoke for his people, a hot-blooded race, in a way that won the hearts of listeners everywhere.

Ralph Kirkpatrick

The quintessential scholar-musician, he brought the harpsichord out of the quasi-Romantic mists of early 20th-century antiquarianism and back into the mainstream of musical life. He assembled the standard catalog of the works of Domenico Scarlatti, edited important keyboard compositions by Scarlatti and Bach, and concertized frequently on the harpsichord (also, on occasion, giving brilliant, memorable performances on the clavichord and the fortepiano). His presence at Yale, where he served on the faculty from 1940 until 1978, was a blessing to several generations of music students there, and his example of fidelity to 18th-century style has guided virtually every harpsichordist performing today.

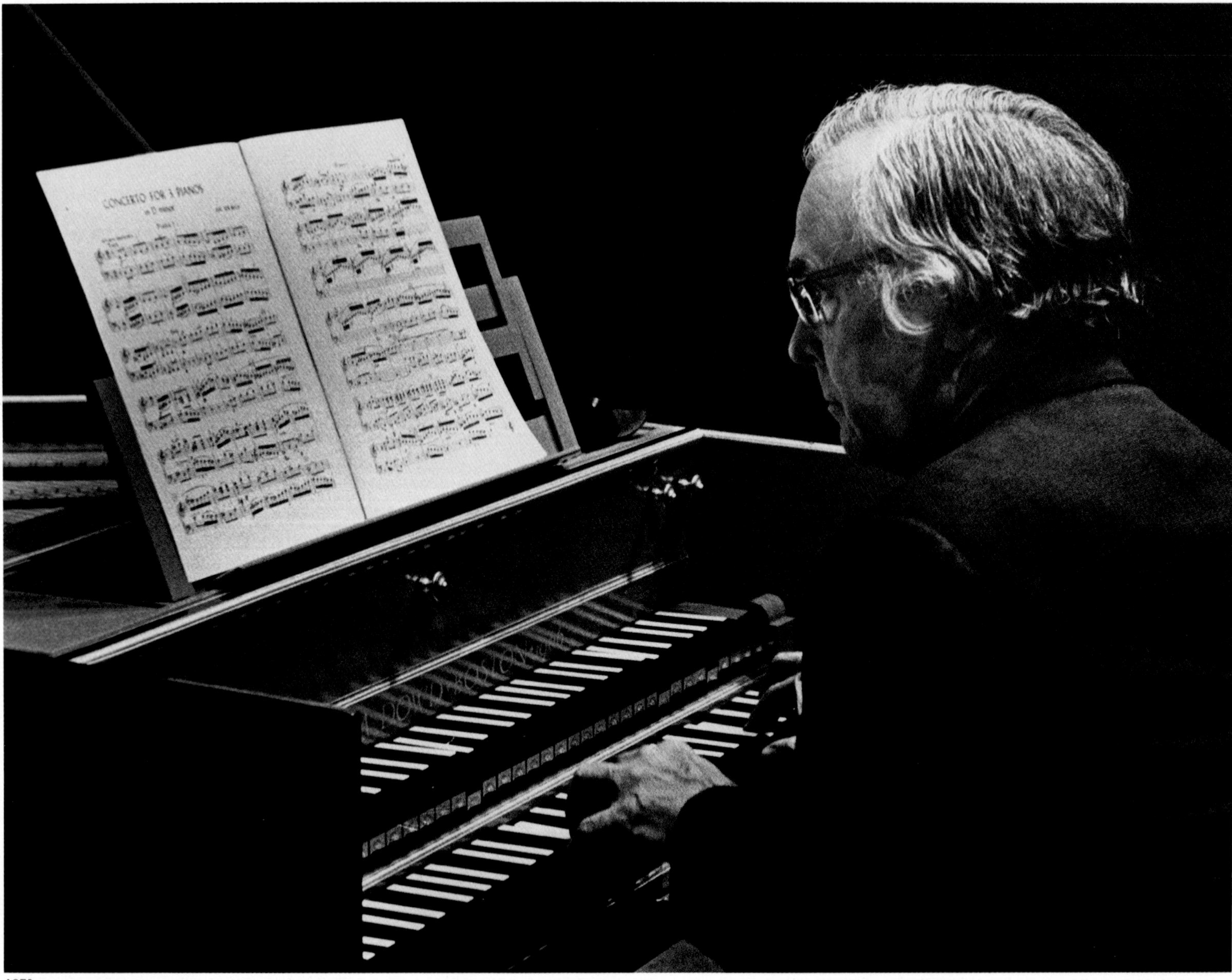

1973

TOSHIKO KOHNO

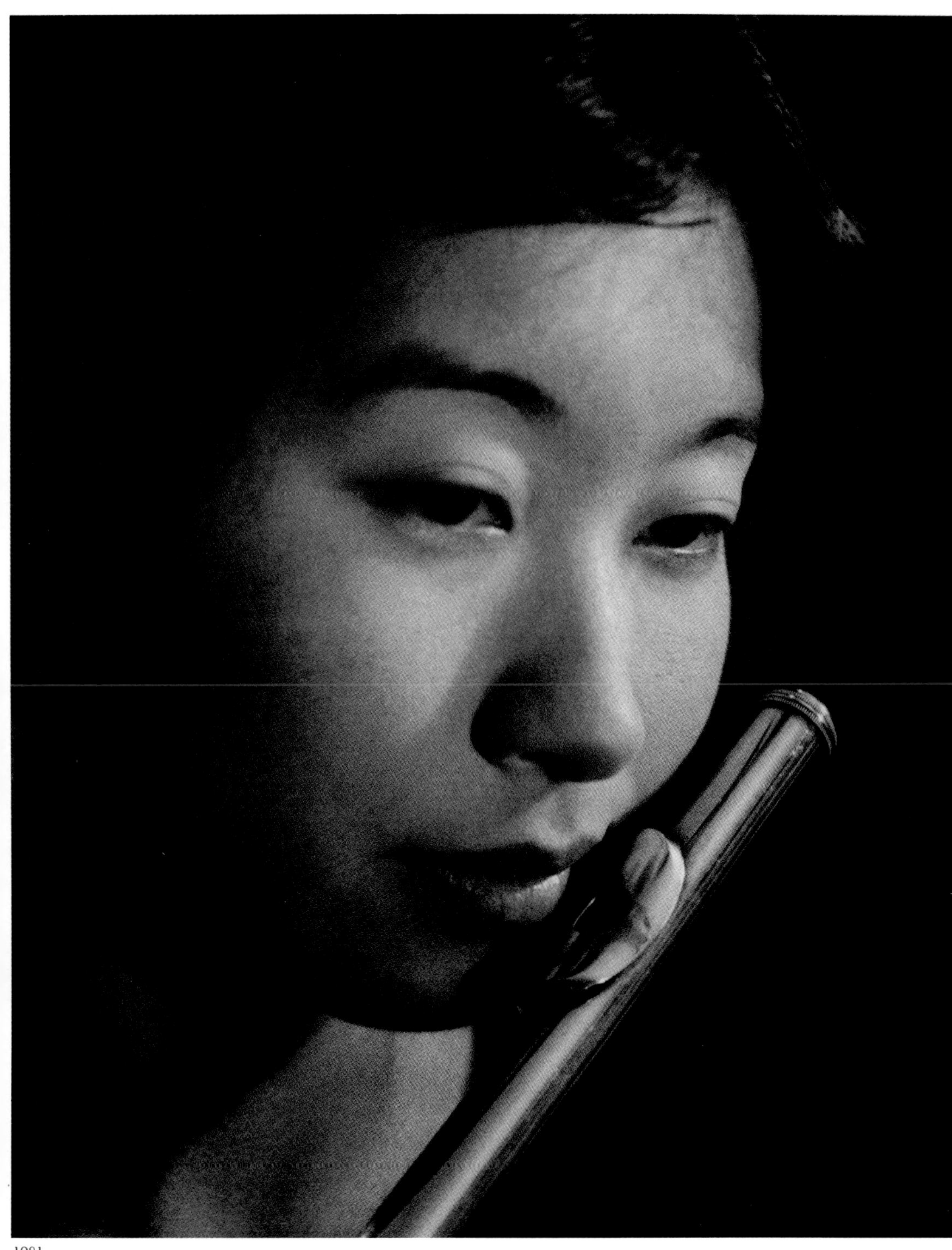

That quiet, young face and delicate presence belie the serious, intense musician who has been the National Symphony's principal flutist since 1979. Her beauty of tone has become one of the hallmarks of the NSO sound, and her virtuosity has stood the ensemble in good stead as it continues its push into the top rank of American orchestras. Always a compliant and sensitive player, each season she grows musically more adventurous and confident.

1981

ERICH LEINSDORF

One of the 20th century's most versatile and proven conductors, he has stood at the crossroads of our musical culture on numerous occasions—in Salzburg as the assistant to Toscanini and Walter in 1934; with the Metropolitan Opera during the golden pre- and post-World War II decades; and as music director of the Boston Symphony from 1962 to 1969. He has guest conducted everywhere, usually to the benefit of the host orchestra ("Playing with Leinsdorf for two weeks is like going back to school," a string player with a major orchestra remarked after one of his engagements), and he knows every nook and cranny of the repertory. Seemingly indifferent, always reined-in, he is the pure antithesis of Leonard Bernstein. He has also written cogently on music and conducting.

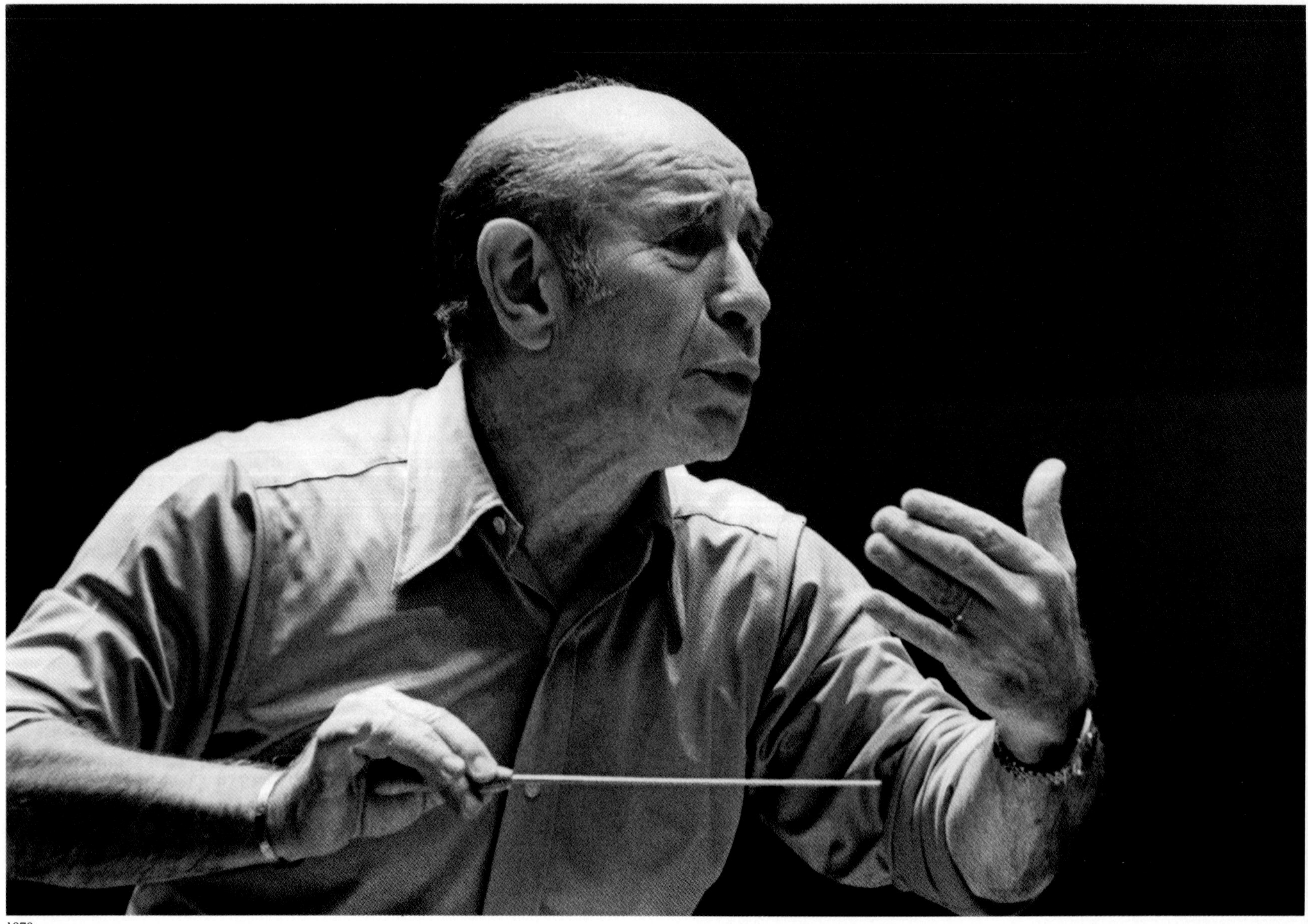

1979

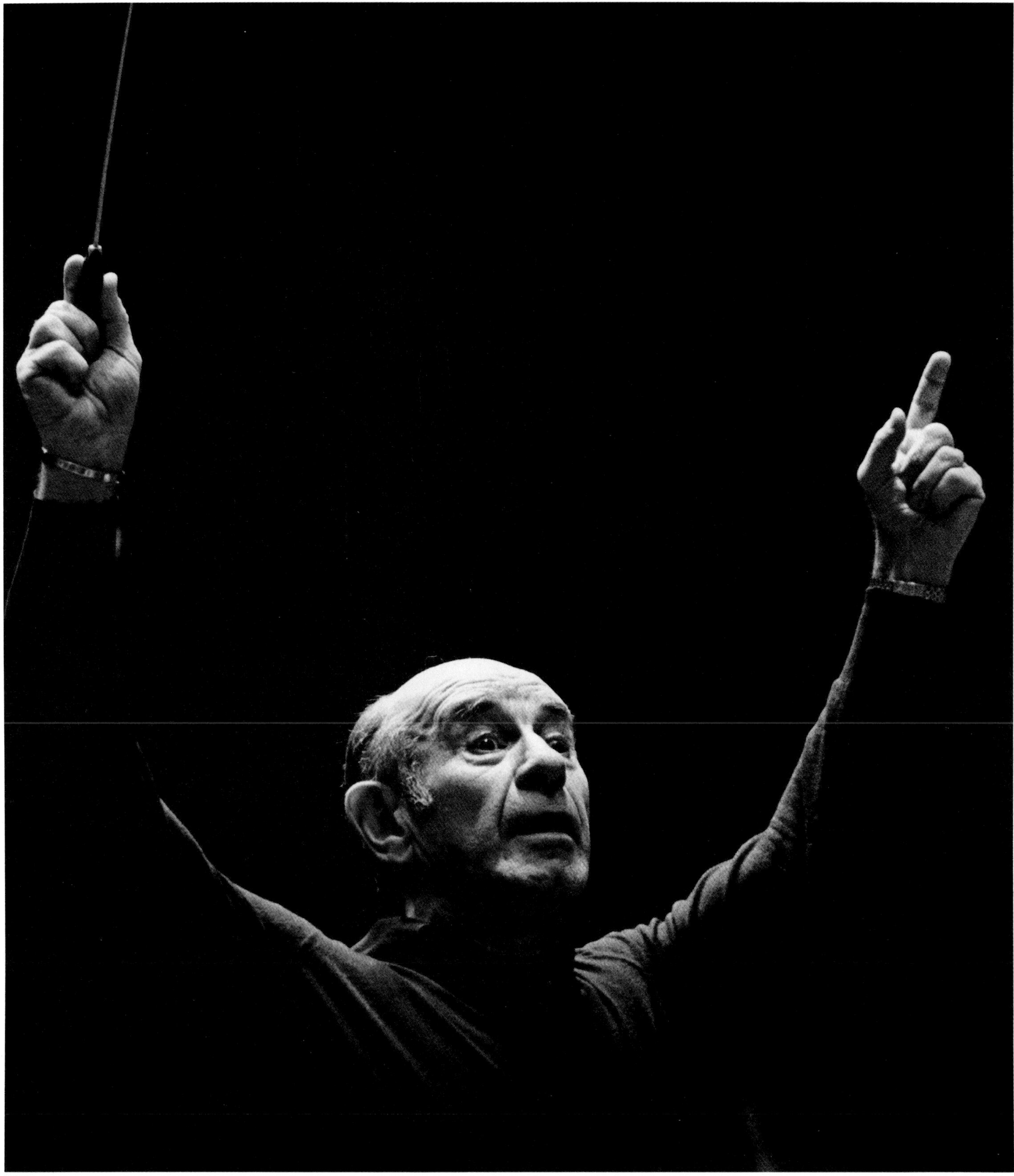

1977

RAYMOND LEPPARD

A specialist in "early music" long before there was an early music movement, Raymond Leppard played a decisive role in bringing the operas of Monteverdi and Cavalli back into the repertory. The London-born harpsichordist and conductor has more recently ventured into the mainstream symphonic repertory, and in 1987 became music director of the Indianapolis Symphony Orchestra. A gifted writer, skillful editor, and noted *bon vivant* with a delightful sense of humor, he is one of the music world's most versatile and cherished talents.

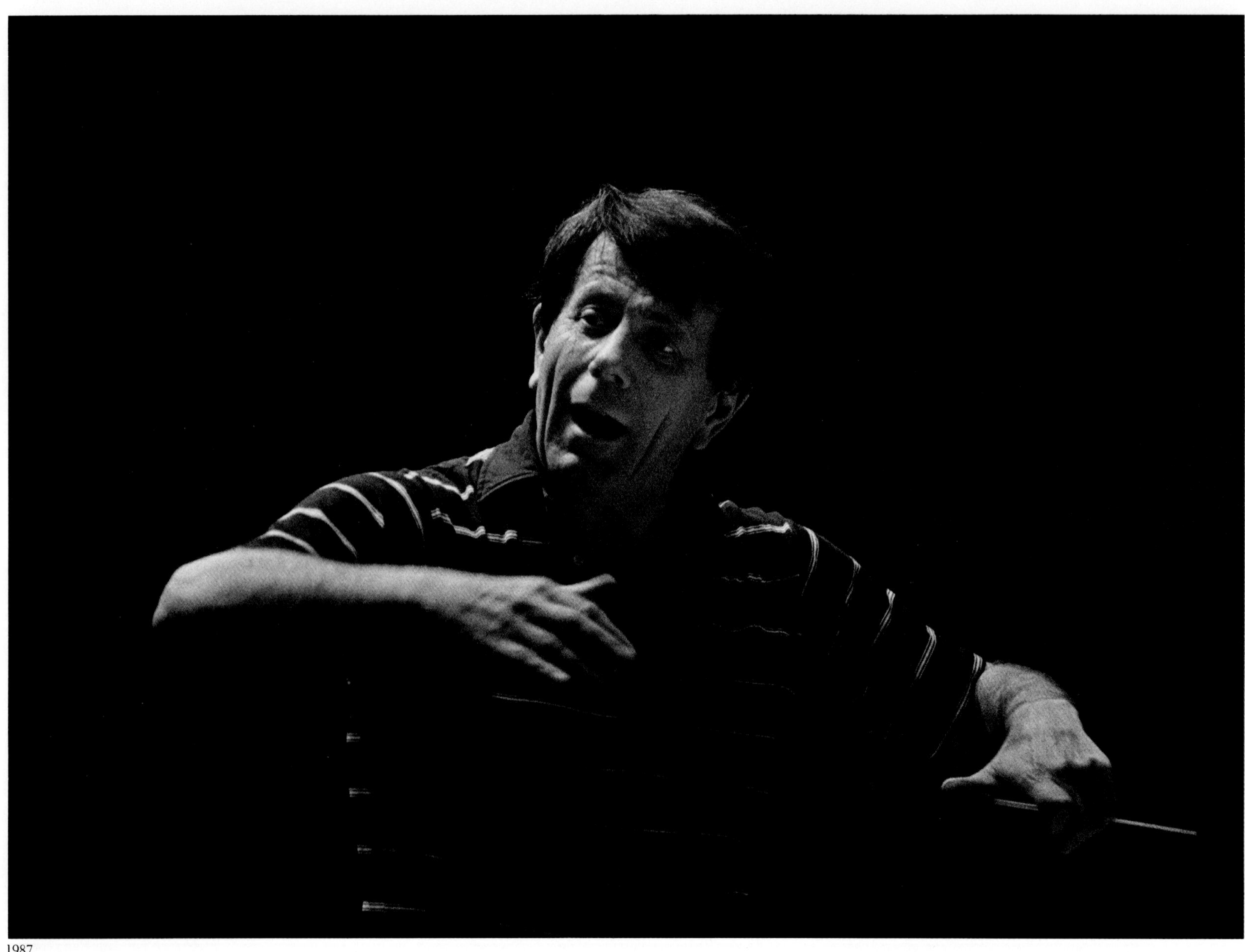

1987

REILLY LEWIS

Reilly Lewis, the founder and conductor of the Washington Bach Consort, is a superb organist and harpsichordist as well as a masterful conductor. His informed and sensitive interpretations of the major choral works of Bach have been among the musical highlights of many Washington seasons. In 1985, Lewis led the WBC on a historic tour of Germany that included a performance in Leipzig as part of the 300th anniversary celebration of Bach's birth.

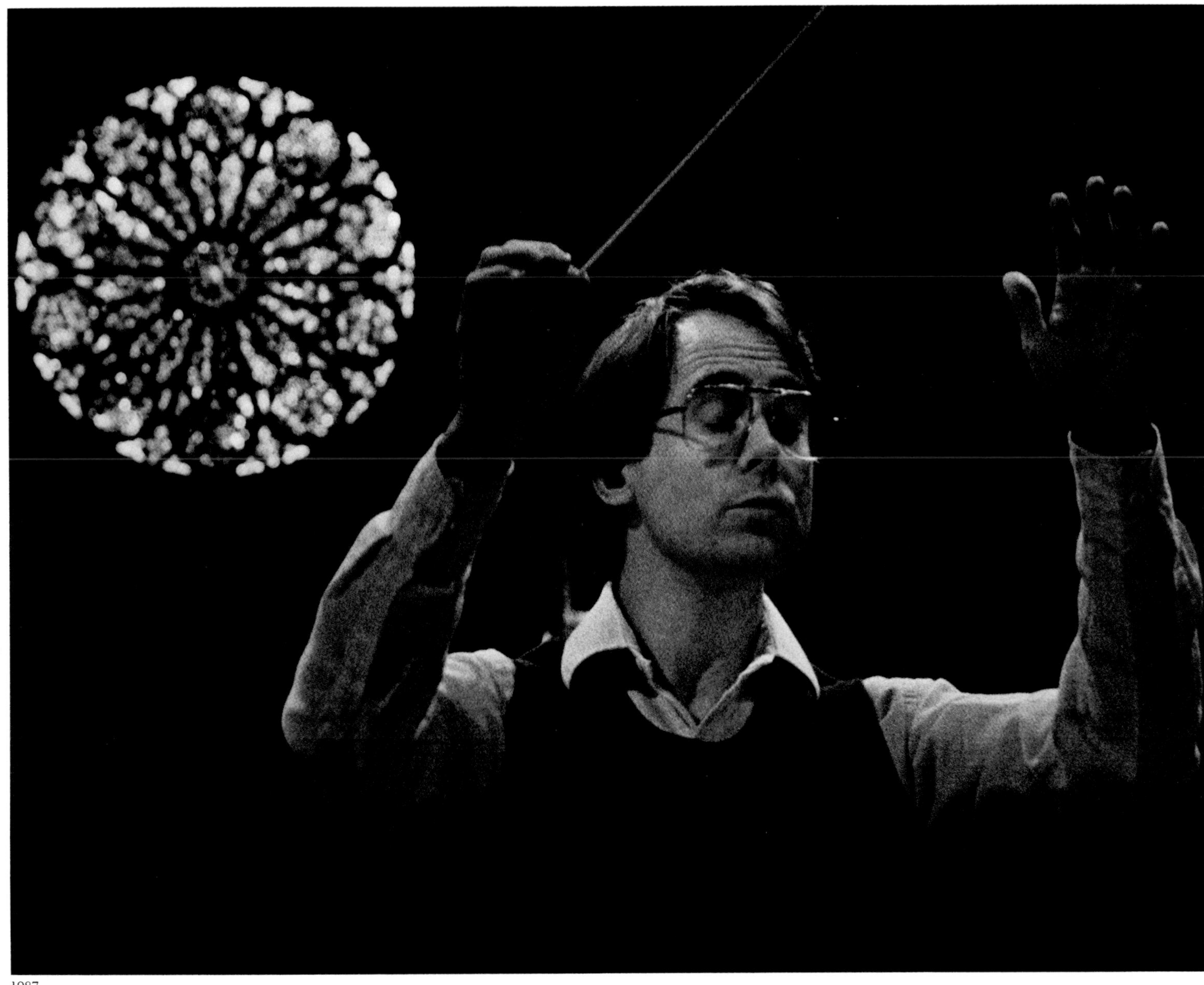

CECILE LICAD

A student of Rudolph Serkin, Cecile Licad was hailed as a major new talent in the early 1980s. She was signed to a recording contract by a major American label, heavily promoted, and encouraged to play repertoire for which she was not ready. Now going through a period of artistic reassessment, she remains an appealing performer with prospects of a solid career.

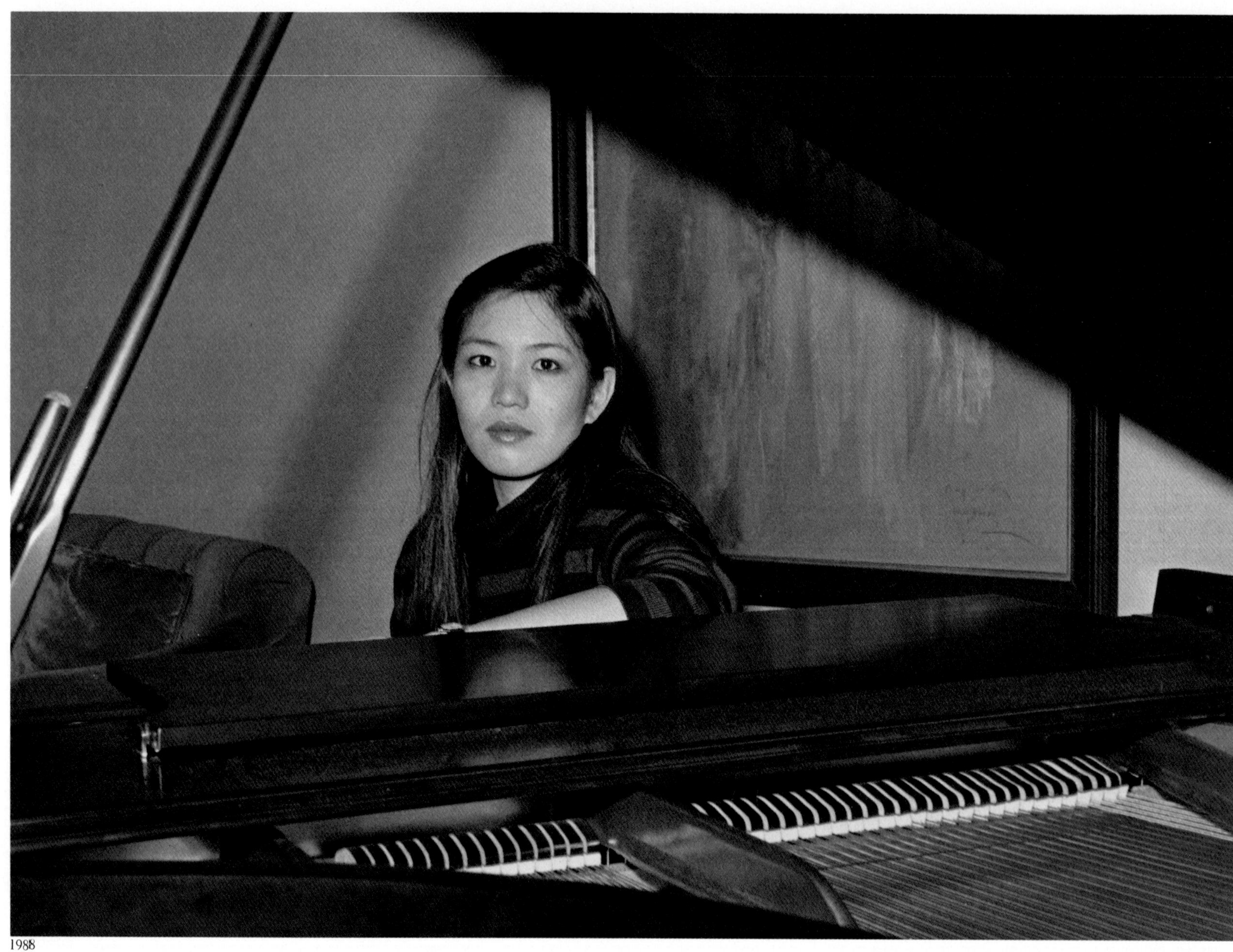

GEORGE LONDON

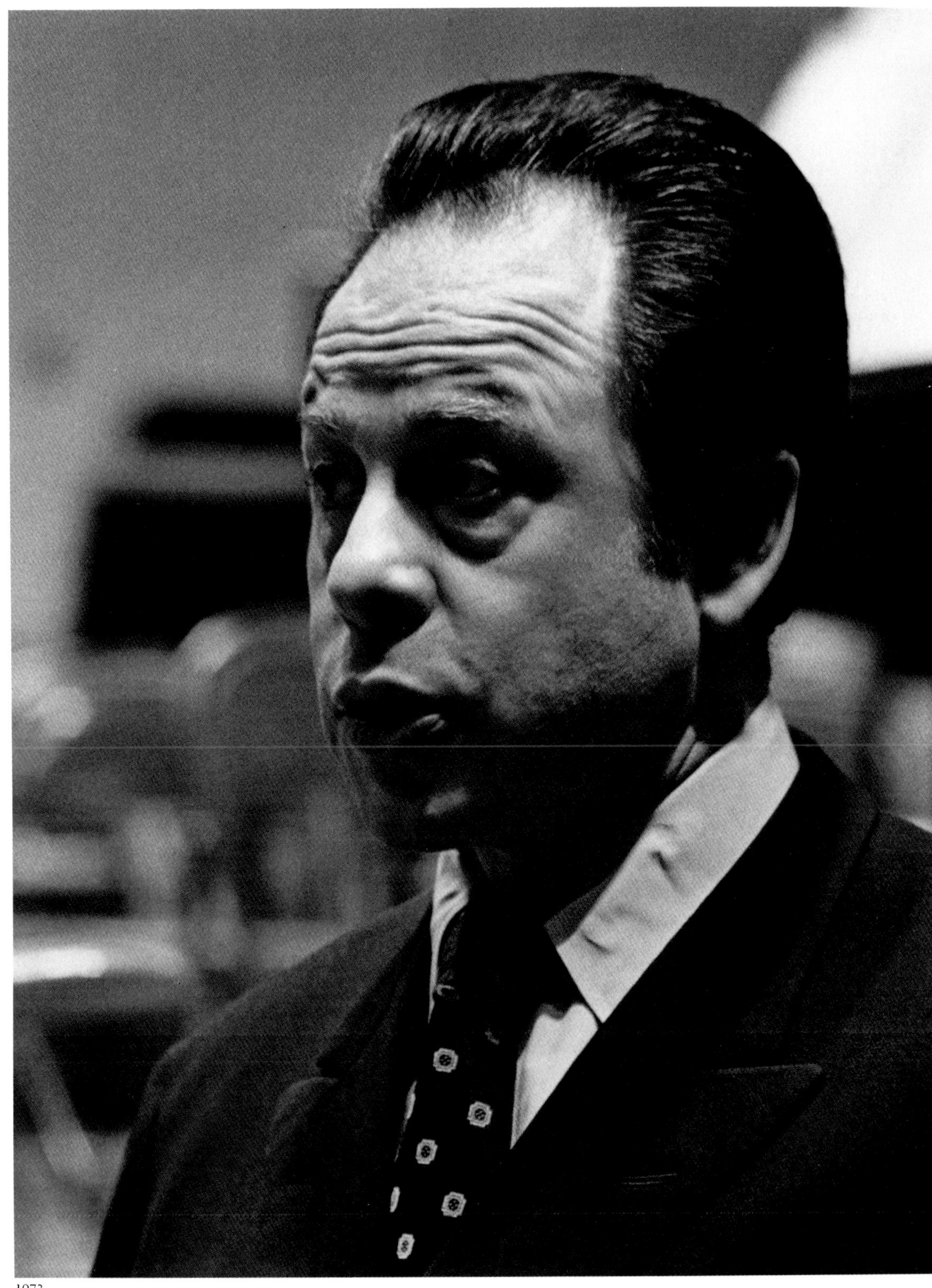

His powerfully theatrical interpretations of such roles as Boris Godunov, Amfortas, Wotan, Scarpia, Figaro, Don Giovanni, Escamillo, and Amonasro established George London as one of the preeminent singers of his generation. He was the first non-Russian to perform the role of Boris at the Bolshoi Theater, and had barely reached the plateau of vocal maturity when paralysis of the larynx tragically ended his career as a performer. He became the artistic director of the Kennedy Center in 1968, and was named general director of the Washington Opera in 1975. In 1977, a massive coronary ended this second phase of his career; he remained an invalid until his death in 1985.

1973

Two of the most powerful and persuasive of today's younger instrumentalists, Ma and Perahia represent what is best in American musical life. Thoughtful, versatile, thoroughly educated musicians, they have developed distinctive performing styles while remaining sensitive to the stylistic demands of the works they interpret. Both are consummate virtuosos, and each, in his way, is a poet: Ma intones dramatically, with epic splendor, while Perahia sings in phrases full of lyric grace.

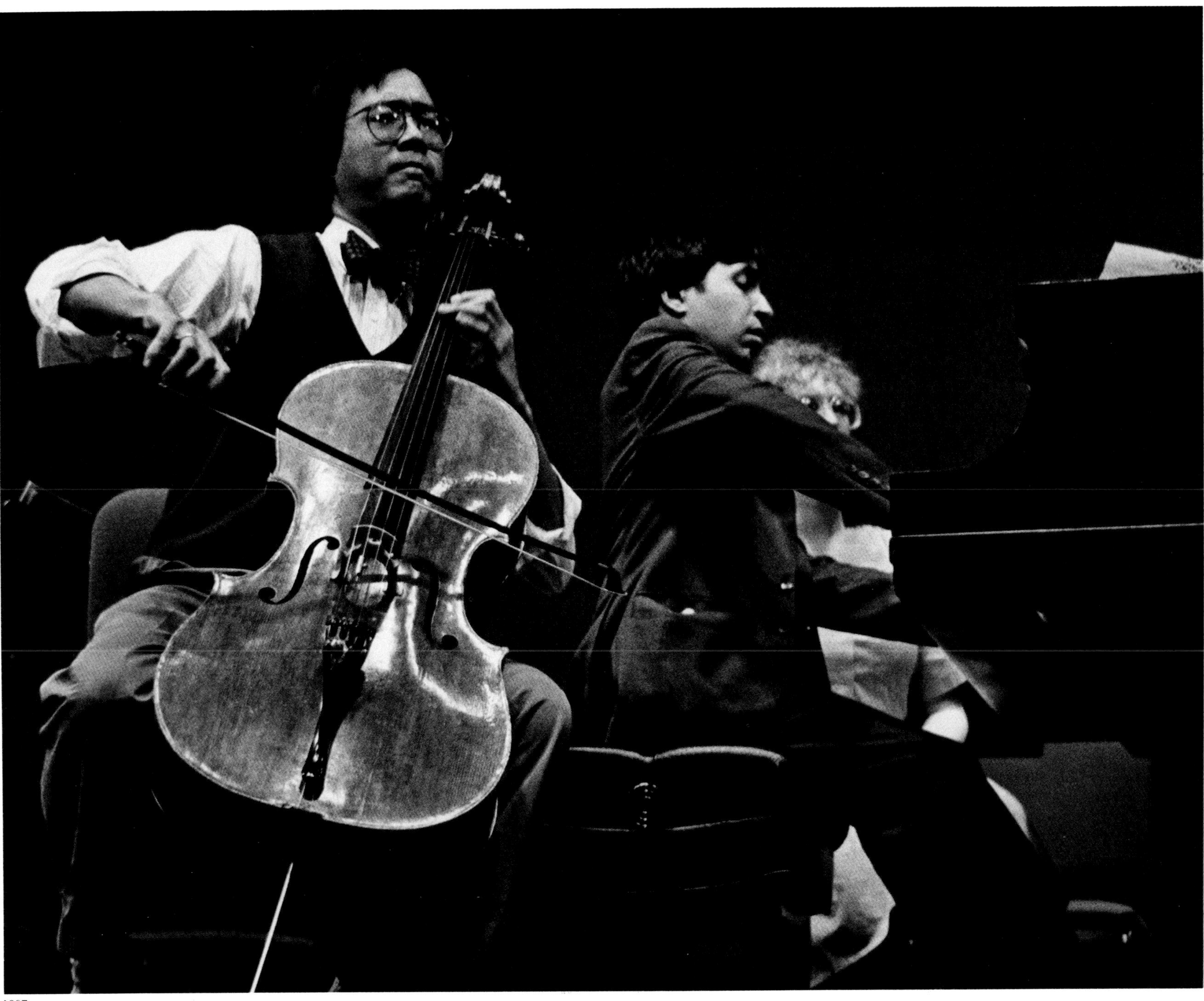

1987

Lorin Maazel

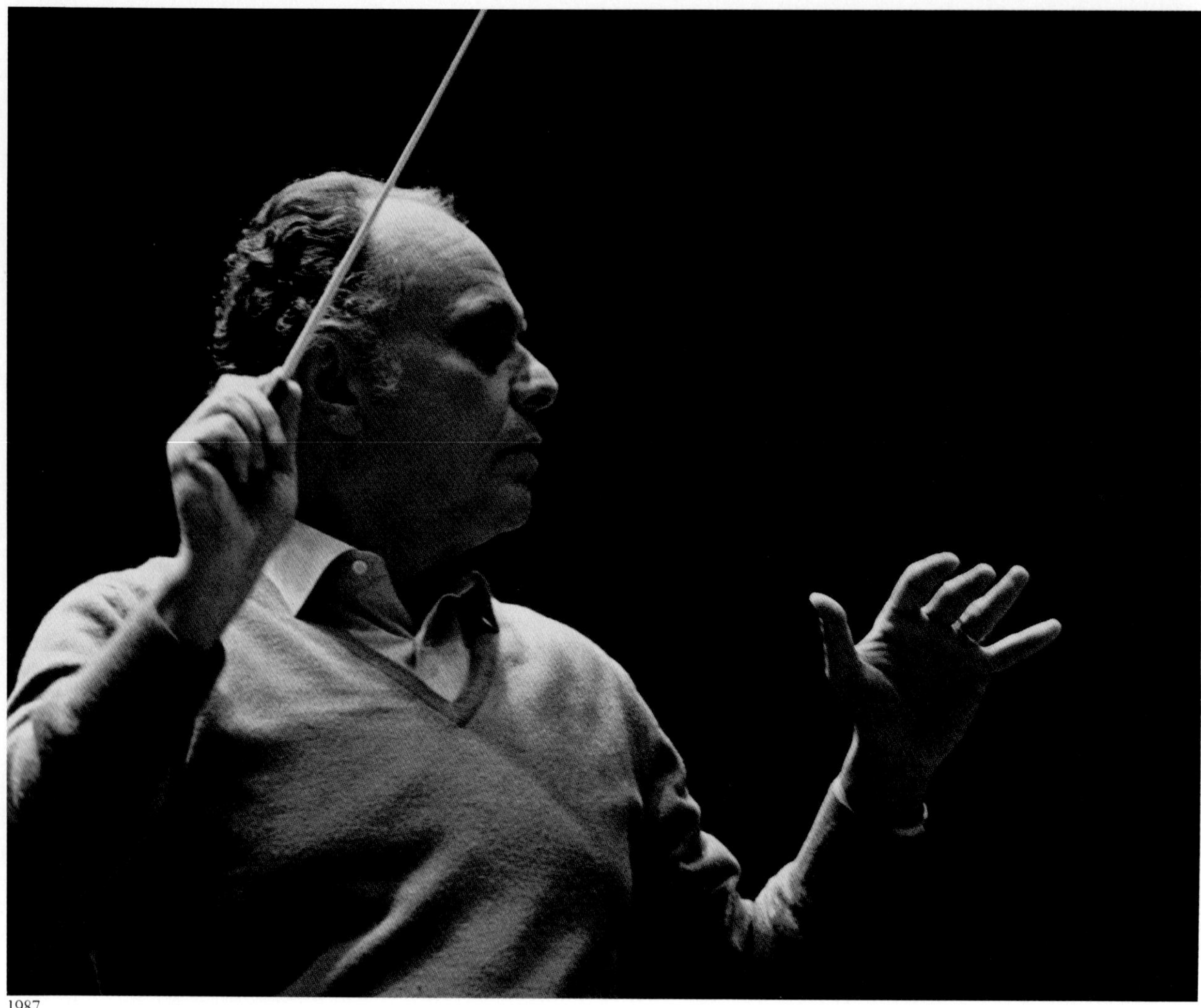

1987

Brilliant, articulate, ambitious, self-assured, and formidably capable, he has emerged as one of the world's leading conductors in a career spanning half a century. It began in 1939 with an appearance at the New York World's Fair. Engagements at the Hollywood Bowl and with Toscanini's NBC Symphony Orchestra soon followed. He attended the University of Pittsburgh and played in the back stands of the Pittsburgh Symphony's violin section, went to Italy on a Fulbright, and continued to polish his skills as a conductor. Work in opera and recordings with a number of Europe's top orchestras firmly established him as a major talent, and in 1972 he was offered the music directorship of the Cleveland Orchestra. In the ten years he was there he maintained the ensemble at the pinnacle of discipline it had attained under Szell, while broadening its repertory and deepening and darkening its sound. He was named director of the Vienna State Opera in 1982, but grew tired of meddlesome ministers, and left after two seasons. He accepted a post as music advisor to his hometown Pittsburgh Symphony in 1984 and will become the orchestra's music director as of the 1988–89 season. Few conductors in the world today possess his combination of experience, ability, and intellect.

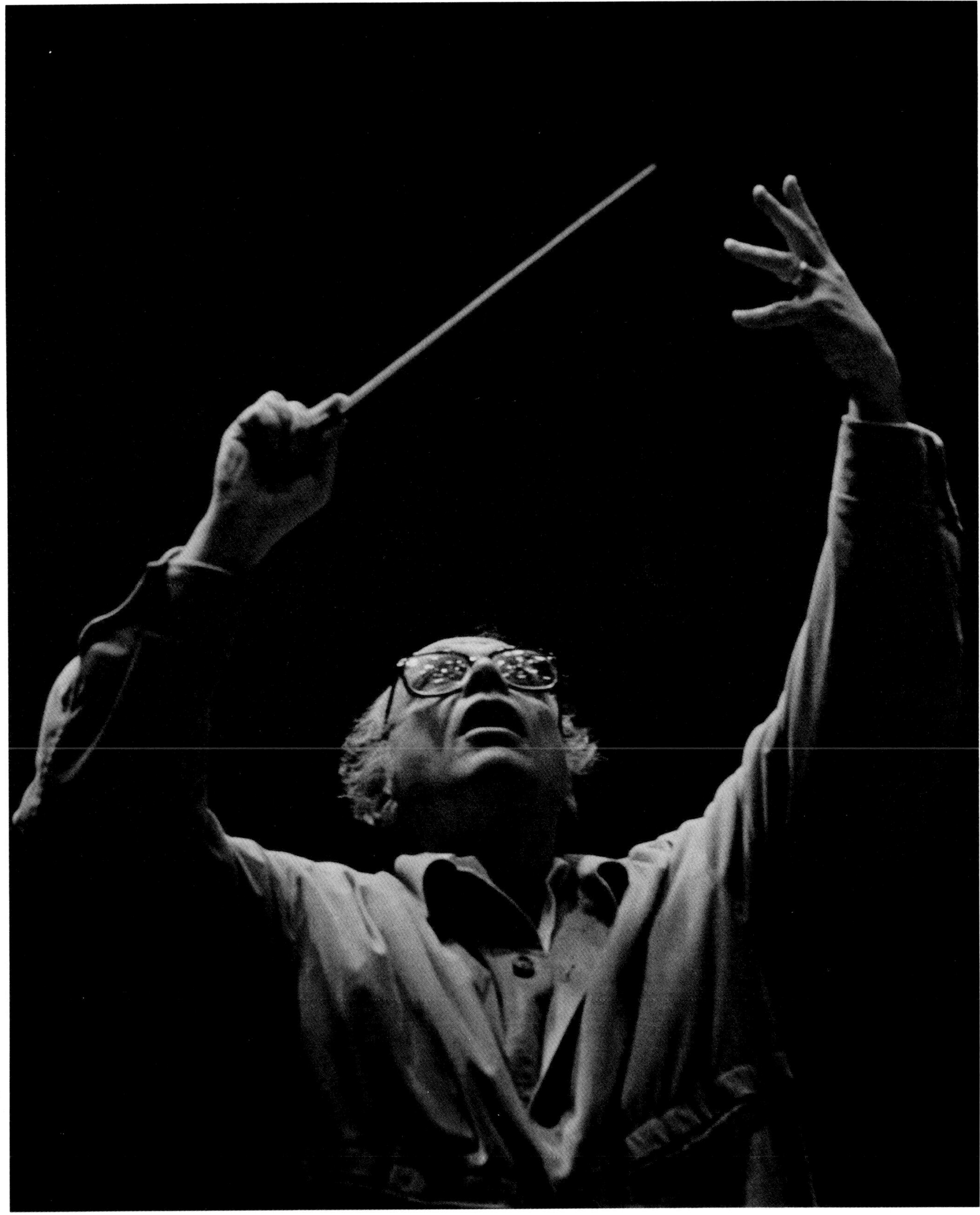

1987

NEVILLE MARRINER

Known to millions through his recordings with the Academy of St. Martin-in-the-Fields, which he organized in 1959, he has distinguished himself in every aspect of the chamber repertory as a conductor of taste and perception. He came up through the ranks, serving as a violinist in the Philharmonia Orchestra and as principal second violin of the London Symphony Orchestra from 1956 to 1968. Knighted in 1979, the same year he was named music director of the Minnesota Orchestra, he has continued to interpret and reinterpret the great symphonic works of the 18th and early 19th centuries with singular success.

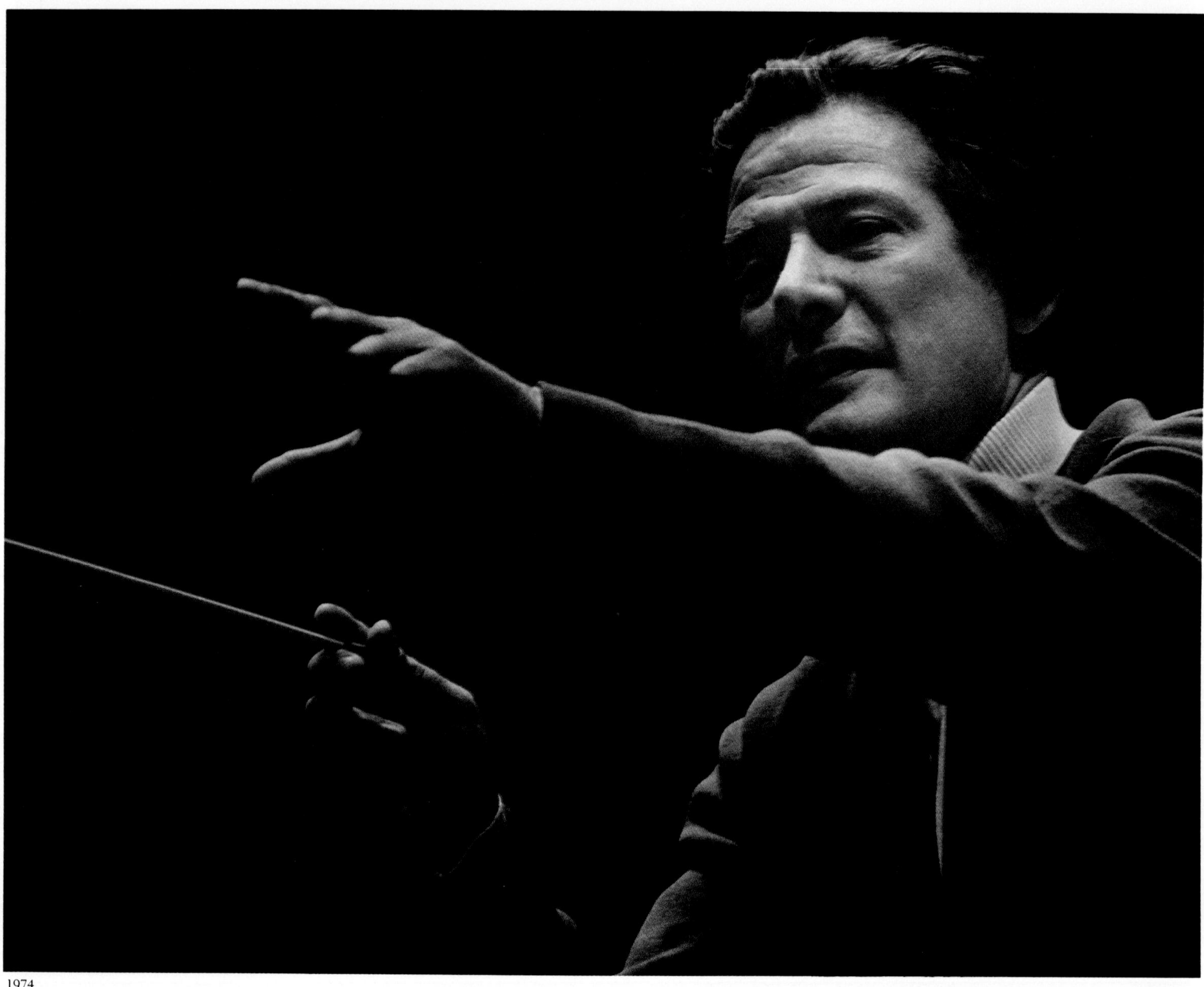

1974

John Martin

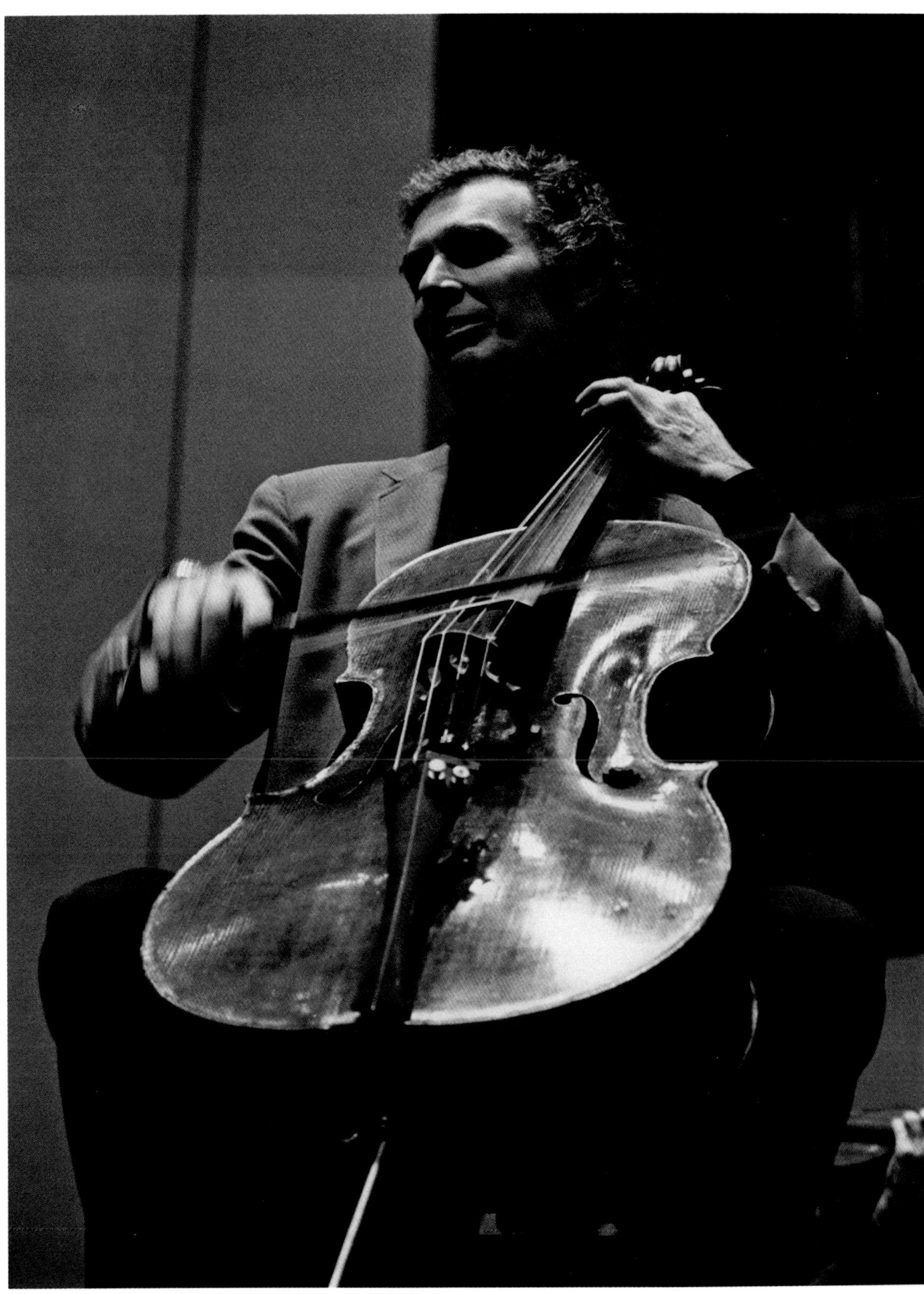

He has been sitting at the center of the National Symphony as its principal cello for more than forty years, and has never grown tired of making music. He possesses the alertness and ingenuity of an athlete, the sureness and concentration of a surgeon, and, above all, that curious blend of restraint and panache that characterizes a section leader. While he can become almost meditative during a performance, he steps easily into the spotlight when a solo comes his way. Soft-spoken, at times even shy, he has a gentle sense of humor and a winning smile. His tone is frequently rather intense, yet his playing has warmth and a true sense of poetry.

1980

Jean Martinon

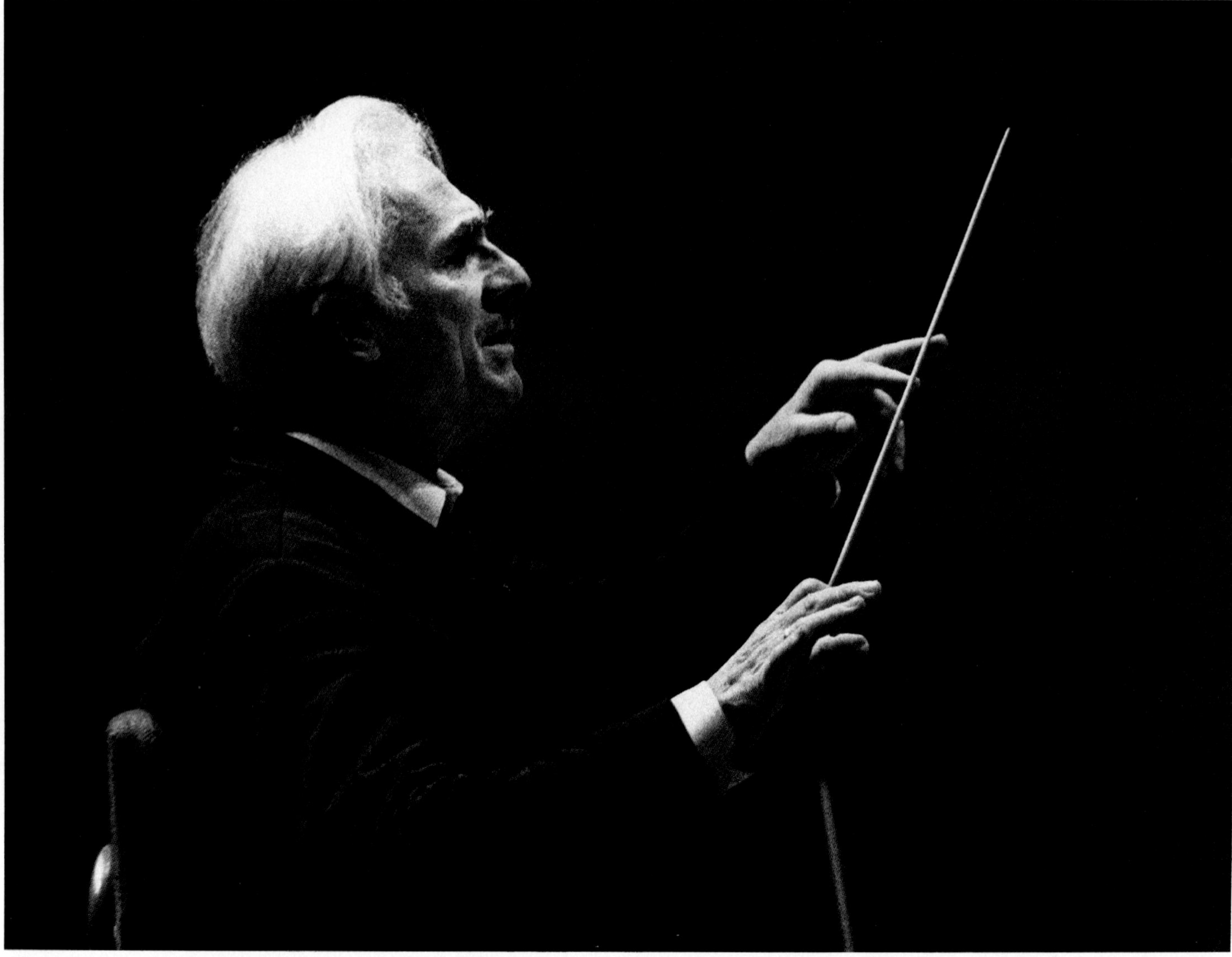

1973

Really a conductor-composer, like Antal Dorati, Jean Martinon graduated from the Paris Conservatoire in 1929 and got both of his careers underway before the outbreak of World War II. During the war, he spent two years in a prisoner-of-war camp. He resumed his conducting career after the liberation, heading various European orchestras before being summoned to Chicago in 1963, following the death of Fritz Reiner. He returned to Paris in 1968 as music director of L'Orchestre Nationale de France, a post he held until shortly before his death in 1976. Jean Martinon possessed a startling mastery of 20th-century music, covering the whole range of styles from Nielsen and Mahler to Ravel, Roussel (one of his teachers), to Varèse, and Bartók. Although his tenure with the Chicago Symphony was relatively brief (1963–1968), his recordings with that orchestra remain among the greatest made anywhere, at any time. His interpretations were marked by an extraordinary blend of intellect, emotion, and Gallic refinement.

MESRU MEHMEDOV

An eloquent conductor who met a tragic end, Mehmedov was a dedicated and serious musician quite removed from any sort of egotistical pretence or show. He died in a plane crash in 1971 while on his way to take up the directorship of the Sofia Philharmonic Orchestra in his native Bulgaria.

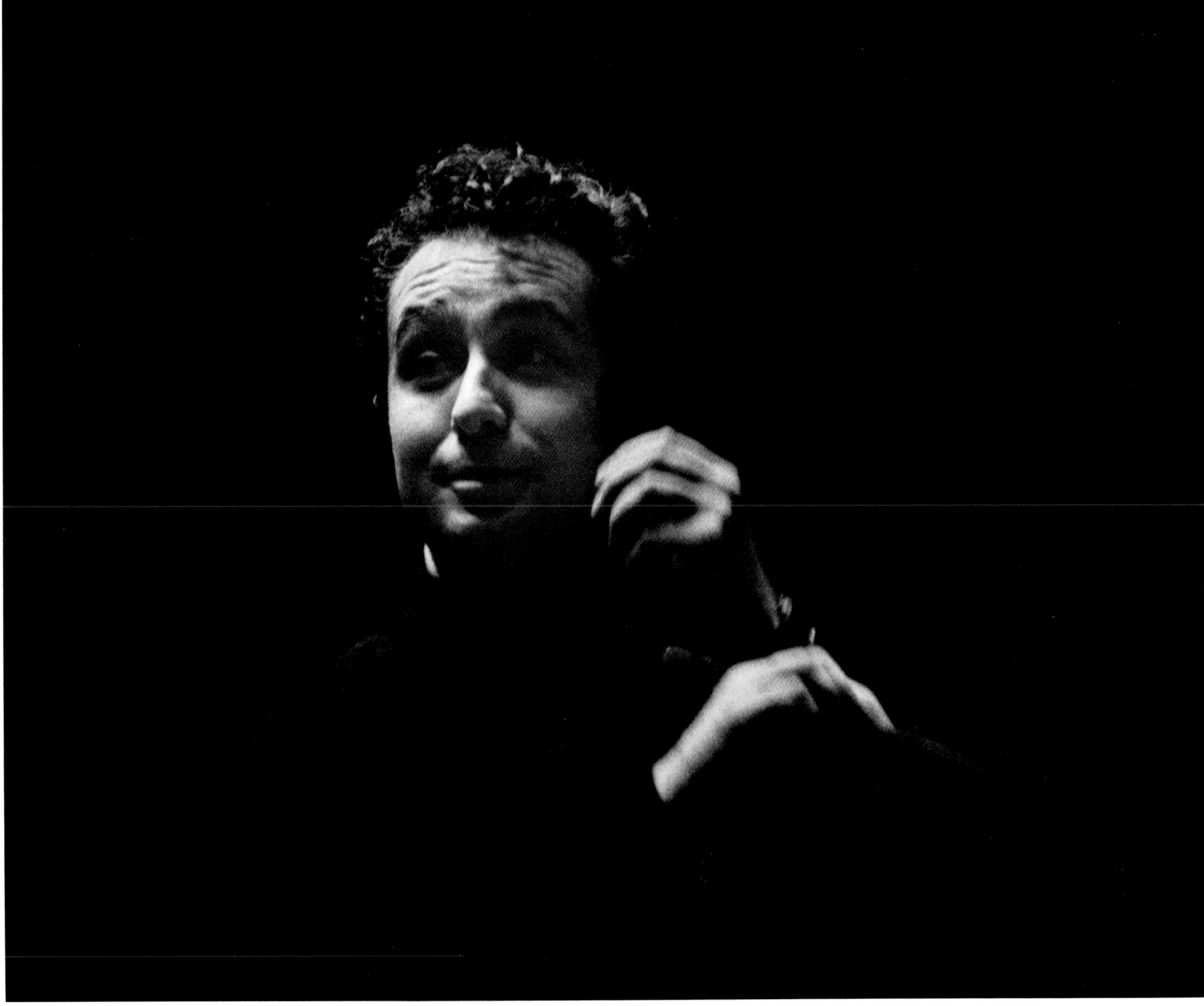

1970

Zubin Mehta

One of the acknowledged stars among present-day conductors, Zubin Mehta is a *wunderkind* who made good, a serious and principled musician who has been conducting the world's top orchestras since he was in his twenties. With his broad sense of culture and history, he is at home in Los Angeles, New York, Vienna, and Tel Aviv; he has traveled everywhere, even to the Antarctic. He is capable of conducting performances of blazing intensity in both the opera house and the concert hall, and is especially noted for his interpretations of Mahler, Strauss, and Stravinsky. Long thought of as a glamor boy of the podium, he is actually a very private person with a generous nature and compelling sense of purpose. Although he has been hounded by the New York press since becoming music director of the Philharmonic in 1978, he has genuine ability and does his homework, rarely stumbling in rehearsal or performance.

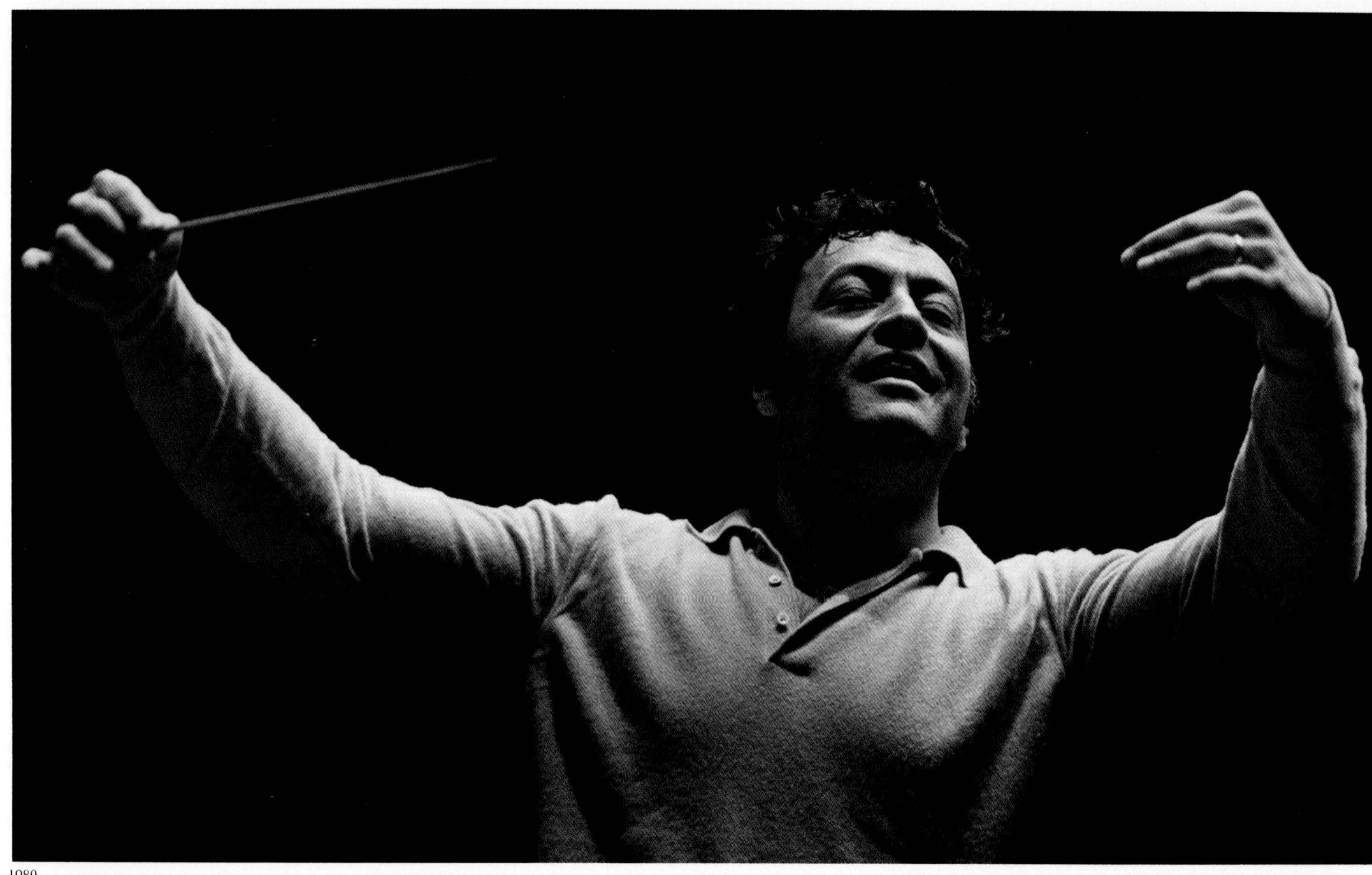

1980

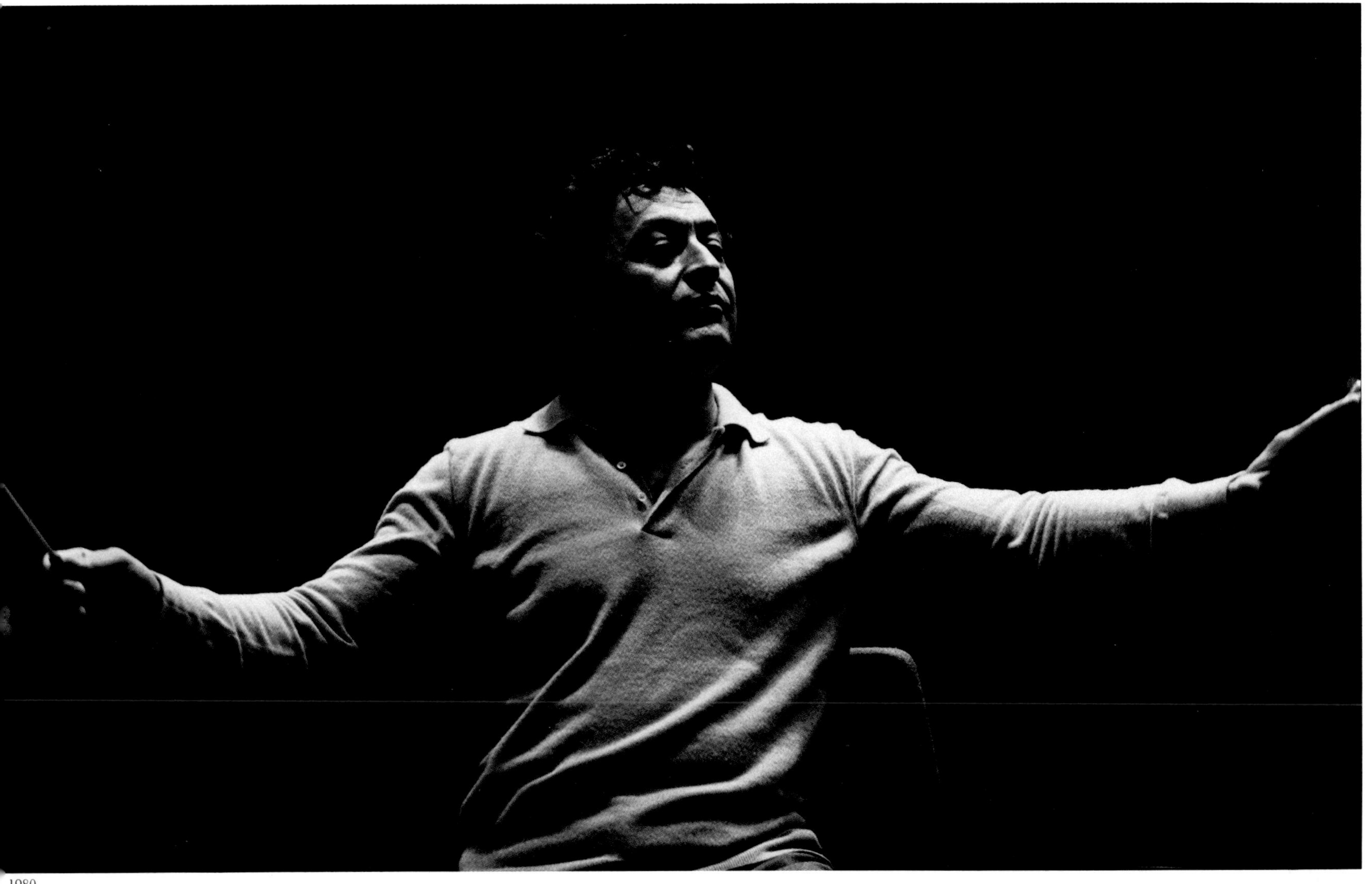

1980

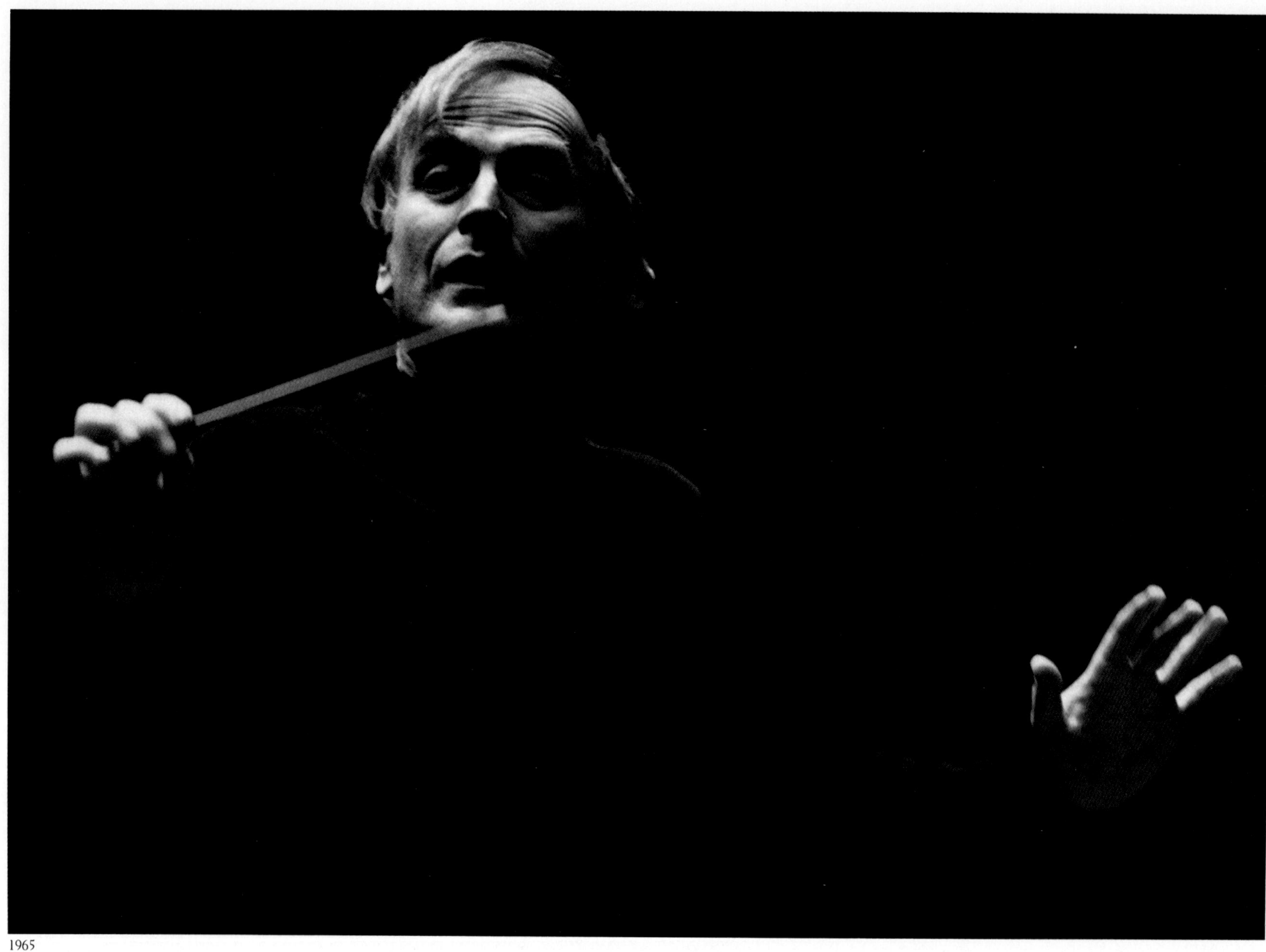

1965

Perhaps the greatest American-born violinist, and certainly one of the great spirits and consciences in the field of music today, Yehudi Menuhin astounded the world with his prodigious accomplishments as a child. During his extraordinary career he has been associated with such legendary figures as Enesco, Elgar, and Bartók (who composed his solo sonata for Menuhin), and has taught and performed in every corner of the globe. A mystical, visionary personality and an extraordinarily precise and articulate manner are combined in him, and can be detected in his approach to all things. His deep convictions concerning world peace and human rights have found eloquent expression not only in his playing but in direct statements that have frequently sounded confrontational, but have always had the force of reason and morality behind them, as when, in the face of great hostility, he defended Wilhelm Furtwängler after World War II. A uniquely thoughtful and widely experienced musician, he has recorded prolifically and remains active as a teacher and writer.

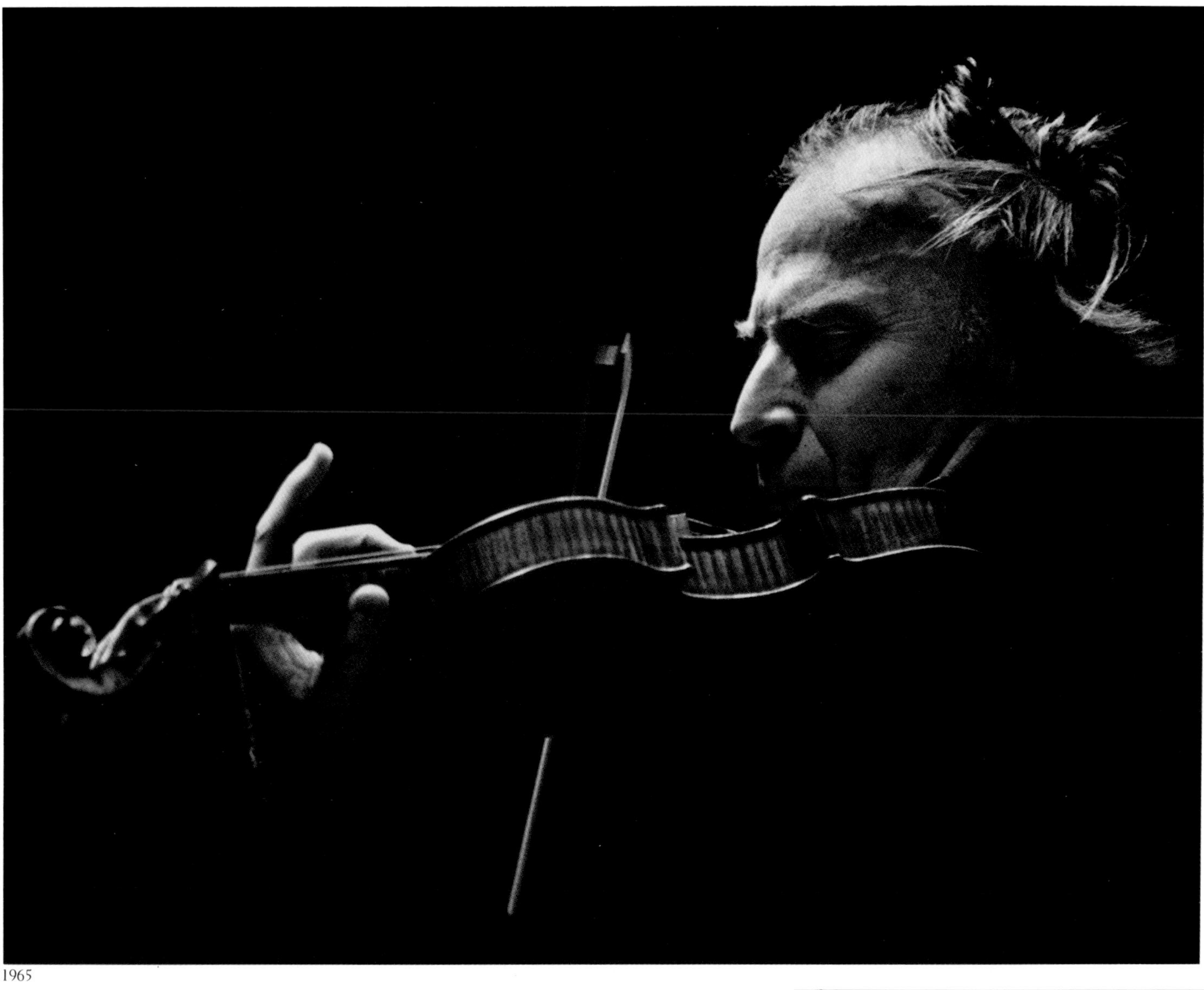

1965

OLIVIER MESSIAEN

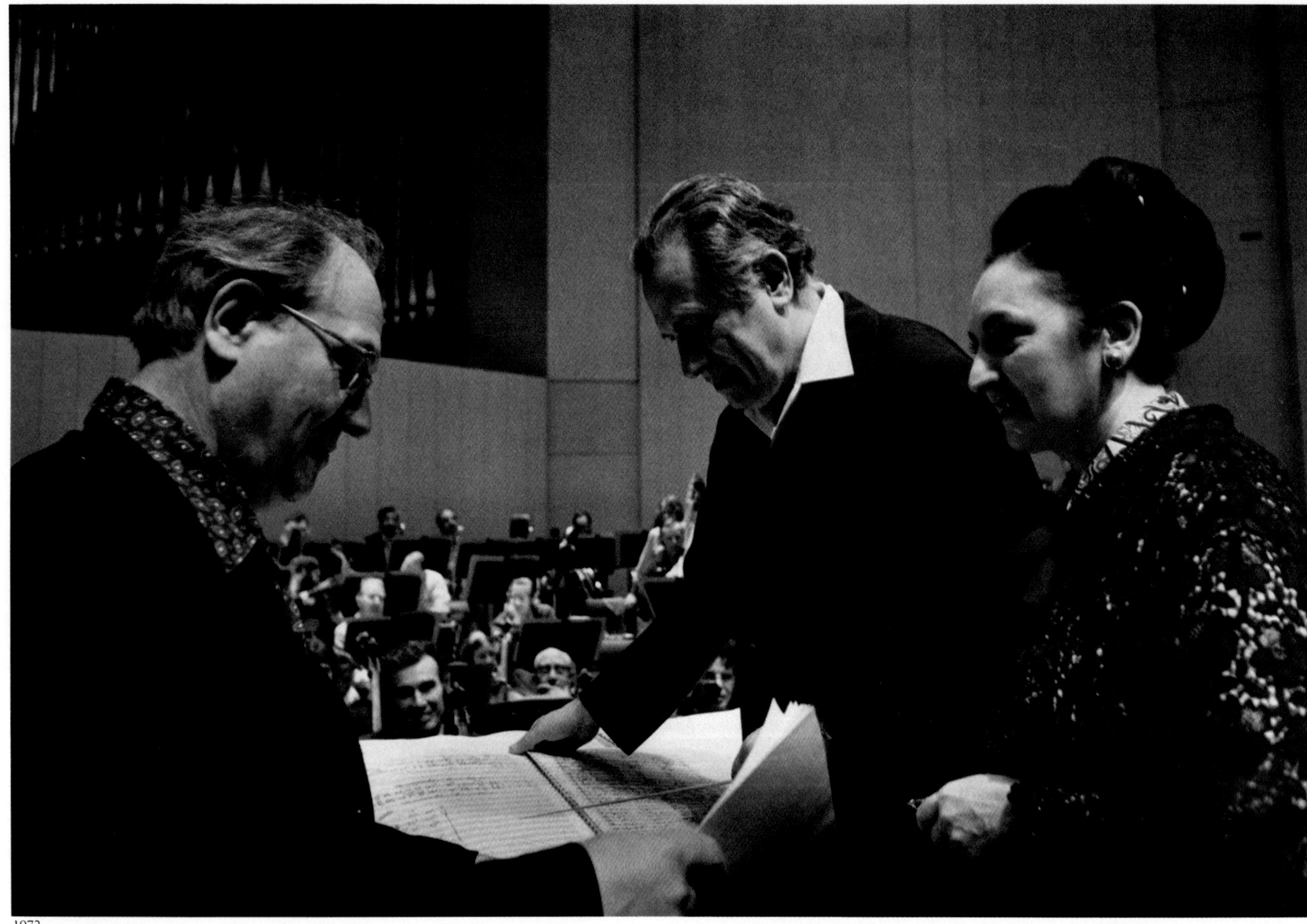

1972

A self-consciously Catholic composer, a mystic and an ornithologist (he is fascinated by bird-song and has frequently used elements of it in his compositions), Messiaen is a seminal figure in 20th-century music and has achieved wide acclaim. Born in Avignon, he passed his early life in Grenoble and the mountains of the Dauphine, which he considers his true home. He is a member of, among other institutions, the French Institute and the American Academy of Arts and Letters. He is pictured here with Antal Dorati and Yvonne Loriod.

Nathan Milstein

Where Heifetz dazzled, Milstein delighted, probing for meaning and emotion without ever losing sight of the musical architecture. A virtuoso with something more—call it warmth, or finesse, or polish—he has been the consummate stylist among the 20th century's great violinists.

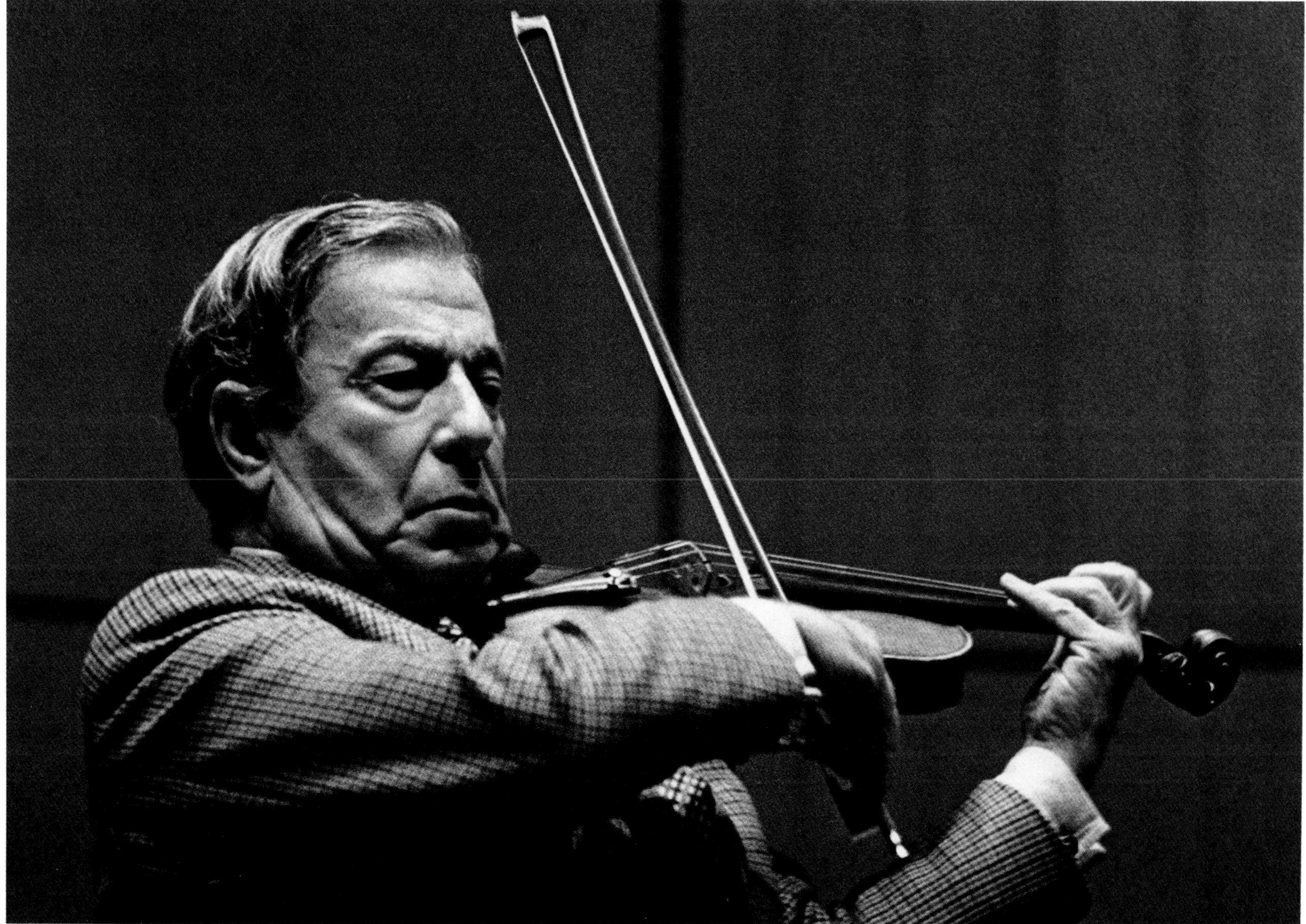

1982

HOWARD MITCHELL

For two decades (1949–1970) he was the man at the helm of the National Symphony Orchestra. A cellist, like three other NSO music directors (Hans Kindler, Antal Dorati, and Mstislav Rostropovich), Mitchell brought the Washington ensemble into the modern age and championed the works of living composers as a balance to the standard Romantic repertory in which he specialized. Following his tenure in the nation's capital, he was named conductor of the National Orchestra of Uruguay.

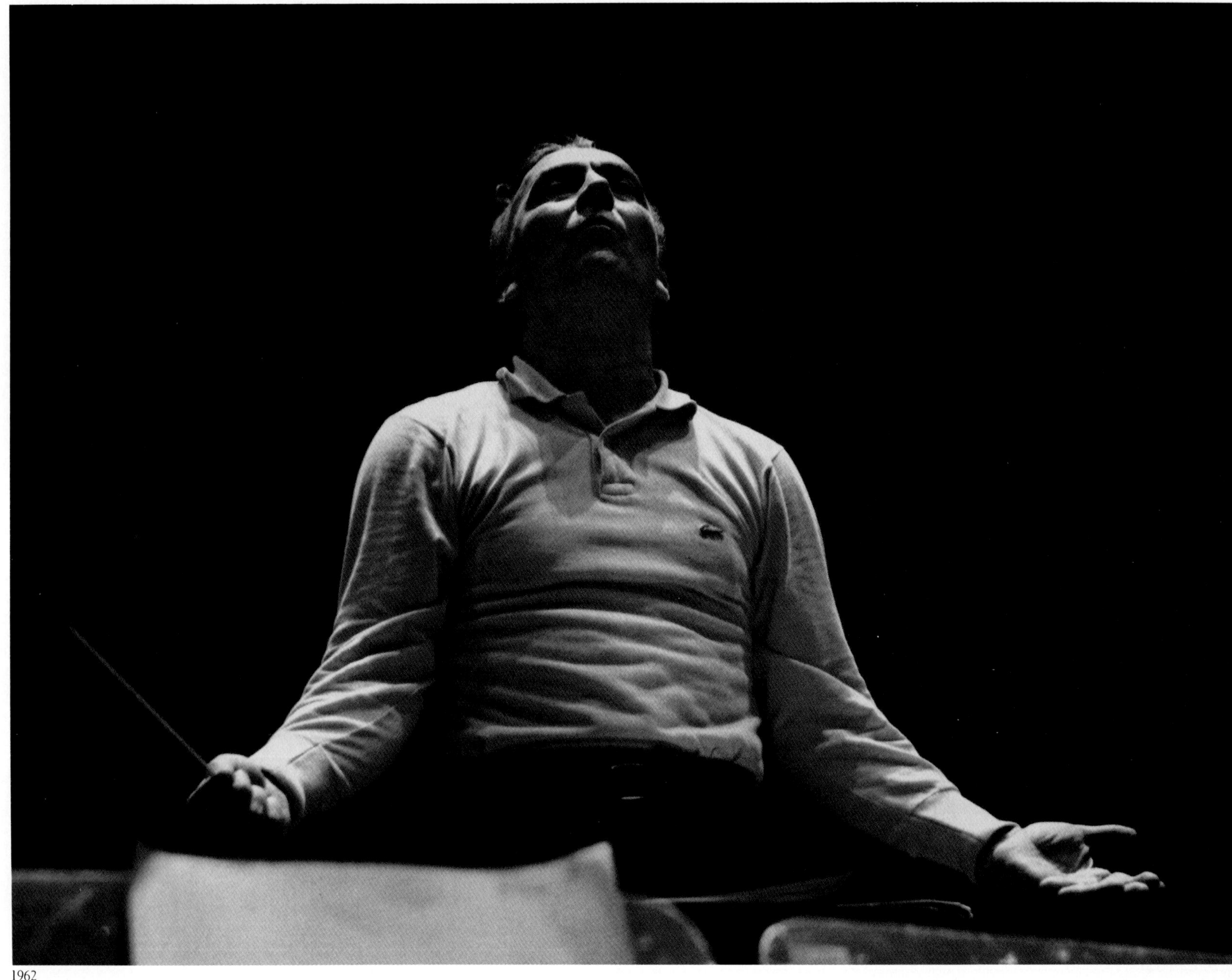

1962

ANNE-SOPHIE MUTTER

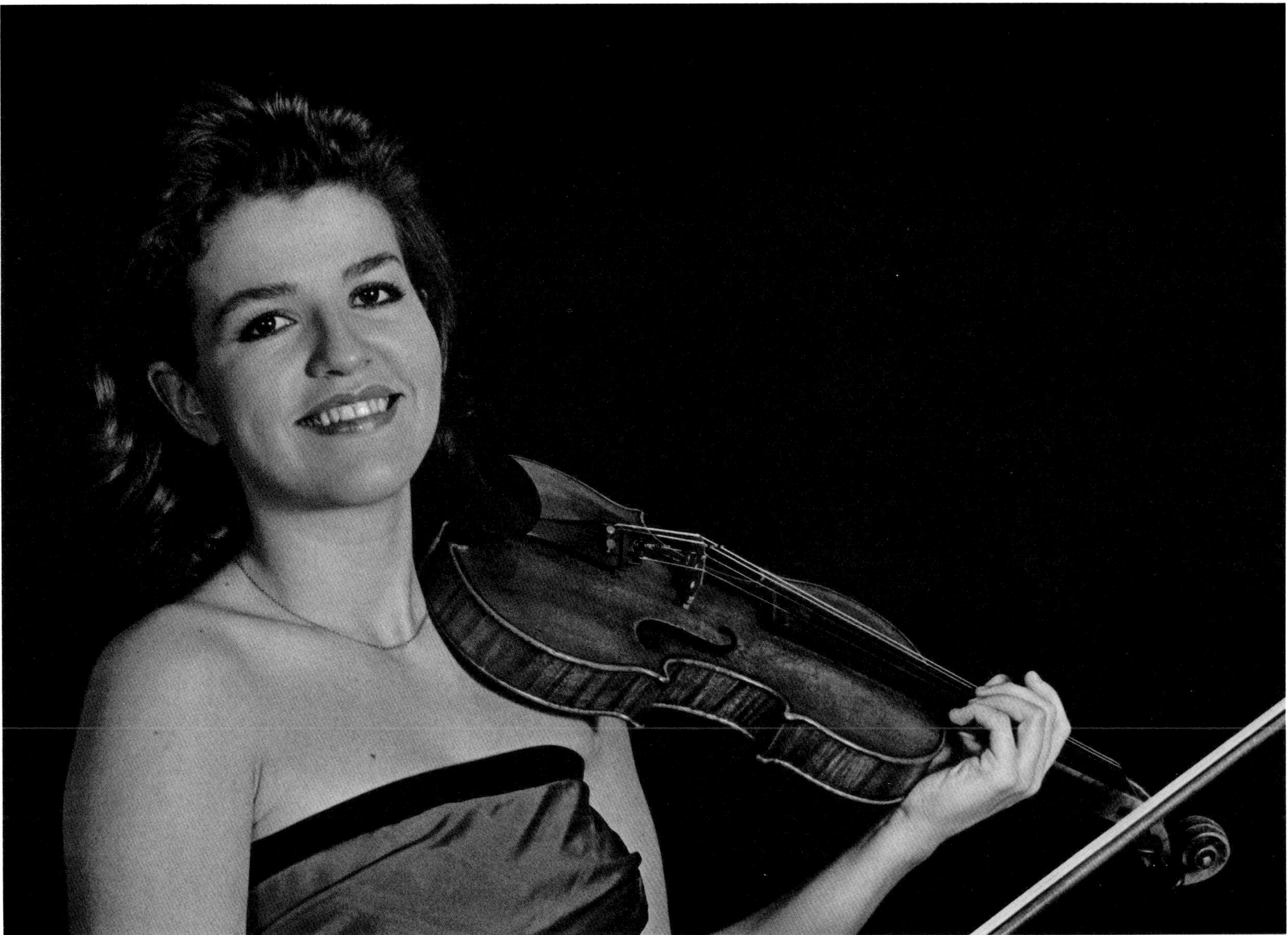

1988

A vivacious and popular performer who displays her art with effortless ease, Miss Mutter has been hailed by Herbert von Karajan as one of the greatest violinists in the world. Noted for her strapless gowns—"with the violin on the skin, the sound is much better"—and for her lack of any pre-performance jitters, she is the recipient of many awards, including the Deutsche Phono-Akademie "Artist of the Year" and the Deutsche Schallplatten Preis. In addition, she is an Honorary Fellow of the Royal Academy of Music and is the first holder of the International Chair of Violin Studies.

DAVID OISTRAKH

The preeminent Soviet violinist of the 20th century. Like many in his generation, he was already a well established and seasoned artist by the time of his American debut, which came, in 1955, at the height of the cold war. He worked closely with the leading Soviet composers of his day, including Prokofiev and Shostakovich; he premiered the latter's two concertos, and the former's second sonata. His playing, always infallibly musical, was marked by sincerity and nobility of expression and by a faithfulness to the written text that few of his colleagues possessed. In particular, his sensitive yet masculine interpretations of the great works of the 18th and 19th centuries stood out as beacons in an age of hyper-Romanticism and interpretive self-indulgence. He taught at the Moscow Conservatory from 1934 and influenced two generations of Soviet musicians. During the final decade of his life he made occasional appearances as a conductor, in which, as in everything else, he was notably successful. His recordings are among the greatest of any violinist of any time.

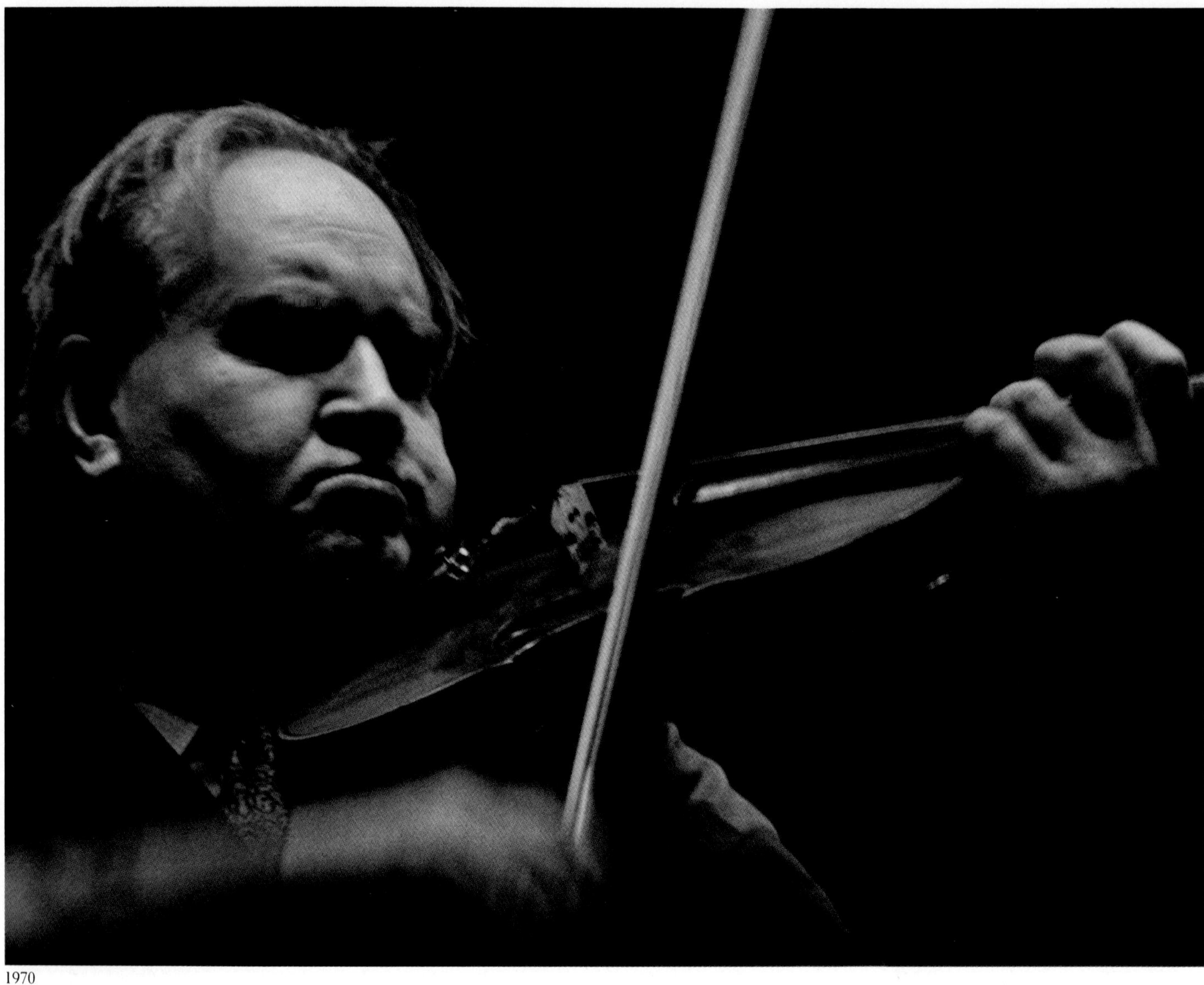

1970

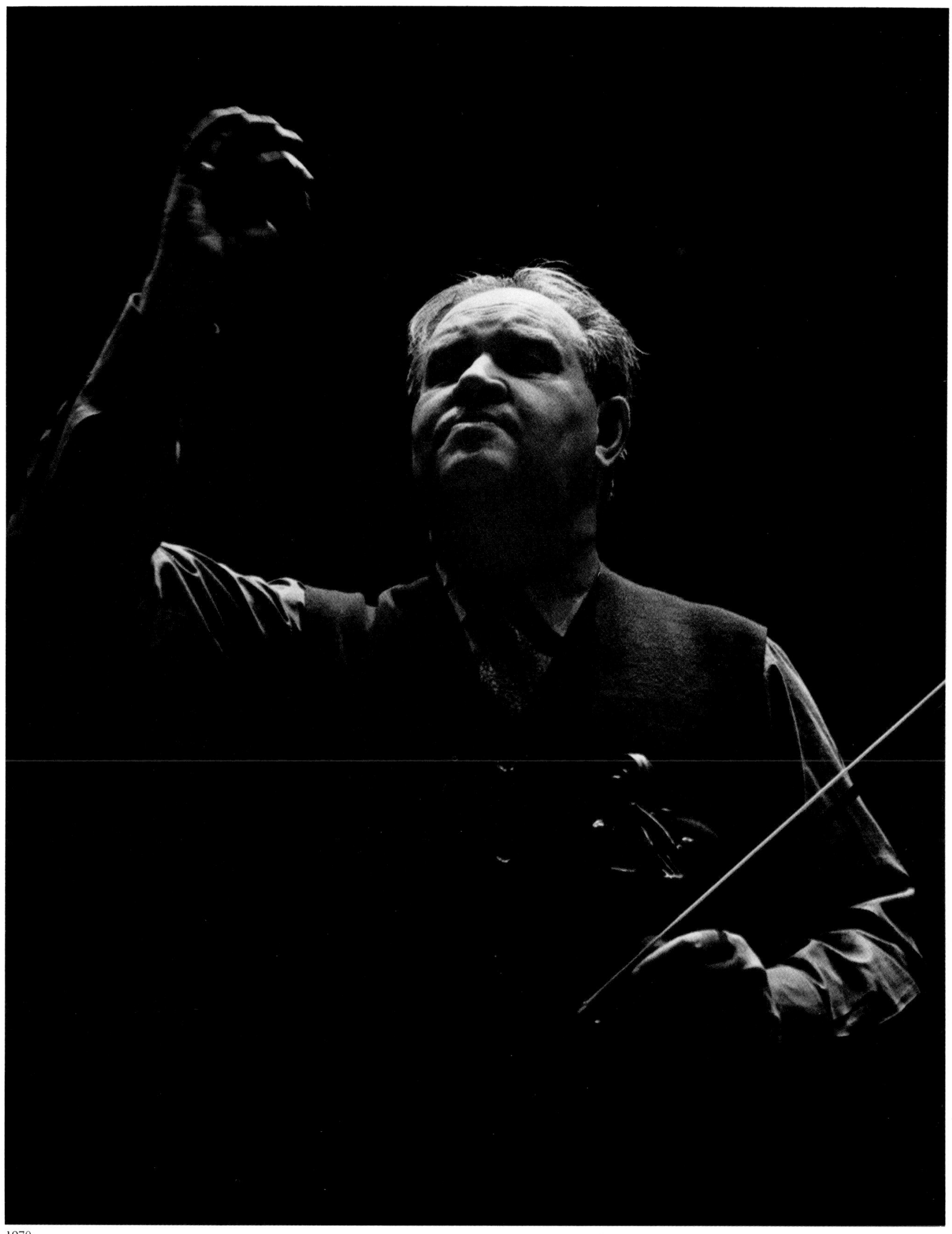

1970

ELMAR OLIVEIRA

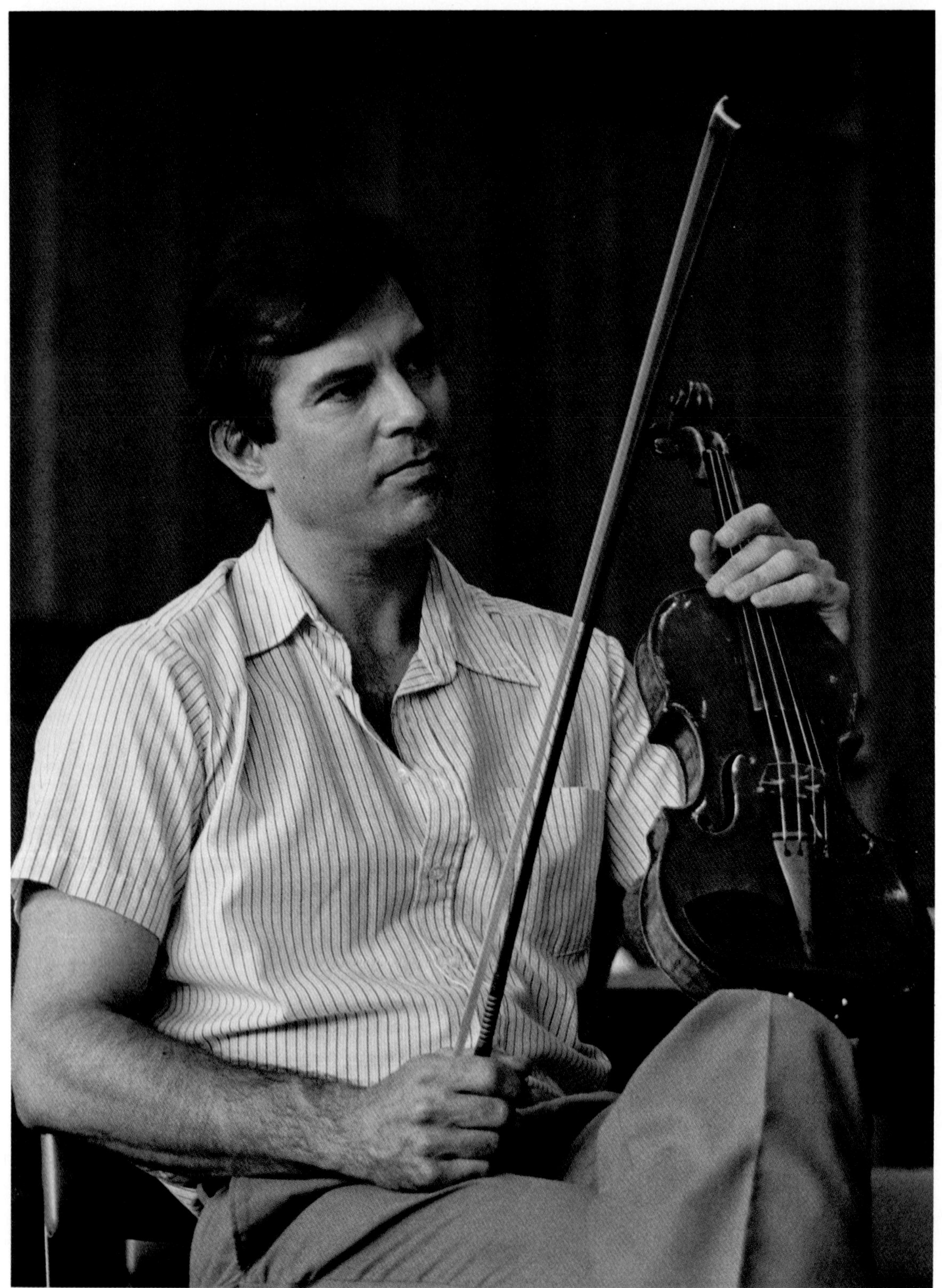

He could be the guy next door, but he is in no sense ordinary. This all-American is one of the world's great violinists, with an almost instinctive musicality and a suave, utterly ingenuous performing manner that communicates directly to an audience. Winner of the gold medal at the 1978 International Tchaikovsky Competition in Moscow, and of the Avery Fisher Prize in 1983, he is a champion of forgotten repertory, American works in particular. His playing as a soloist is warm but always controlled, and he has proven himself a capable recitalist and chamber musician as well.

Eugene Ormandy

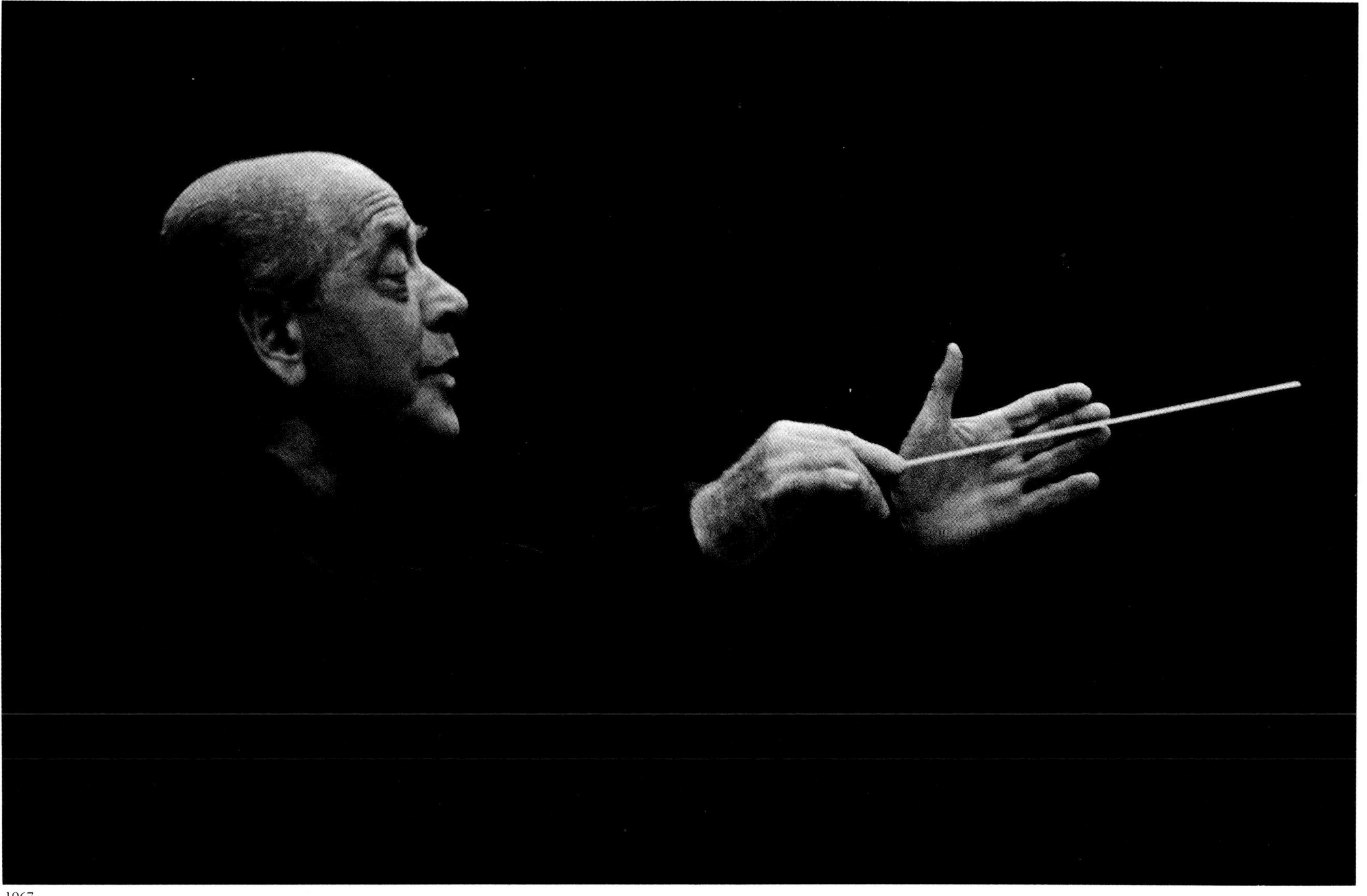

For 44 years the Philadelphia Orchestra was Eugene Ormandy's orchestra, and in the opinion of many, it was the greatest orchestra in the land. By the time Ormandy retired, in 1980, there was not one player in the ensemble he hadn't auditioned, and he rightfully claimed that the "Philadelphia sound" was really the "Ormandy sound." He was all business in rehearsal and performance, a thorough, meticulous craftsman with the sharpest of ears. While passion rarely showed in his conducting, it was always present in the music he made.

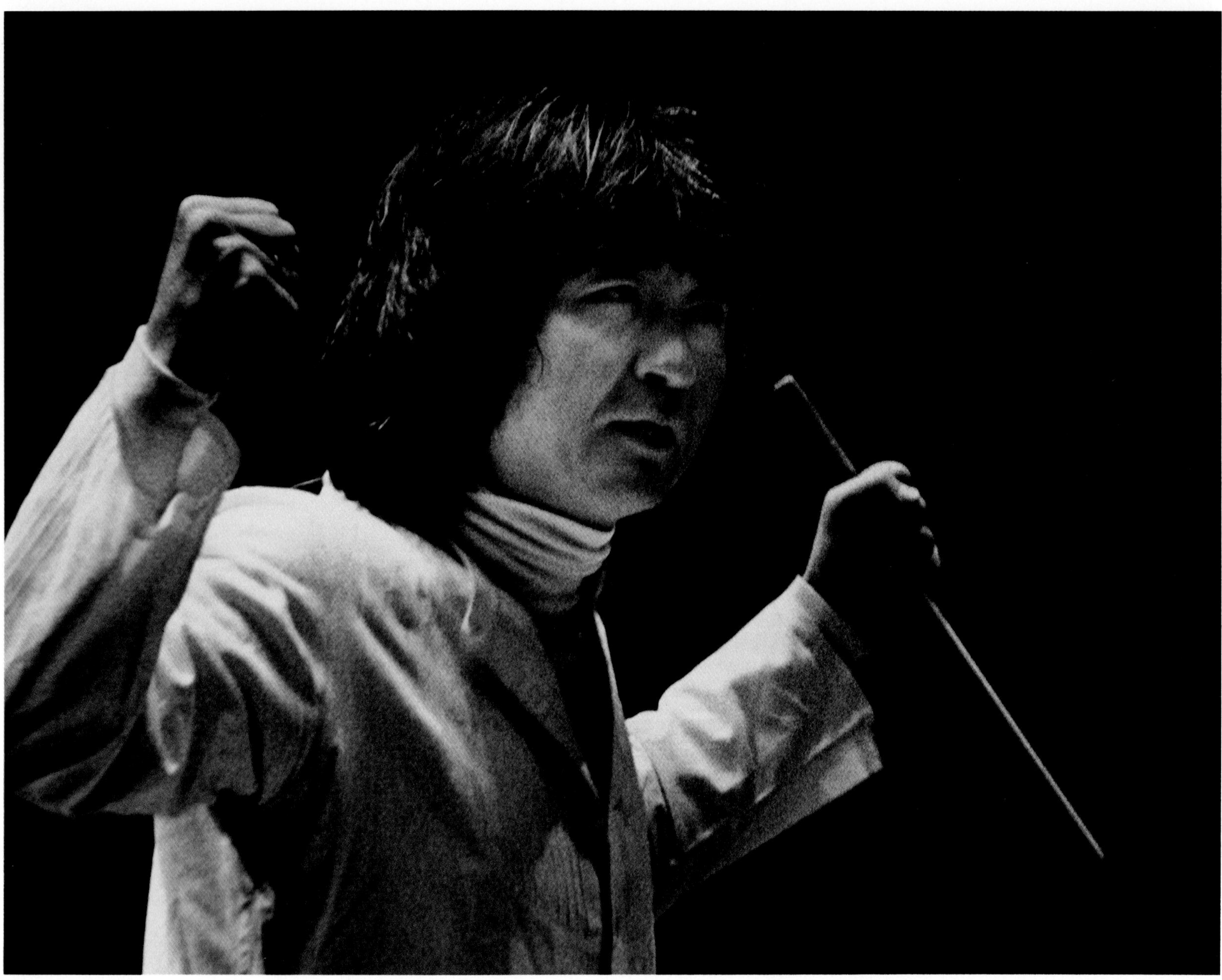

1978

Another of that remarkable crop of young conductors who emerged from Tanglewood in the late 1950s and early 1960s, Seiji Ozawa possessed athletic grace and extraordinary mental and musical aptitude from the beginning, but it was his singular determination to become a conductor that made the difference. After training in Japan, he was discovered at the competition for conductors in Besançon in 1959, and quickly came under the wing of Charles Munch. Successive mentors included Herbert von Karajan and Leonard Bernstein, and he quickly joined the ranks of those making frequent appearances with the world's top orchestras. Music directorships in Toronto, San Francisco, and Boston have been the pillars of his career, but he has also been active in Europe and has made occasional but highly successful forays into the opera pit. A master of technique, possessing a choreographic flamboyance and control of gesture that are second to none, he is at his best in the coloristic, virtuoso repertory of the late 19th and early 20th century. His insights into the standard repertory have deepened with experience, and he has established himself as a major champion of contemporary figures such as Messiaen and Sessions.

CARLOS PAITA

Carlos Paita, a native of Buenos Aires, developed his talents in his home town, conducting the orchestra of the Teatro Colón, the National Radio Orchestra of Argentina, and the Buenos Aires Philharmonic. He made his European debut in 1966 in Stuttgart; since then he has performed with a number of London orchestras and guest-conducted several ensembles on the continent as well. In 1981, the Swiss recording firm Lodia signed Paita to an exclusive contract, under which he has produced several records that have attained a cult following.

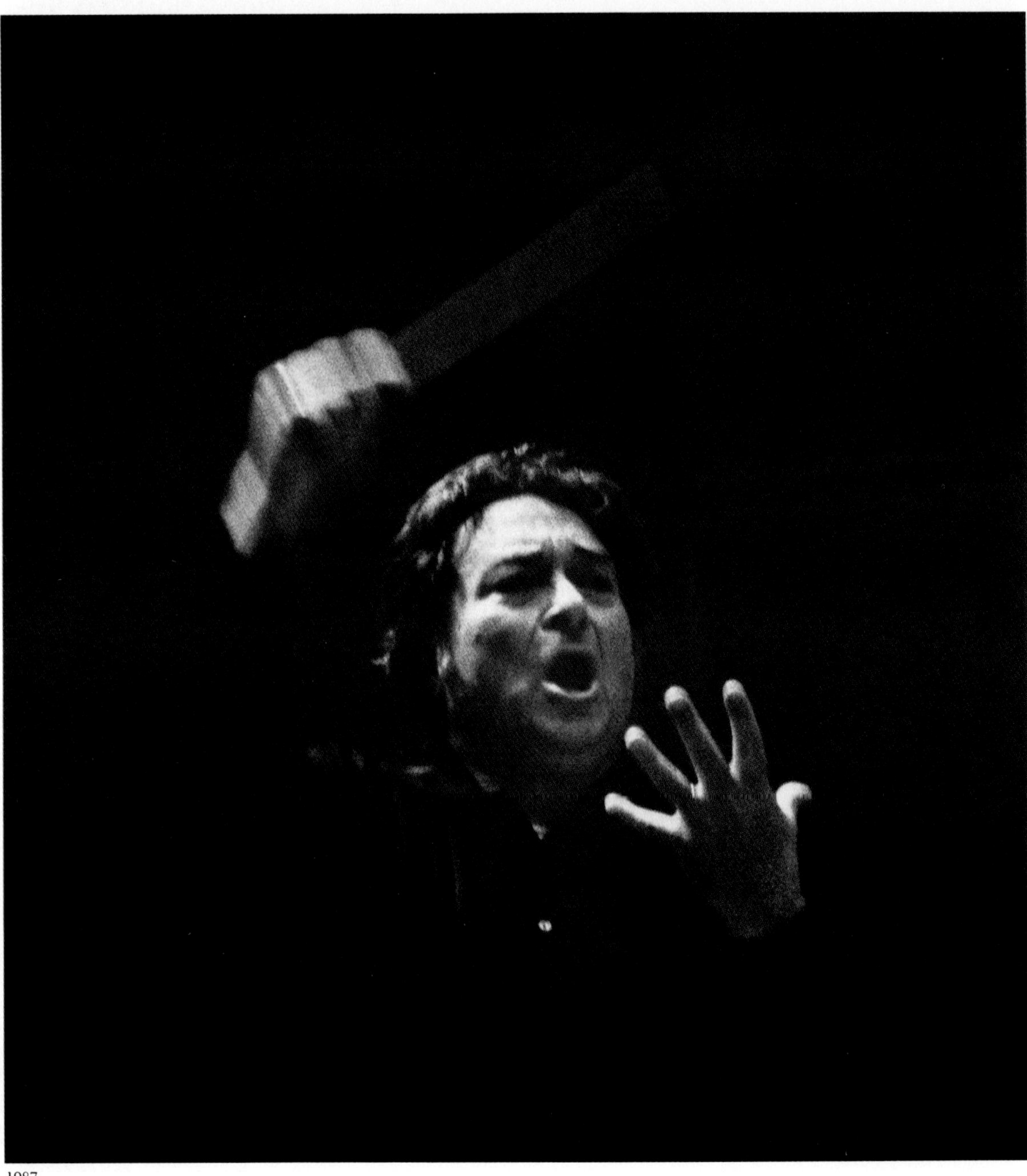

1987

Paul Paray

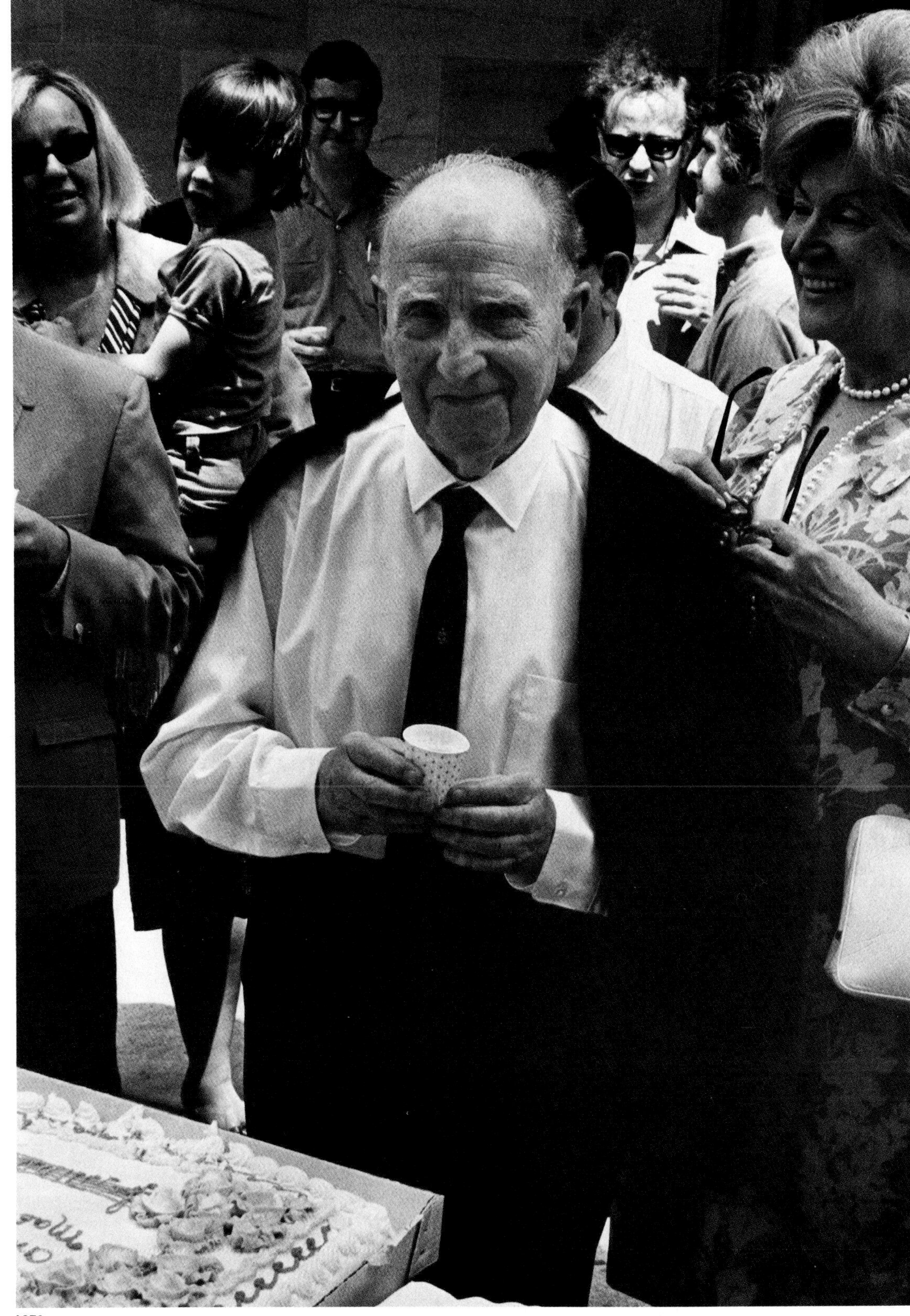

A master whose energy continued undiminished into his nineties, Paul Paray (shown at right at his 85th birthday celebration) was one of the century's great exponents of French music, both in France and abroad, and an inspiring interpreter of the mainstream symphonic repertory. To hear him conduct Rossini's *William Tell* Overture with the Detroit Symphony (whose music director he was from 1951 to 1963) was to hear something very close to perfection—a performance so good it made you wonder why anyone would want to interpret the piece again. He was a figure of elegance, exuberance, and extraordinary generosity. And he remained a teacher to the last: his final appearance in the United States, which he made at the age of 92, was at the head of the orchestra of the Curtis Institute of Music.

1970

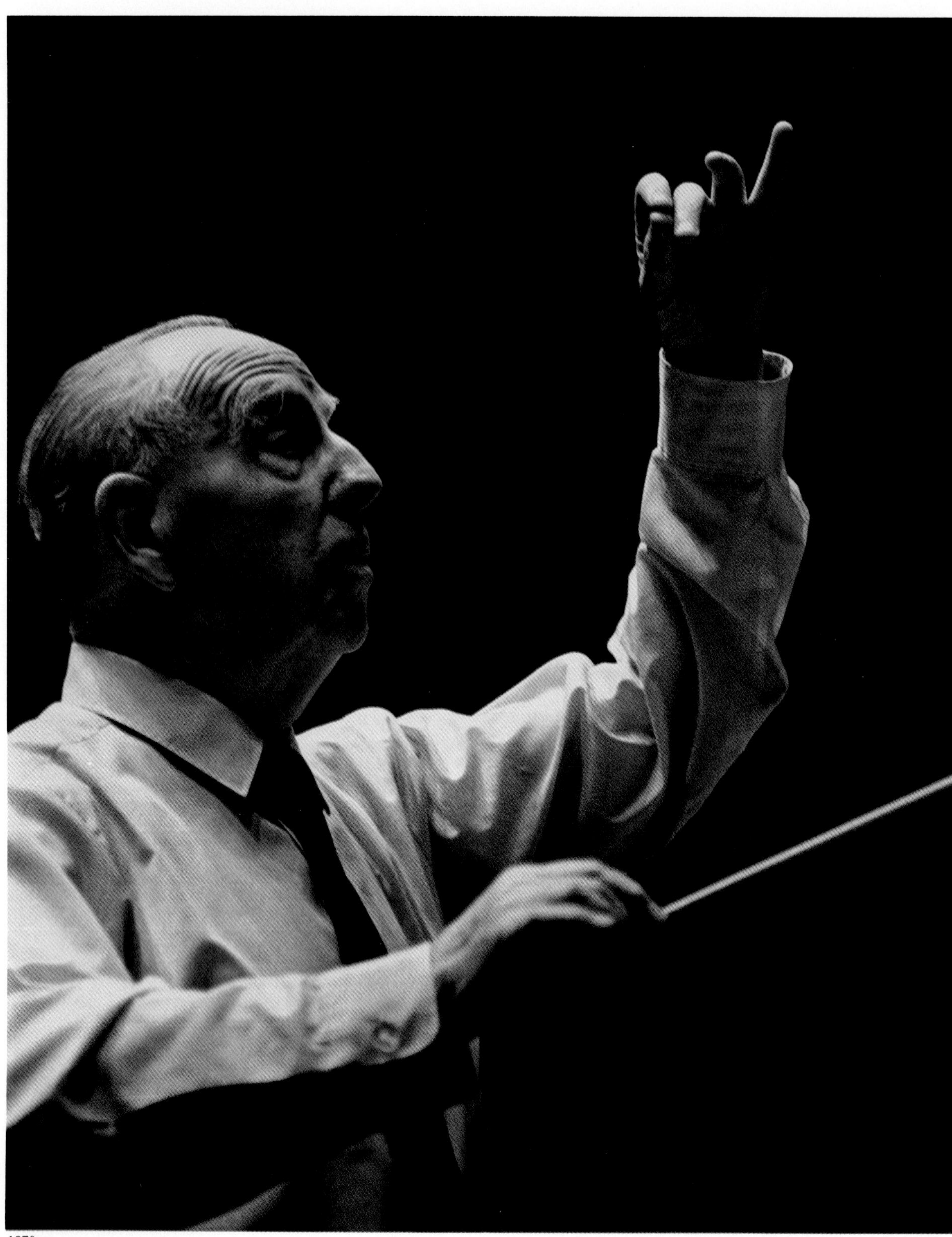

1970

JON KIMURA PARKER

A native of Canada, Jon Kimura Parker came to international attention when he won the first prize in the 1984 Leeds International Piano Competition. The 1984–85 season saw him make his recital debuts in New York, London, and Frankfurt, and included a Royal Command Performance for Queen Elizabeth II.

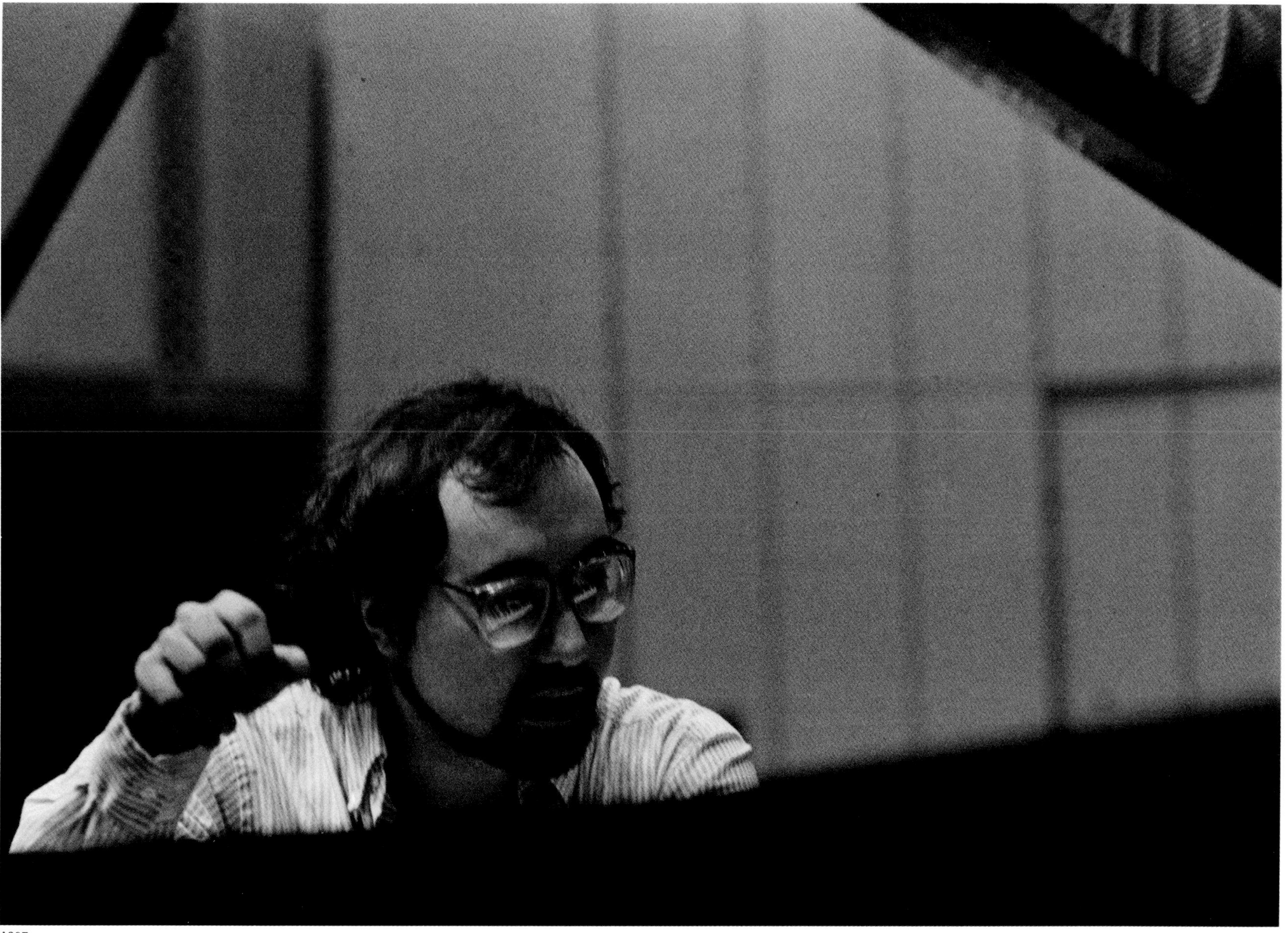

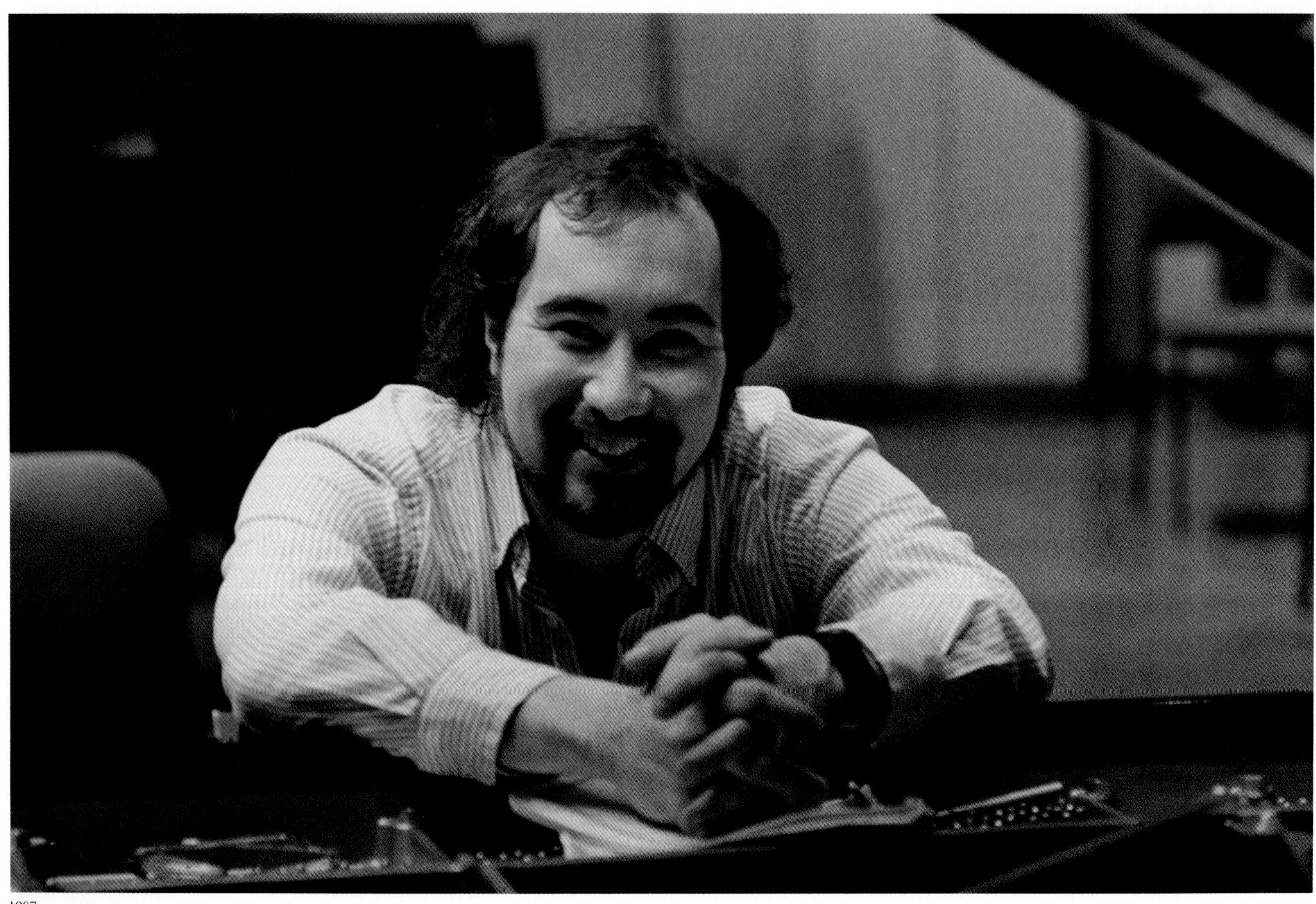

1987

RICHARD PARNAS

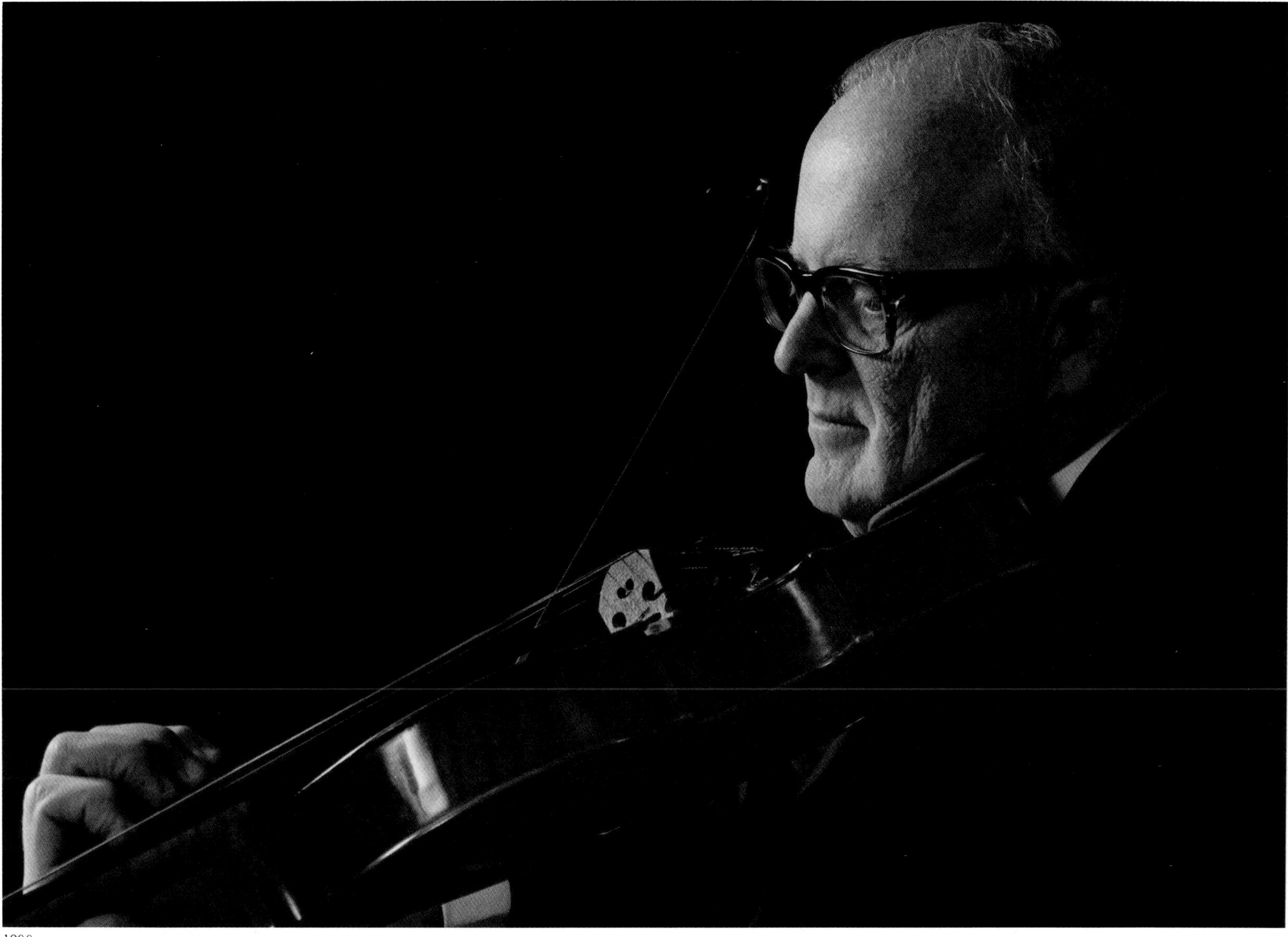

1988

Richard Parnas is the principal violist of the National Symphony Orchestra. He joined the NSO in 1955, after four years as a member of the United States Navy Band and one season with the St. Louis Symphony. Parnas takes an active part in the musical life of the nation's capital, performing with area chamber orchestras and teaching at Catholic University, George Washington University, and George Mason University.

Krzysztof Penderecki

A paradoxical and brilliant composer of some of the 20th century's most powerful music, Penderecki leapt to the forefront of the post-war *avant-garde* when he was barely 25, with his extraordinary *Threnody for the Victims of Hiroshima*. Fascinated by sonority, he has produced a remarkable body of breathtakingly innovative works for choral and orchestral forces, in which can usually be found a striking rhythmic complexity, an intense expressiveness, and, often, profound religious feeling. Although he began as one of the most adventurous of young compositional Turks, Penderecki has turned increasingly toward an assertion of tonality in his recent scores. While he may only have meant to be provocative when he said, "We must go back to Mahler and start over," he has clearly embraced a variety of neo-Romanticism in the last few years. In spite of this unusual turn, his is one of the world's most adventurous musical minds.

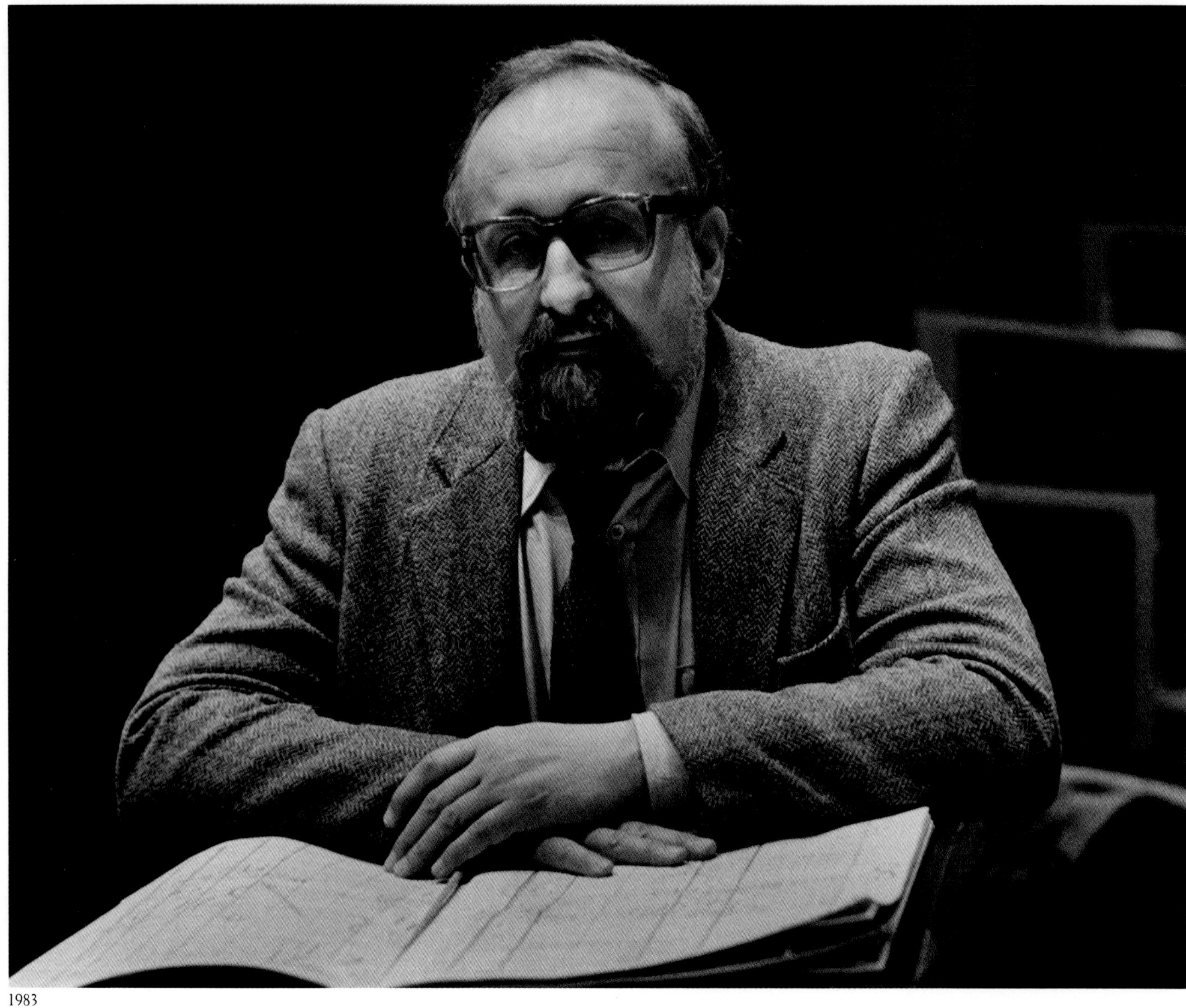

1983

RUGGERO RAIMONDI

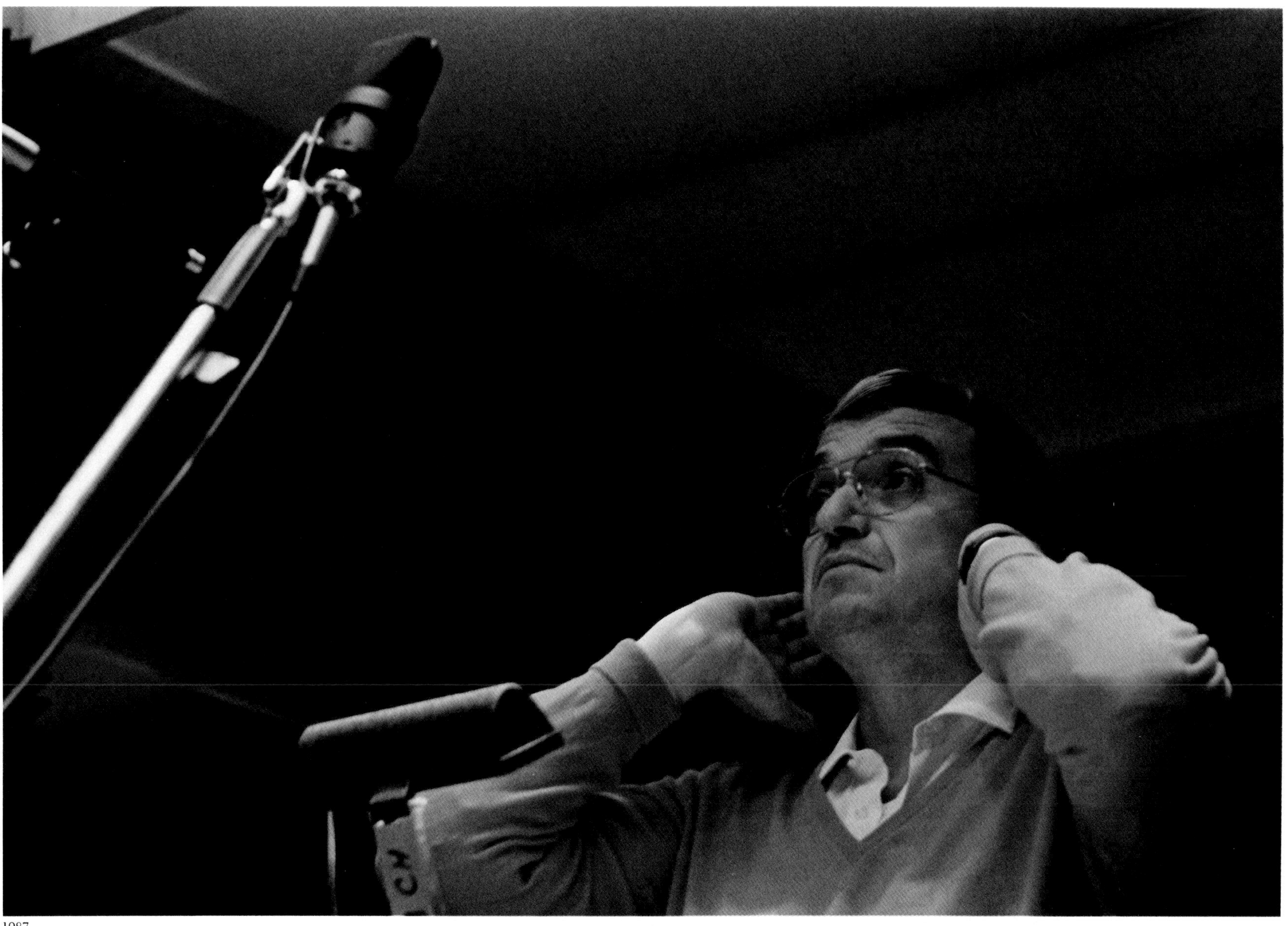

1987

A versatile bass, Ruggero Raimondi exudes a remarkable energy on stage and has a unique tone quality that enables him to personify the more "serious" roles in the repertory. He has had particular success with Don Giovanni, Escamillo, and Boris Godunov, all three of which he has realized on film. In addition, his Figaro in Mozart's *Le Nozze di Figaro* is a standout.

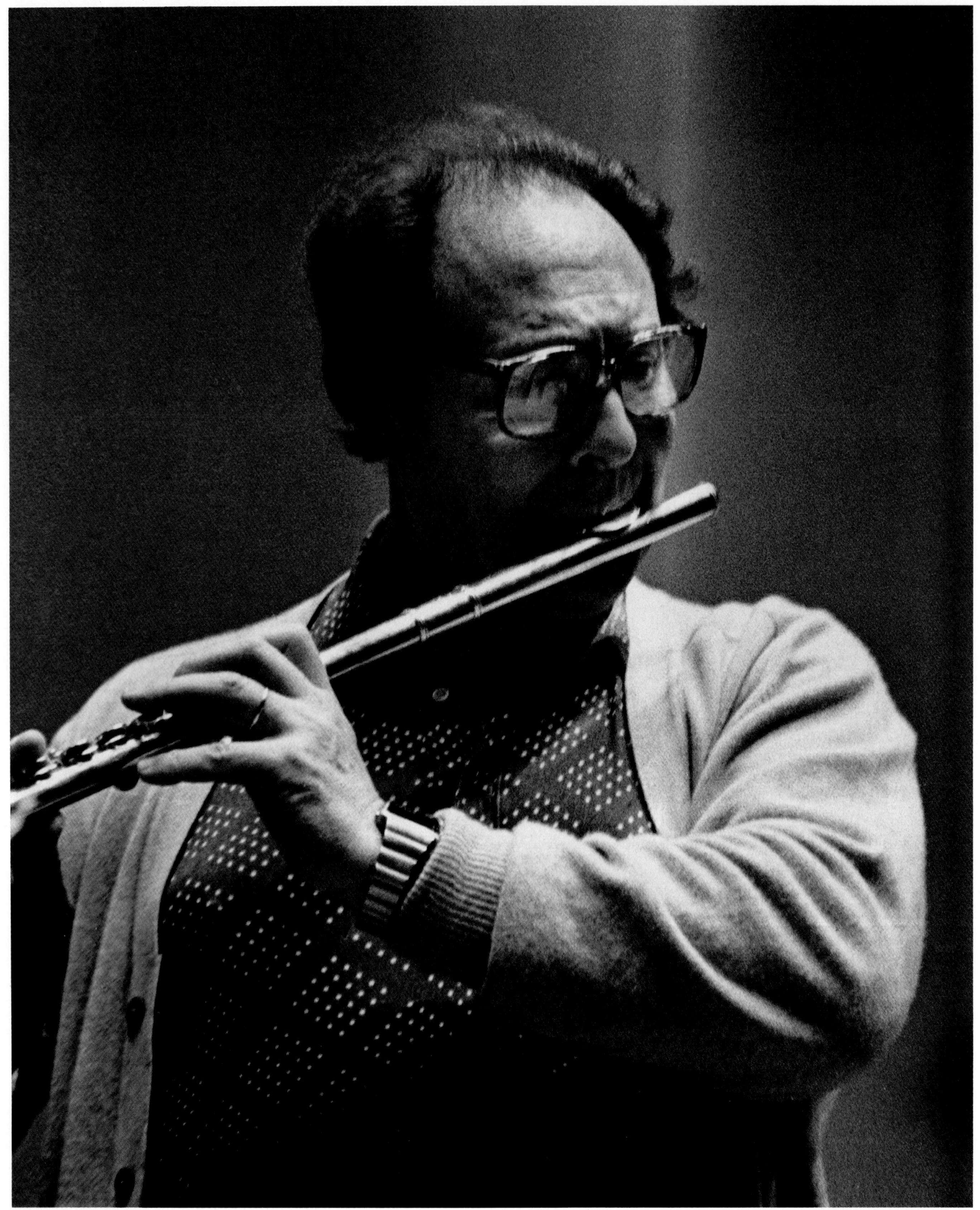

1983

Jean-Pierre Rampal

The prince of flutists in the 20th century, he has brought the instrument international popularity and restored it to a place of honor among solo vehicles, something it had not enjoyed in nearly two centuries. Still one of its most eloquent exponents, he plays with an amplitude and suavity of tone that have never been matched. Among the works that have been written for him are concertos by Jolivet, Martinon, Rivier, and Francaix, and, most precious of all, the Sonata for Flute and Piano by Francis Poulenc. During his extraordinary performing career of more than four decades he has taught numerous students, explored fascinating corners of the repertory, built a monumental discography, and maintained a concert schedule that covers most of the globe each year. As delightful offstage as on, he is a gourmet, *bon vivant*, and a model of Gallic charm.

KURT ROGER

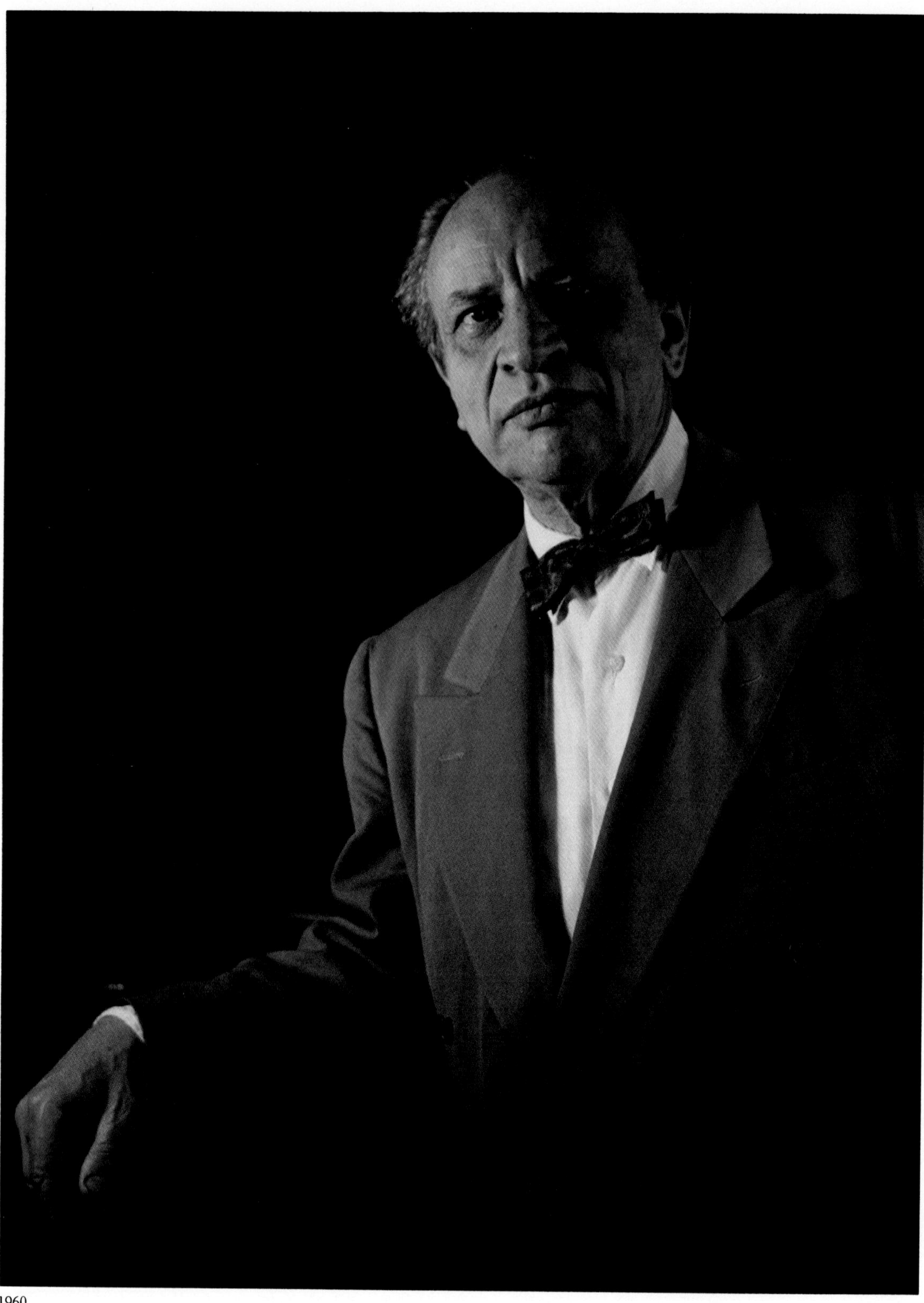

A native of Vienna, he taught theory and composition there from 1923. Following the *Anschluss,* he left Austria, settling first in New York, later in Washington. His works—traditional in form and content but bearing a thoroughly personal melodic stamp—were championed by Rafael Kubelik and Erich Leinsdorf during their associations with, respectively, the Chicago Symphony and the Rochester Philharmonic.

LEONARD ROSE

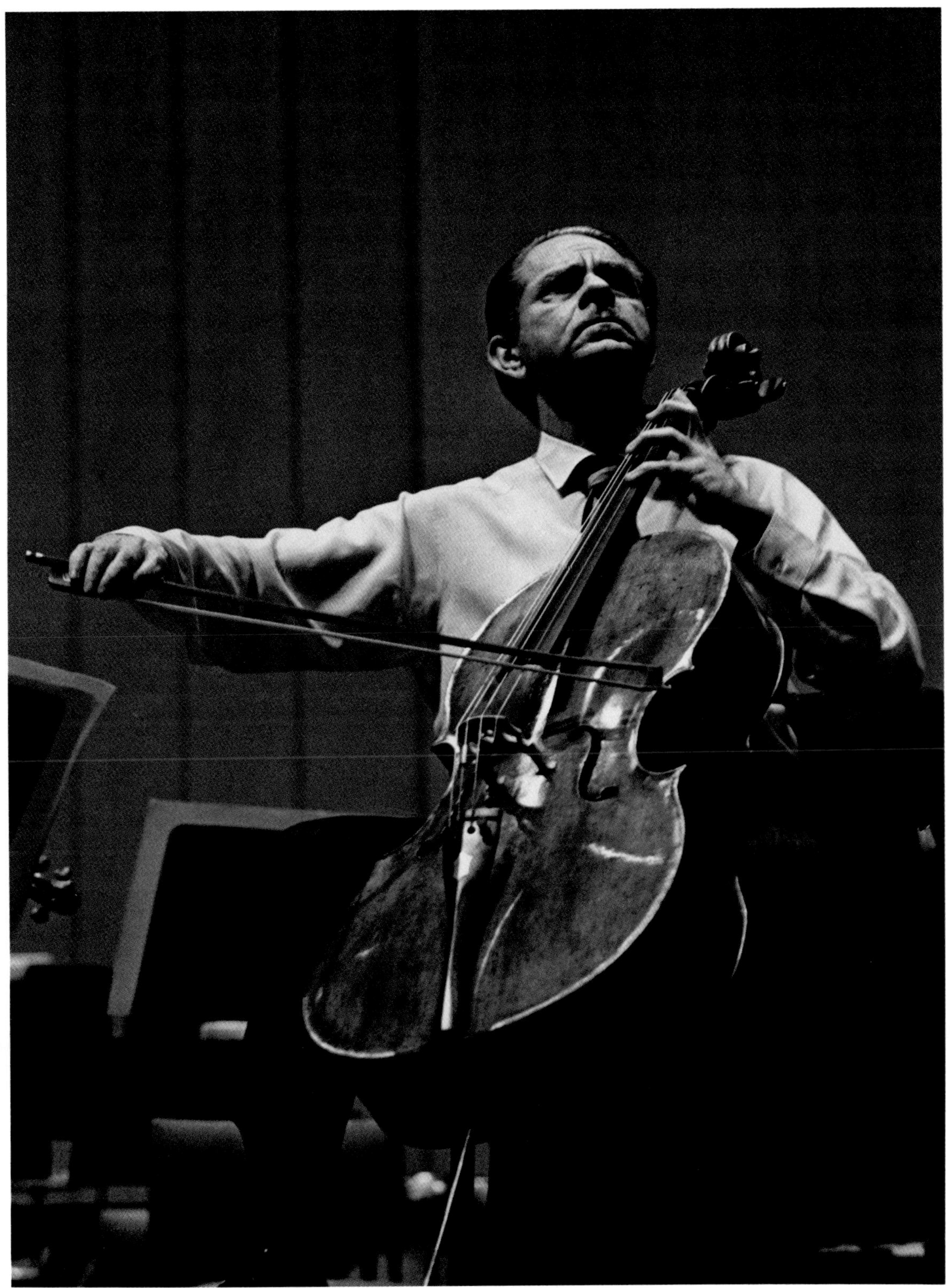

Born in Washington, D.C., he studied in
New York with Frank Miller, and at the
Curtis Institute with Felix Salmond.
Following his graduation in 1938, he spent a
single season in the cello section of the NBC
Symphony under Toscanini. He held the
principal chair with the Cleveland Orchestra
from 1939 to 1943, and with the New York
Philharmonic from 1943 to 1951. Thereafter
he devoted himself to a distinguished career
as a soloist and member of the Stern-Rose-
Istomin Trio. He was also a fine teacher who
numbered among his students Lynn Harrell,
Stephen Kates, and Yo-Yo Ma.

1973

MSTISLAV ROSTROPOVICH

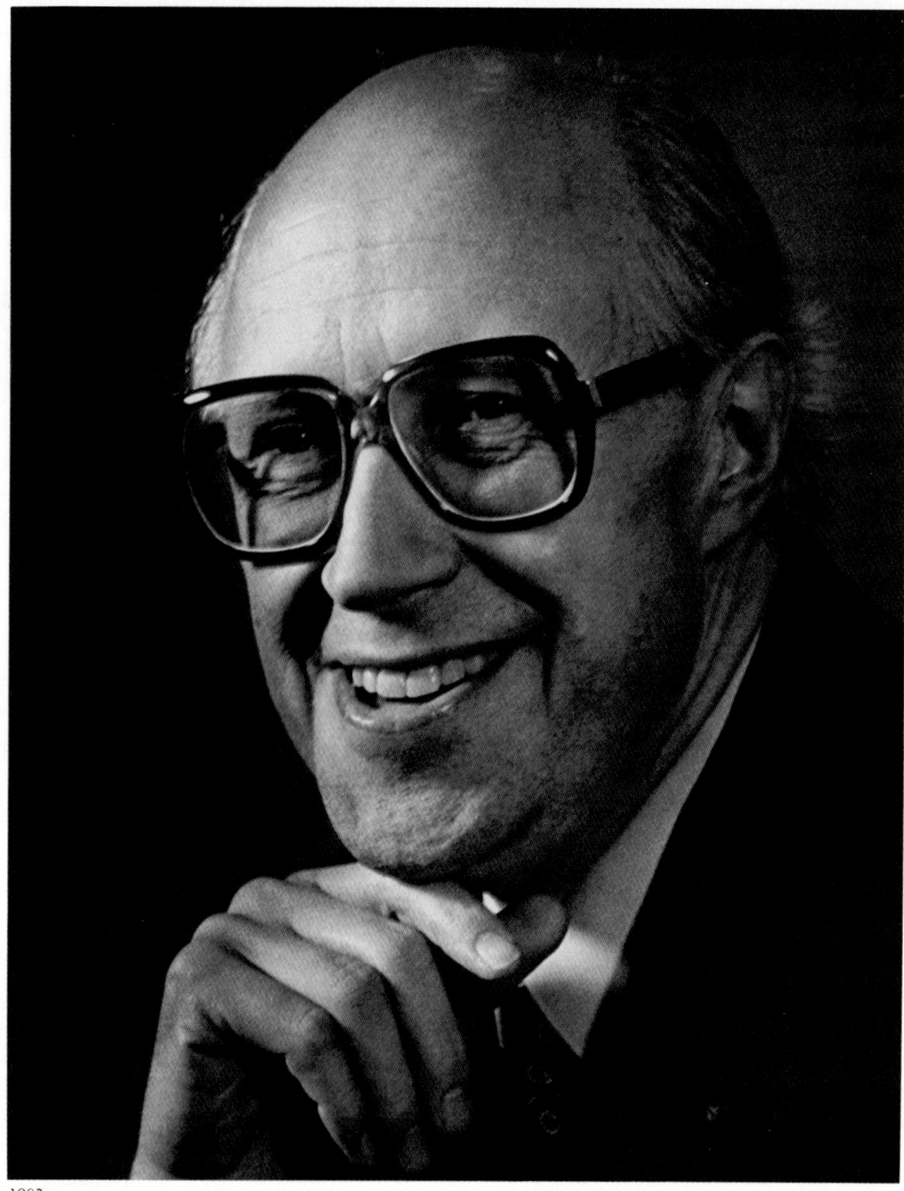

1983

Who else besides "Slava" has been awarded the Officer's Cross of the Order of Merit of West Germany, the Commander of France's Legion of Honor, the Honorary Knight Commander of the Most Excellent Order of the British Empire, the Presidential Medal of Freedom, *and* the Stalin Prize and the Order of Lenin. And who else has been a defender of Alexander Solzhenitsyn, has had works written for him by Shostakovich, Prokofiev, Britten, and Bernstein, *and* has distinguished himself as a pianist, as perhaps the world's finest living cellist, and as the music director that has made the National Symphony Orchestra one of America's top orchestras. He has, of course, also won several recording prizes, including the Grammy Award and the Grand Prix du Disque, is the holder of more than thirty honorary degrees, and received the 1974 Annual Award of the International League of Human Rights and the 1985 Albert Schweitzer Award. The National Symphony Orchestra is justly proud of its maestro.

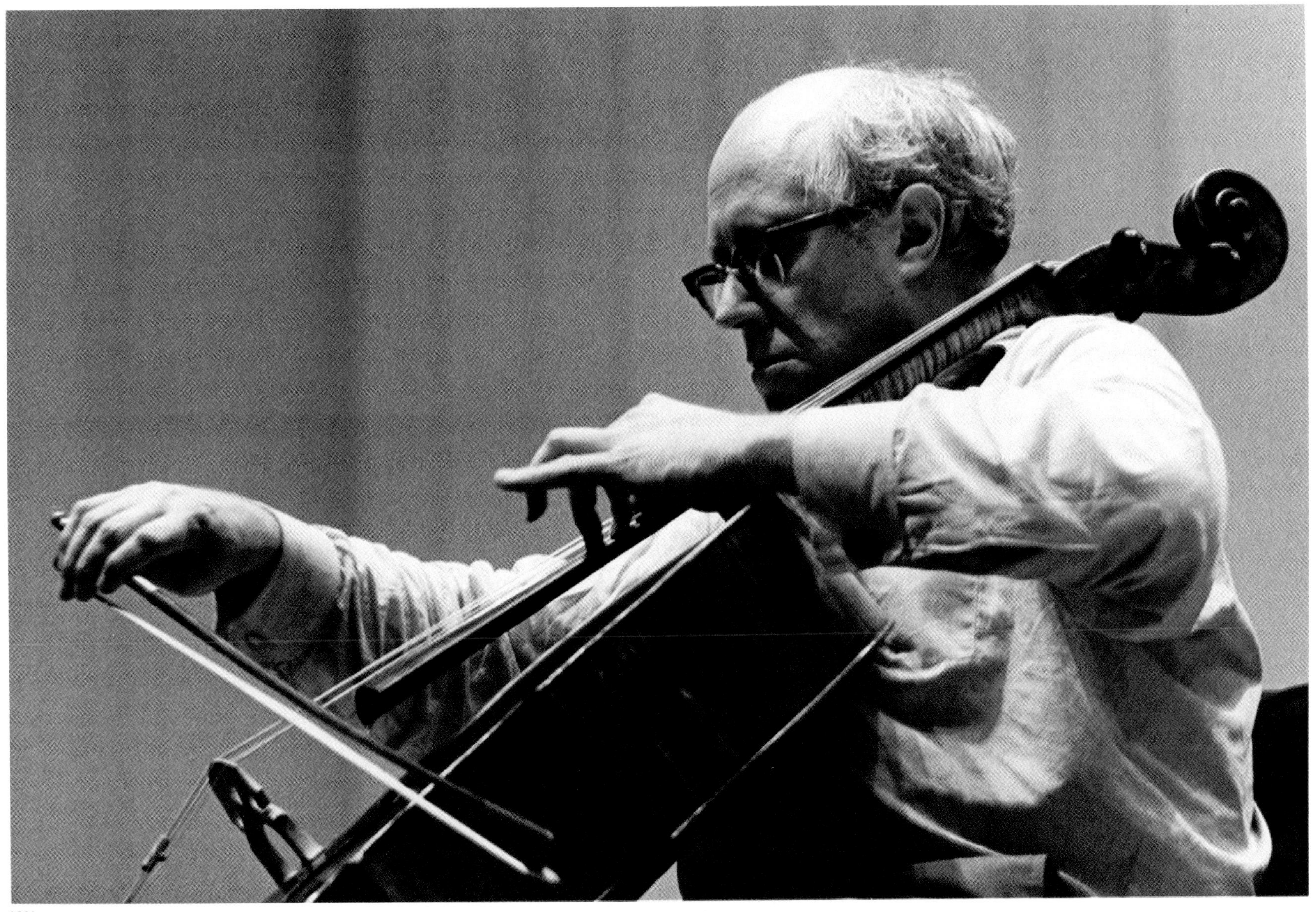

1981

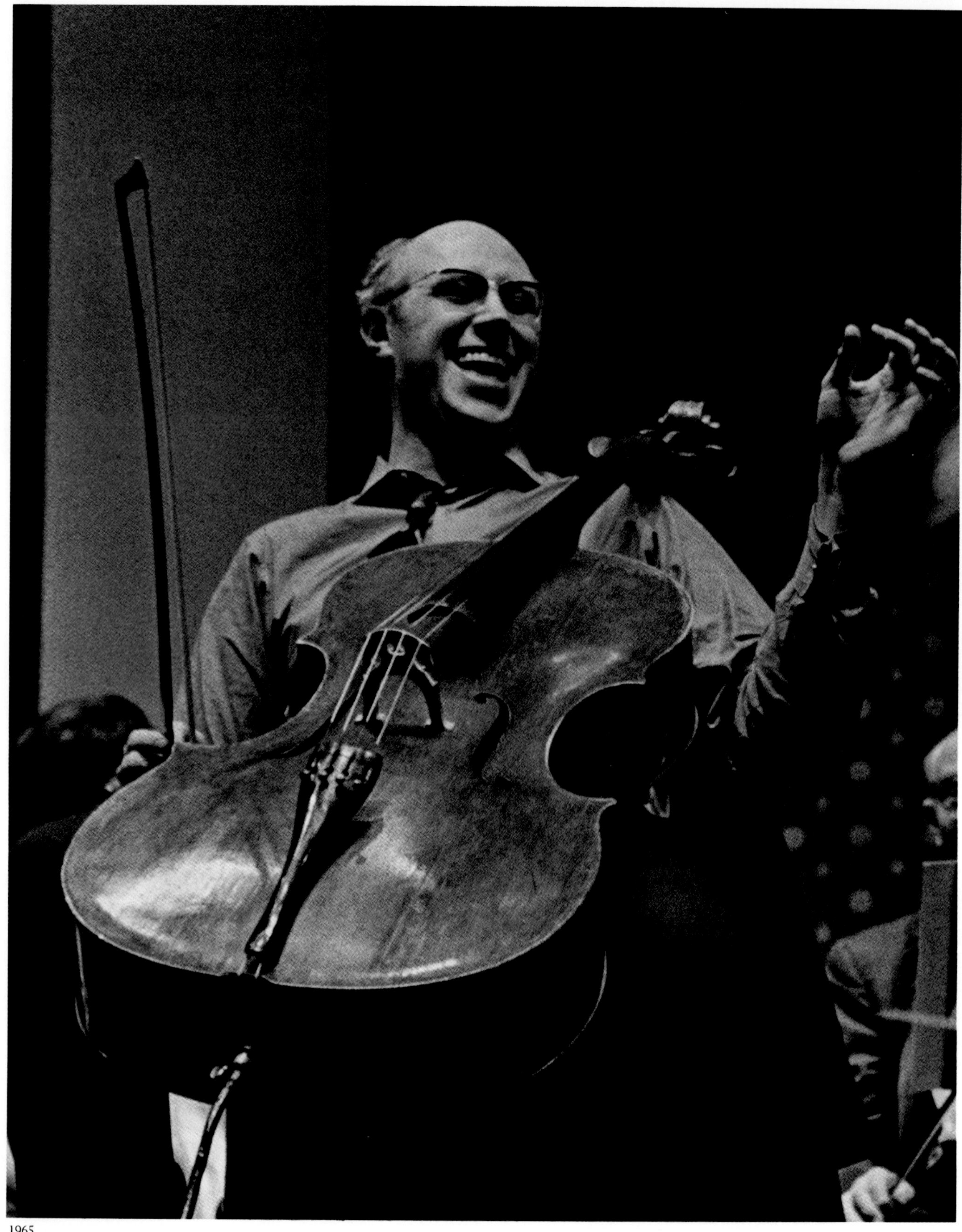

1965

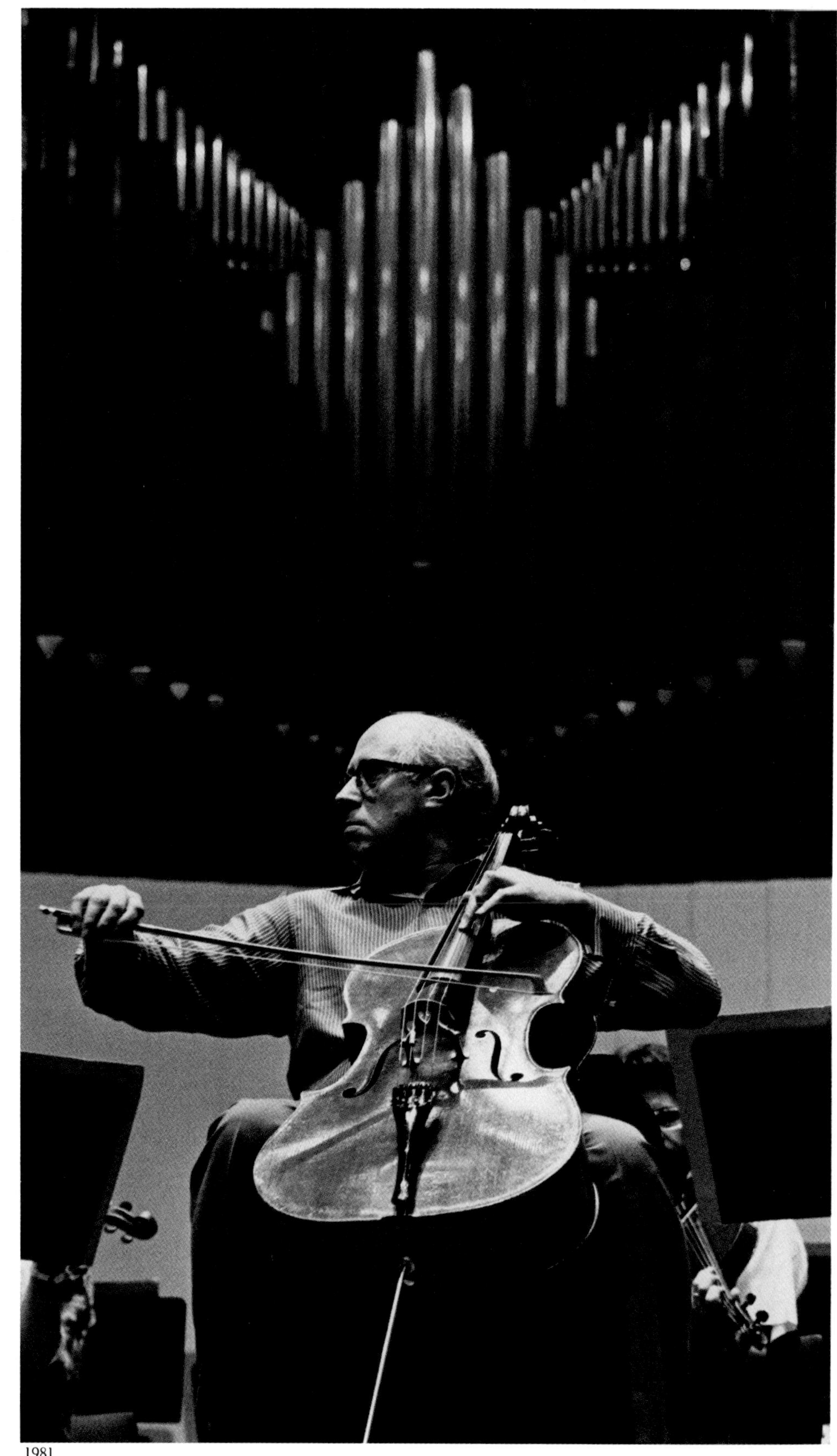

1981

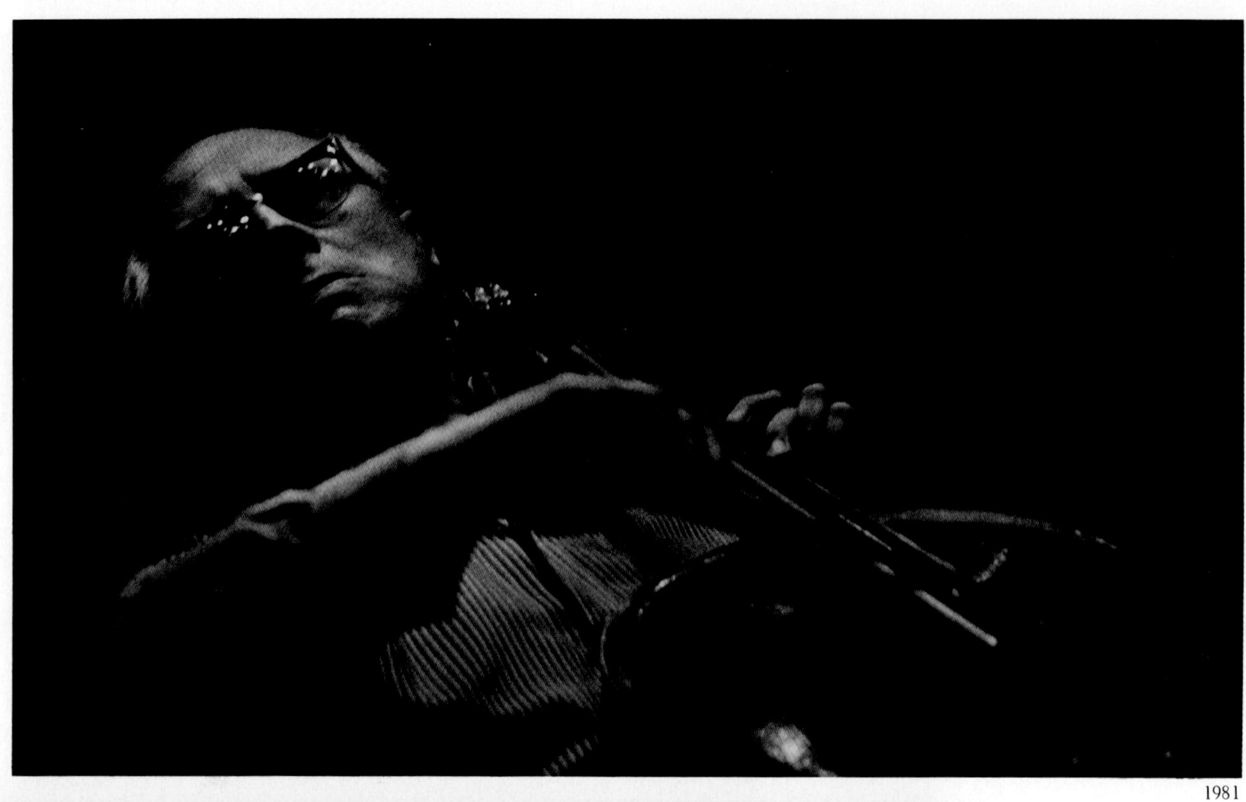

1981

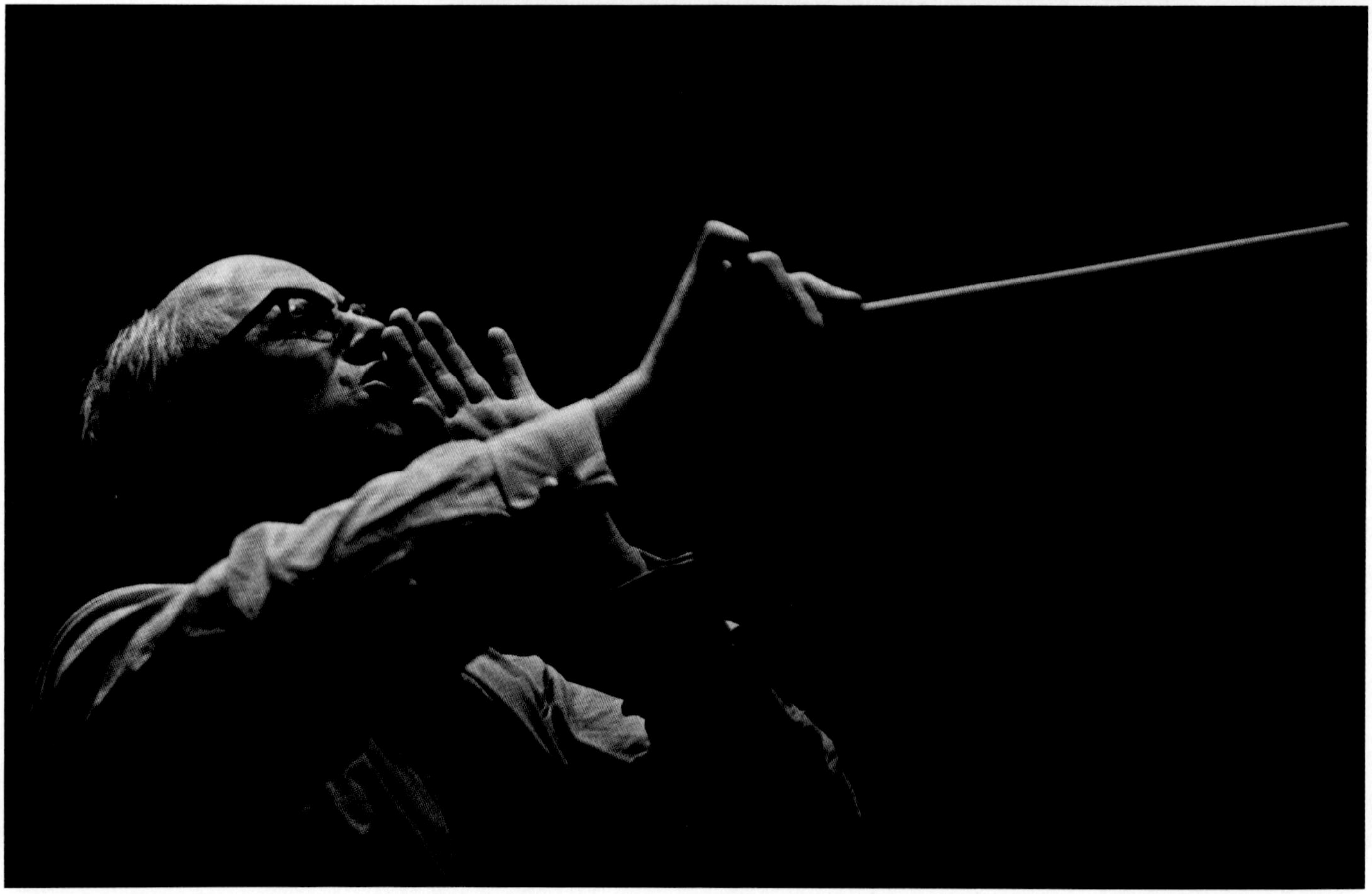

1968

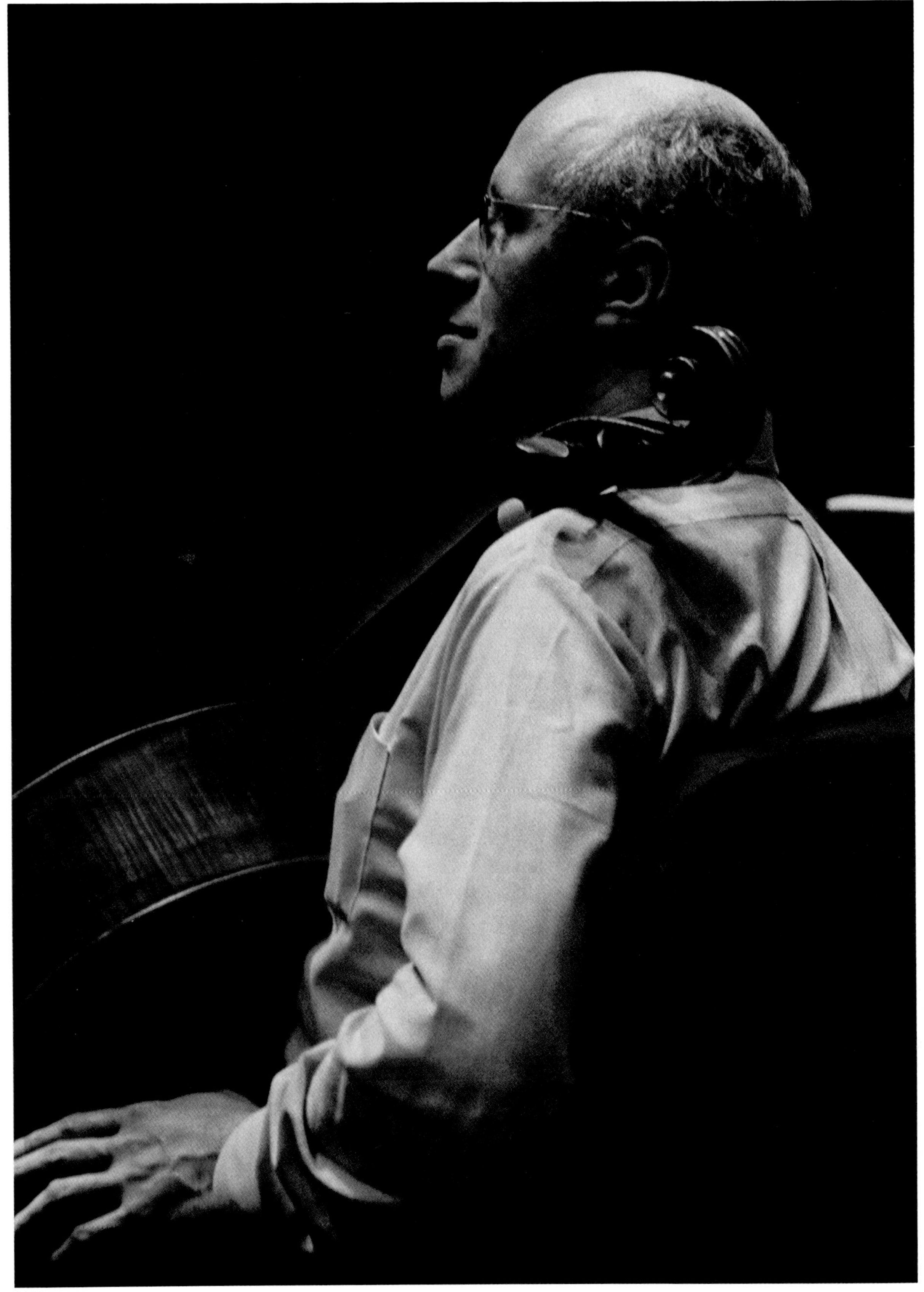

1968

Artur Rubinstein

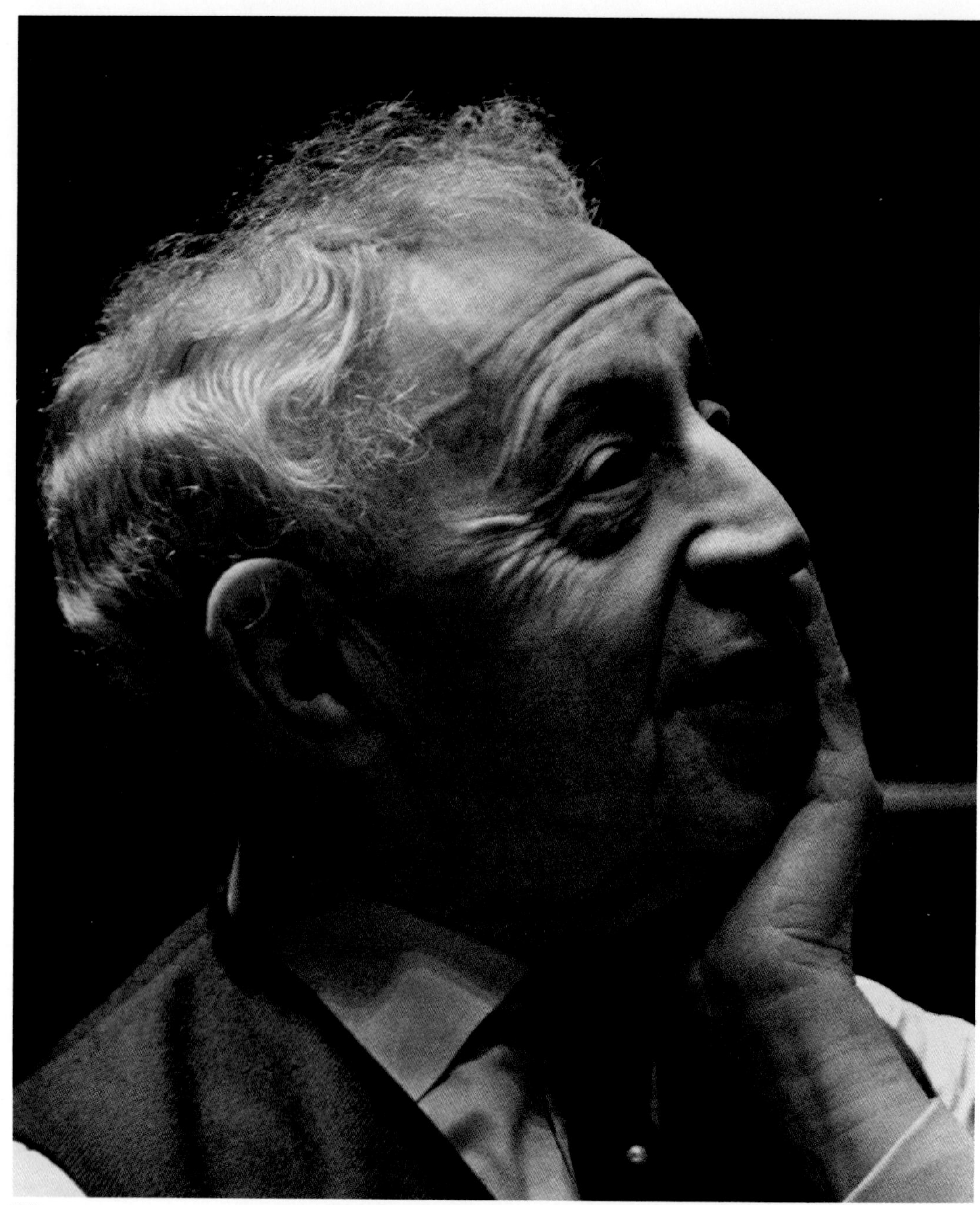

1968

The great wizard of the keyboard, a performer of indefatigable warmth and energy, and a man who loved life and lived it fully, Rubinstein was one of the most inspired and distinctive musicians of the century. A master interpreter of Chopin, and of much other 19th- and 20th-century repertory (his scope as a performer was enormous by today's standards), he concertized for more than 80 years, proving during that extraordinary career that he was truly in a class by himself.

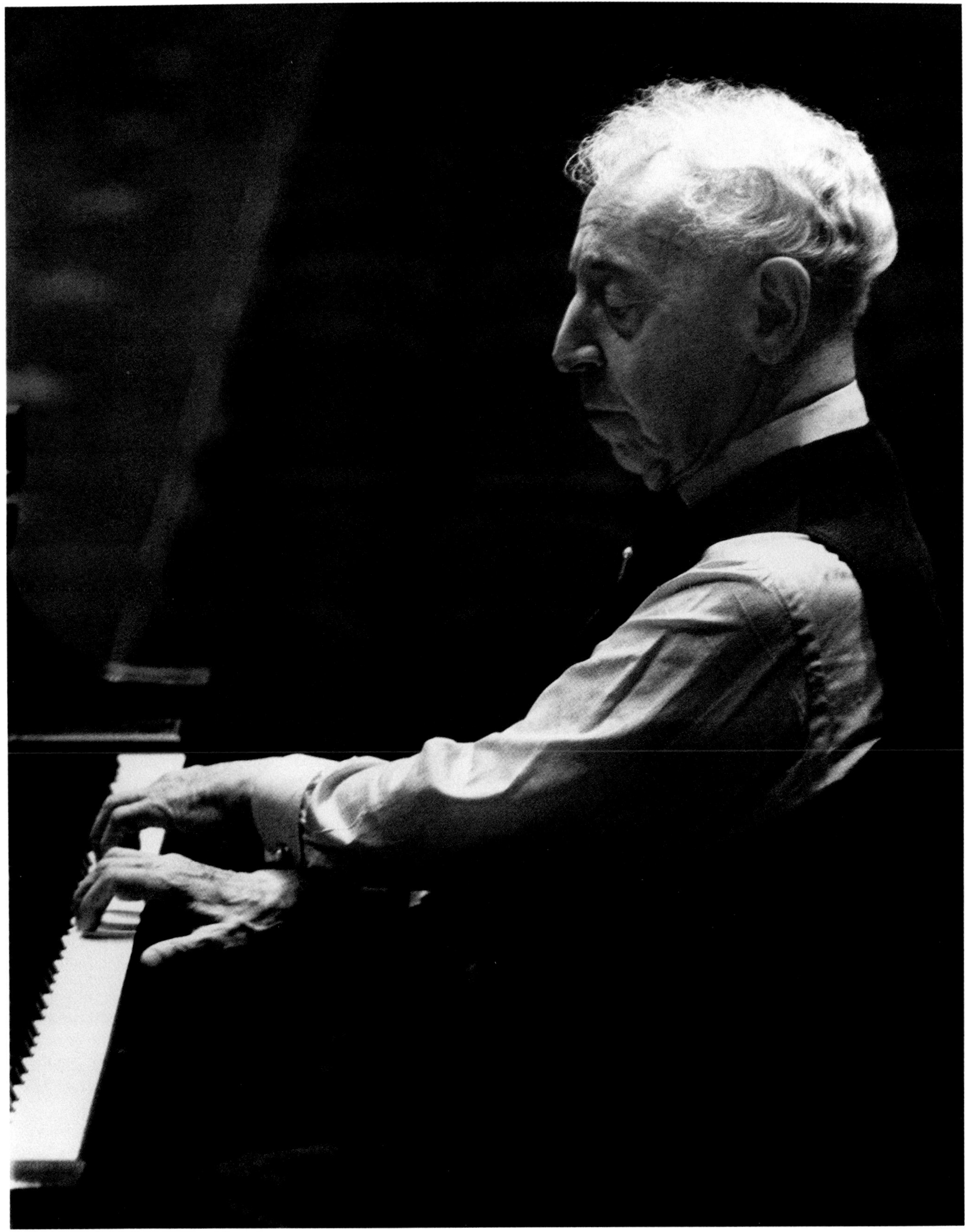

Julius Rudel

This versatile, Viennese-born conductor is a proven genius in the opera pit. His energy and resourcefulness helped establish the New York City Opera as one of the country's leading houses during a halcyon period in the 1960s and 1970s, and his curiosity, quickness, and creative temperament continue to make him one of the country's most valuable musicians. His repertory is extraordinarily large, and he remains a living link to pre-war performance traditions of the Austro-Germanic school.

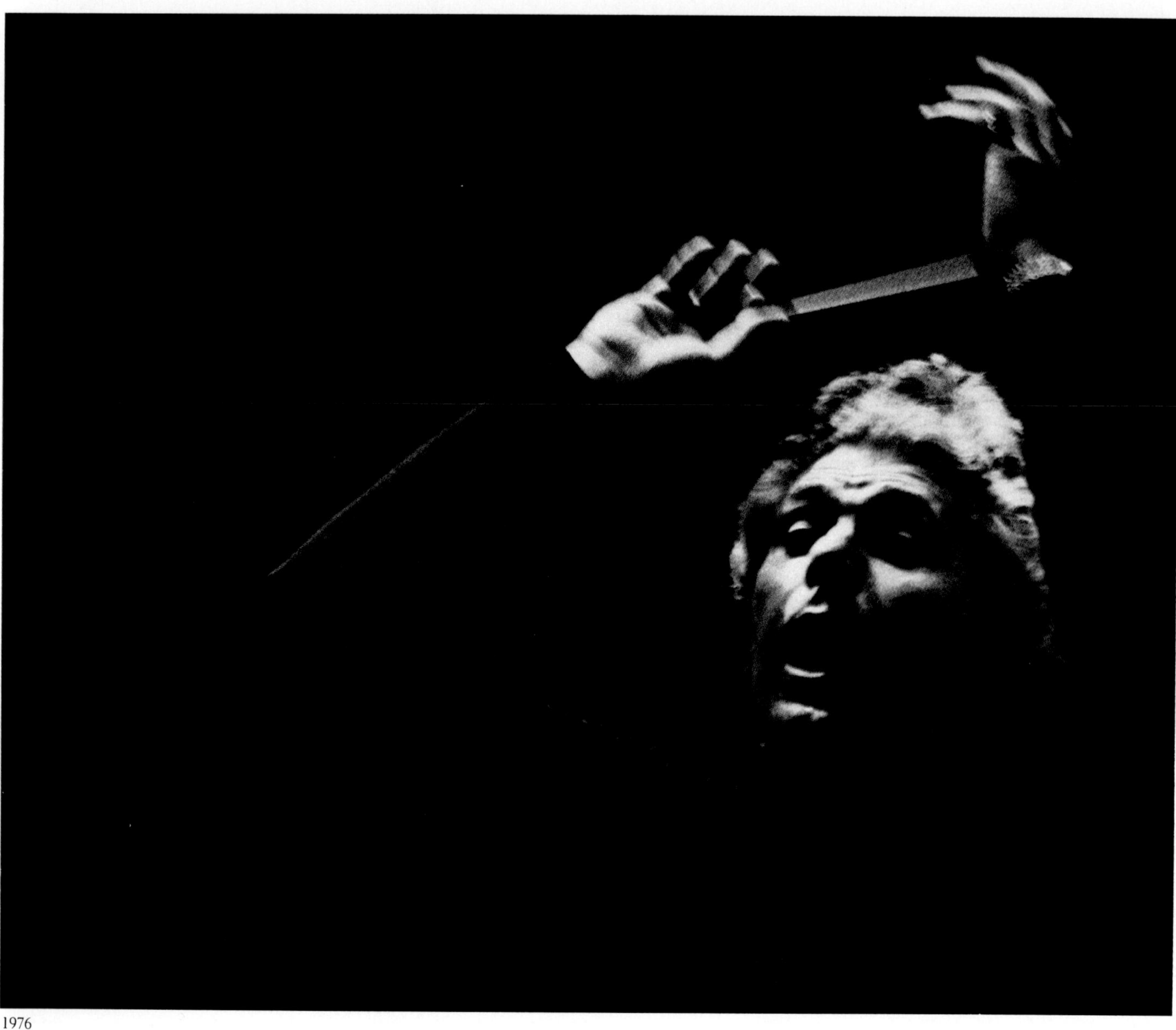

1976

MAX RUDOLF

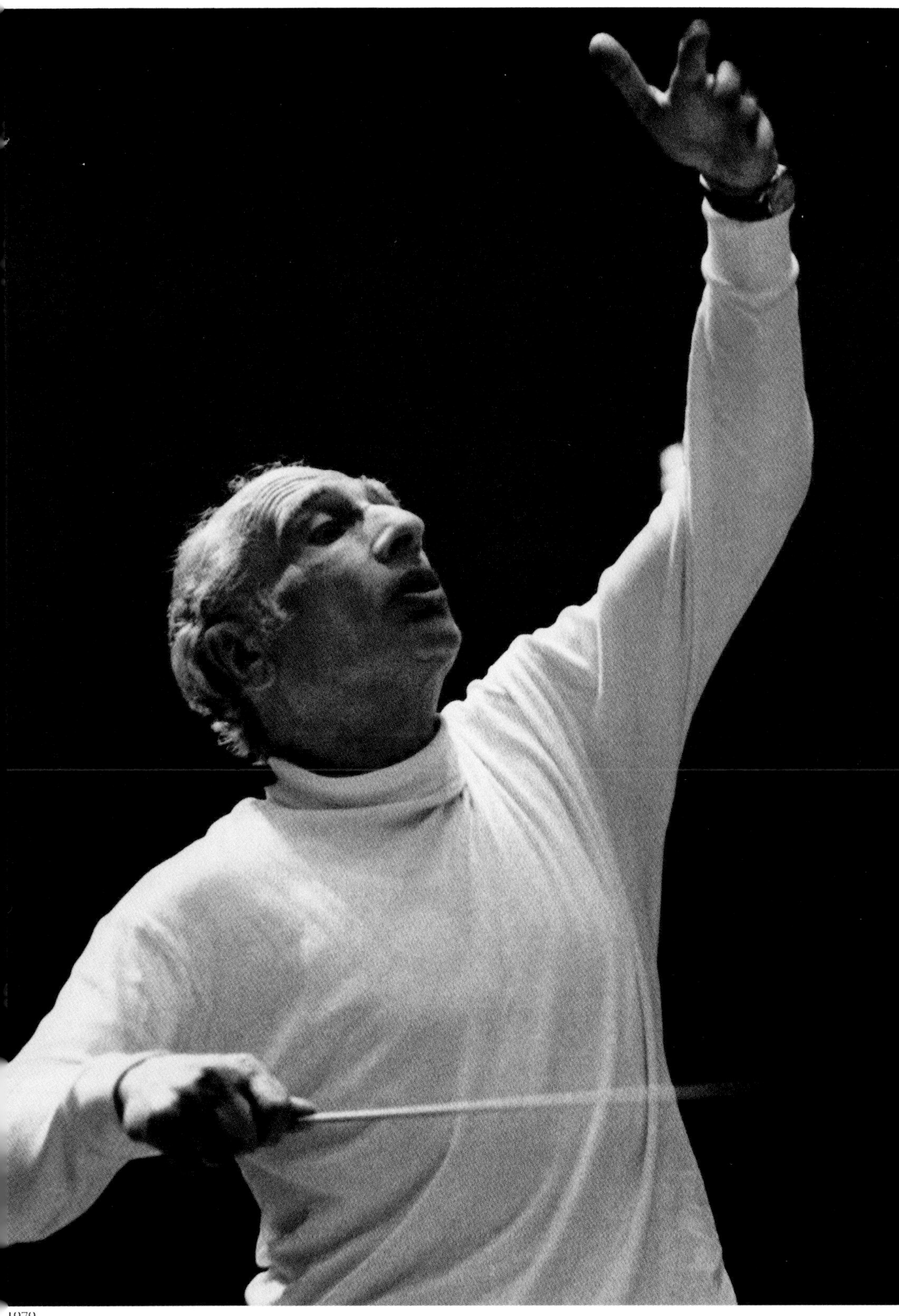

1979

Max Rudolf's wonderfully creative, kinetic performances broke most of the rules that his book *The Grammar of Conducting* laid down, but made you realize things about the music that no book could have told you. To hear a Mozart symphony with Rudolf conducting was to realize that the music, while most elegant, was also muscular. He was a superb collaborator and accompanist, and could have written books on conducting concertos and opera if he had wanted to.

Kurt Sanderling

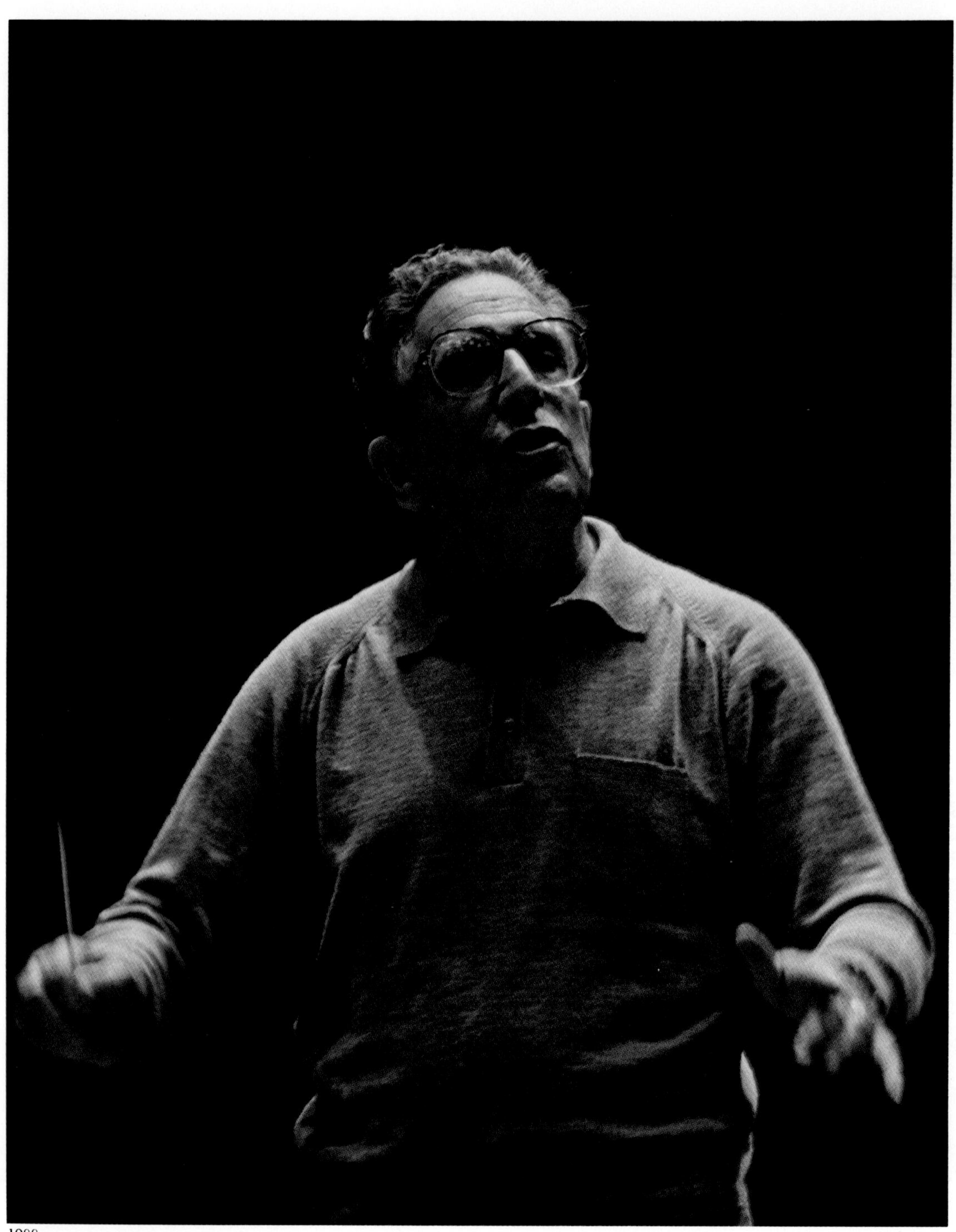

1988

Heavily influenced by the conductors he observed in the inter-war Berlin of his youth, Kurt Sanderling is a conductor of impressive abilities. After emigrating from Germany in 1936, he became an assistant conductor of the Moscow Radio Orchestra, then music director of the Kharkov Philharmonic, and eventually permanent conductor of the Leningrad Philharmonic, an appointment shared with Evgeny Mravinsky. He has toured widely in Europe, Japan, North America, and Australia, and has worked frequently during the past decade with London's Philharmonia Orchestra. In 1977, Sanderling became music director of the Berlin Symphony, but he has continued his schedule of guest conducting in this country with the orchestras of Los Angeles, San Francisco, New York, and Boston.

Hermann Scherchen

A musician of notably wide-ranging interests, he conducted the established repertory with conviction and authority and gave ground-breaking interpretations of many contemporary scores. He was also active throughout his career as an author and as editor of several musical journals. German by birth, he left the Third Reich in 1933, eventually settling in Switzerland.

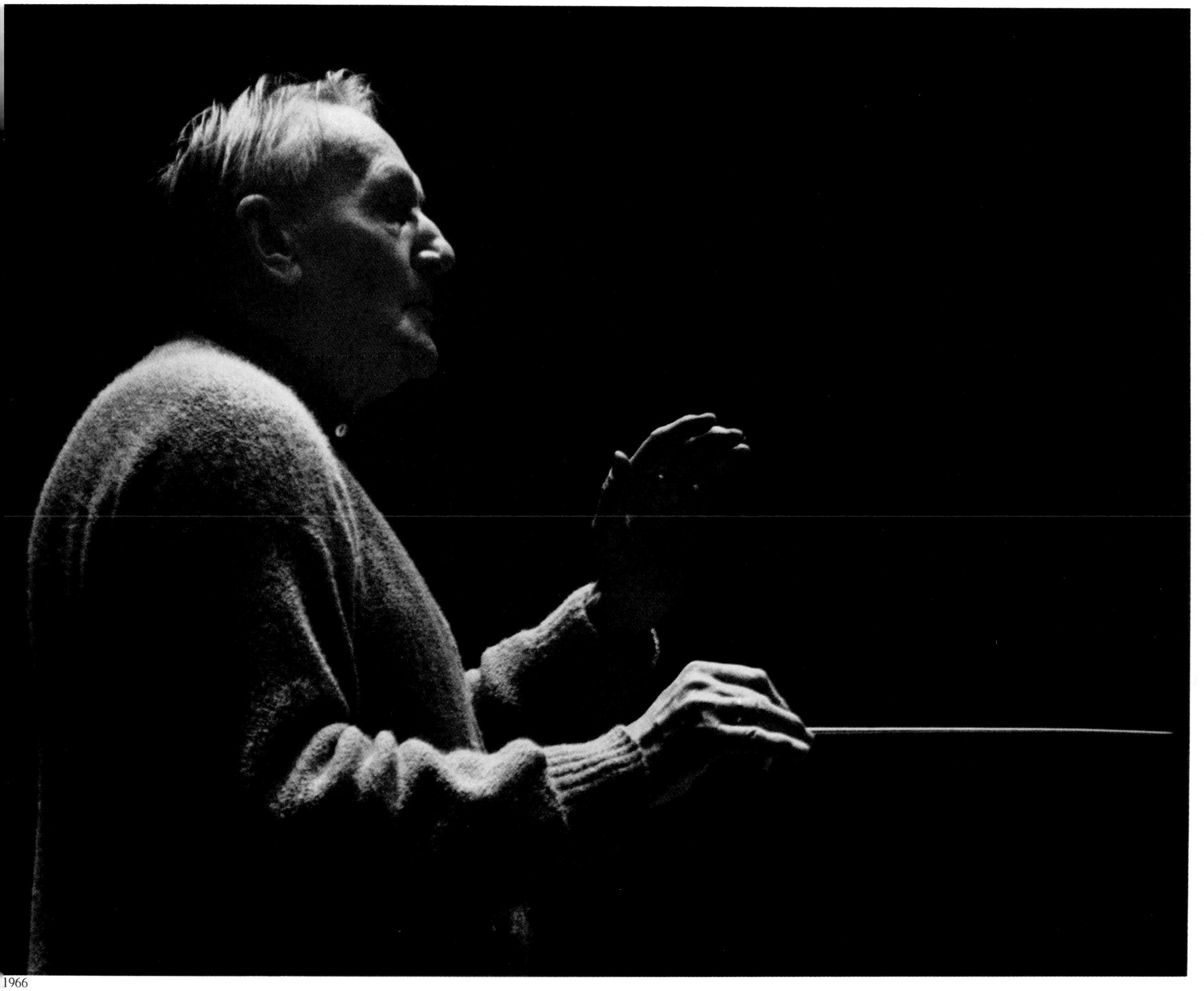

1966

GUNTHER SCHULLER

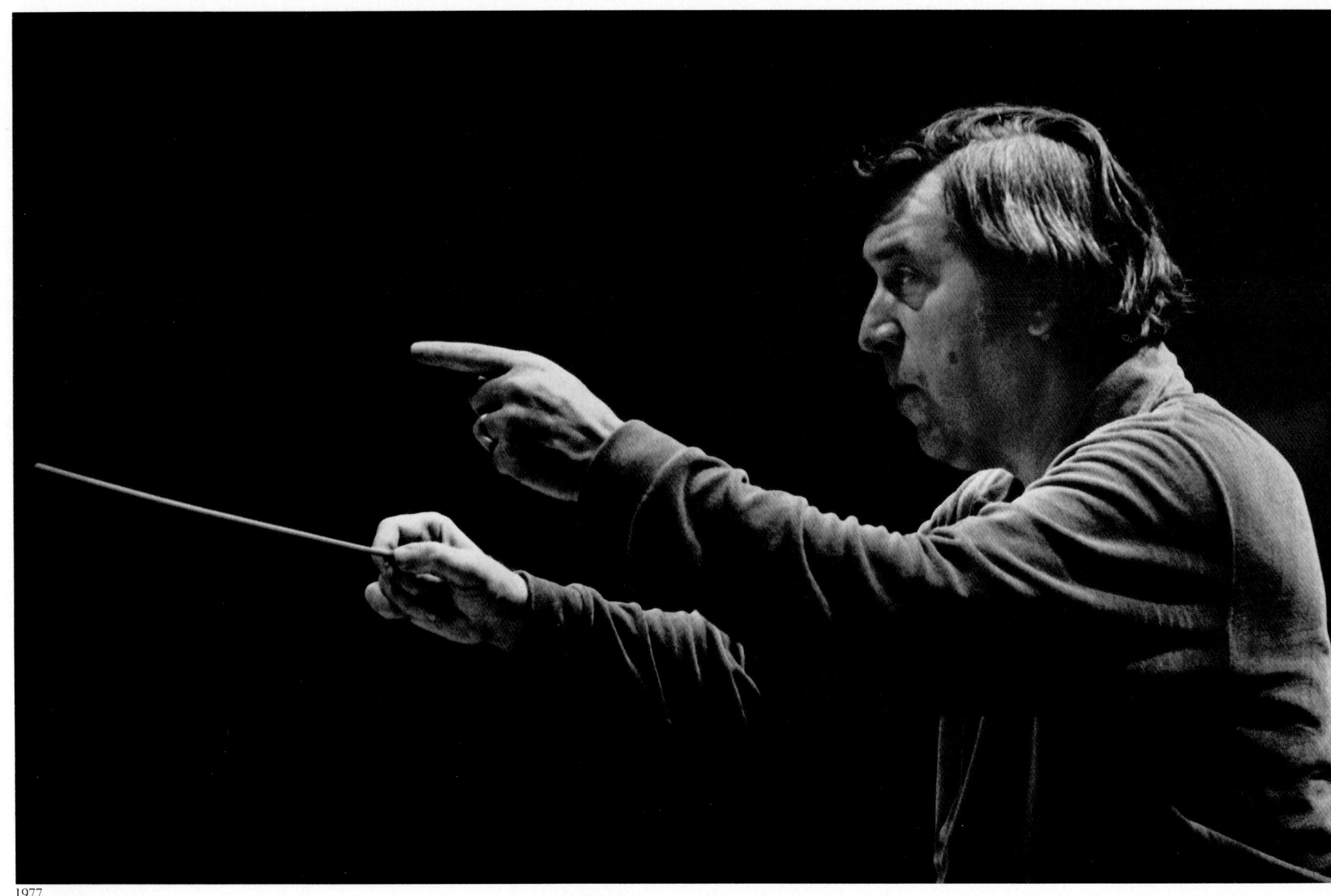

1977

A jack of all musical trades, Gunther Schuller played horn in the Metropolitan Opera Orchestra from 1945 to 1959, simultaneously carving a niche for himself in jazz circles and earning a reputation as a composer of classical, jazz, and "third stream" (a term he coined) works. Noted for his eclectic sensitivities, his alert and receptive mind, and his talents as an educator and administrator, he is one of the music world's most honored activists. When all is said and done, he remains one of its finest creators as well: a composer of *real* music and a willing explorer of new sounds.

NORMAN SCRIBNER

"You're not together," he will tell his chorus. "You sound like a bunch of beans going down a funnel." With his attention to detail and unorthodox rehearsal techniques, Norman Scribner has made the Choral Arts Society of Washington into one of the country's premiere vocal ensembles and brought a special animation to the capital's musical life. He has also prepared choruses for numerous other conductors, having developed particularly close working relationships with Leonard Bernstein and Mstislav Rostropovich.

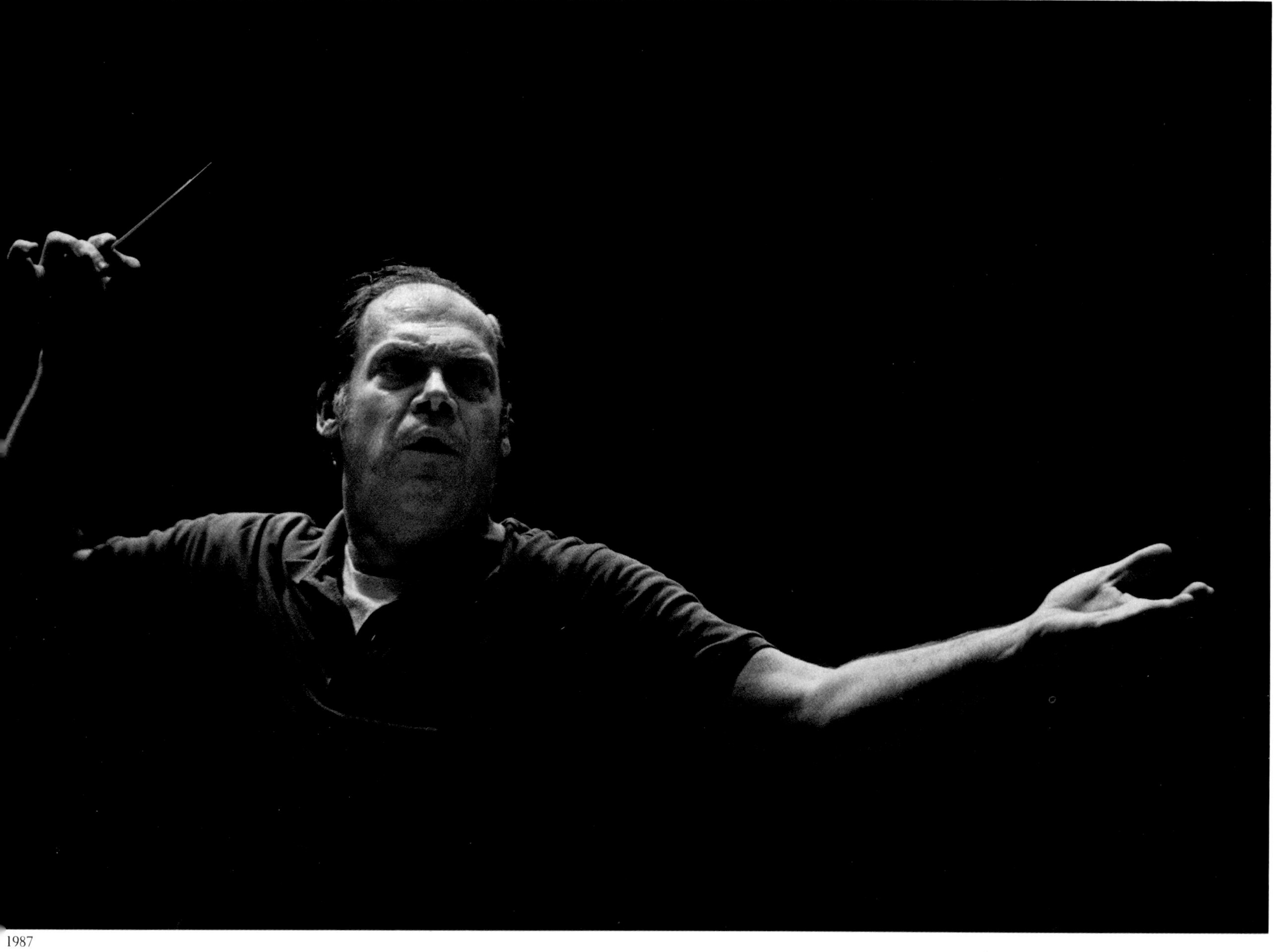

1987

"Each of us is but an island," he said near the end of his long life. "Music is the ocean." He established the guitar as a concert instrument, rescuing it from neglect and creating a new technique, a new repertory, and a new style of playing. Yet he remained as inimitable as the sun or the mountains of his native Spain.

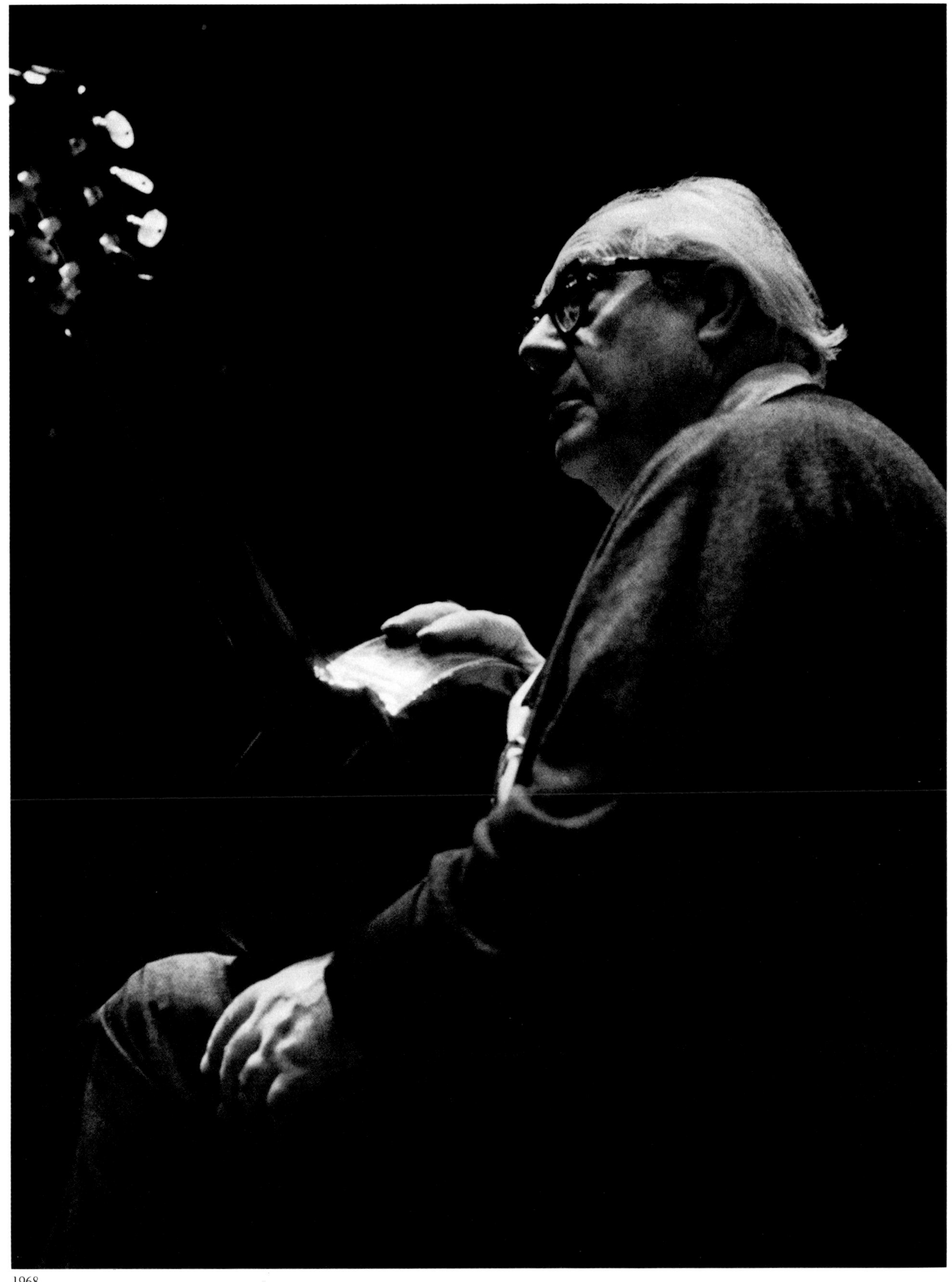

PETER SERKIN

A superb case of following in your father's footsteps while not following at all. Adventurous, offbeat, unconventional, he is a brilliant musician, as thoroughly attuned to the music of the present as to that of the past. He has championed contemporary composers of diverse outlooks, played Beethoven on the fortepiano, and concertized—with equal ease—as a chamber musician and as a soloist with the country's major orchestras. Nothing is beyond his reach, yet he is so introspective as to sometimes seem introverted, even detached.

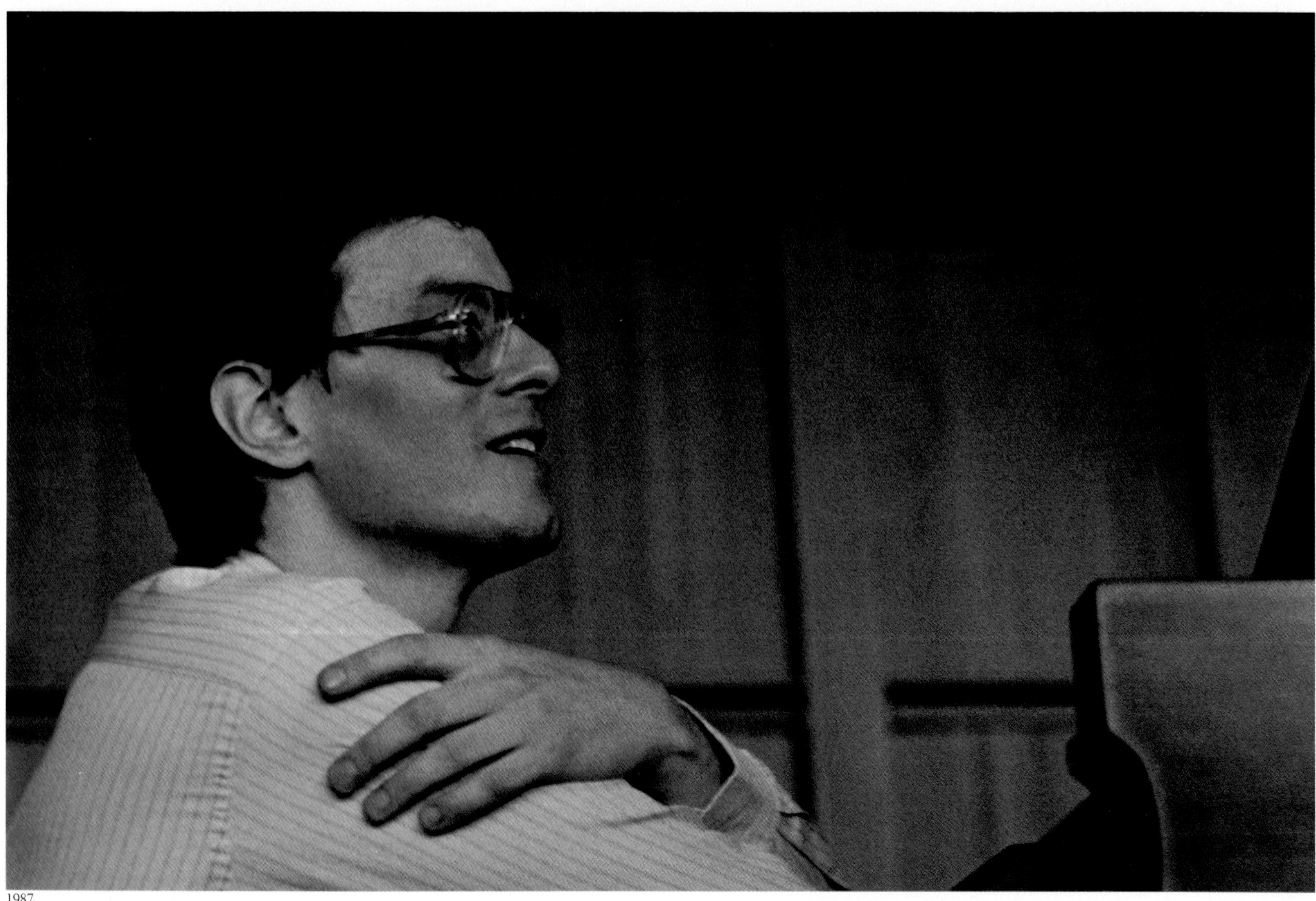

1987

DOC SEVERINSEN

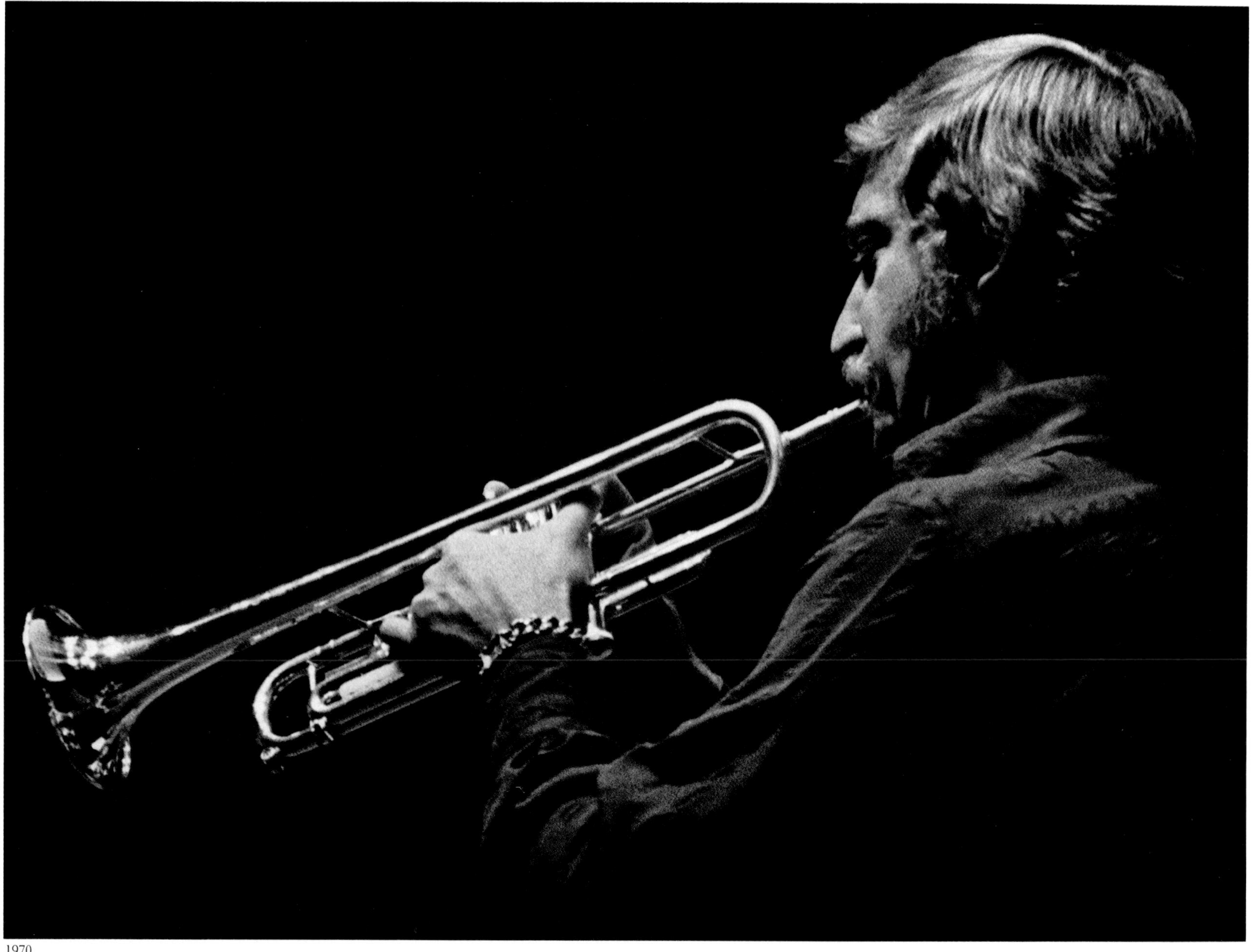

1970

Johnny Carson's musical lieutenant, leader of the band on "The Tonight Show," and
one of the jazz world's great trumpeters, here's . . . Doc!

DMITRI SHOSTAKOVICH

Dmitri Shostakovich, like his father Maxim and his grandfather, the composer Dmitri Shostakovich, has made a name for himself as a pianist. The fact that he could play the piano well enough to perform on tour with the Soviet orchestra that his father conducted enabled both of them to defect in 1981. They were quickly invited to perform with the National Symphony Orchestra, and on that occasion, Dmitri played the piano concerto that his grandfather had written for his father to play as a young man.

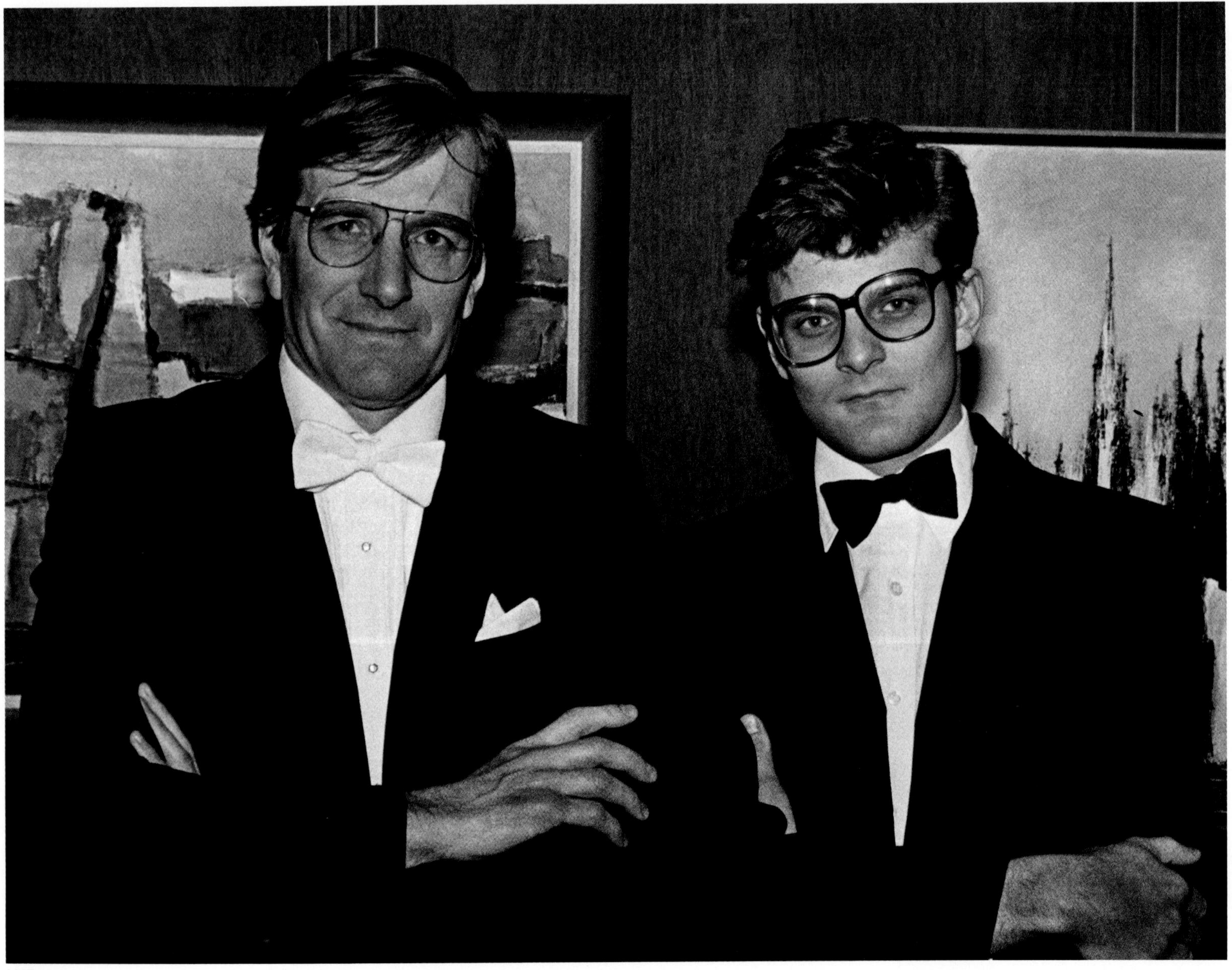

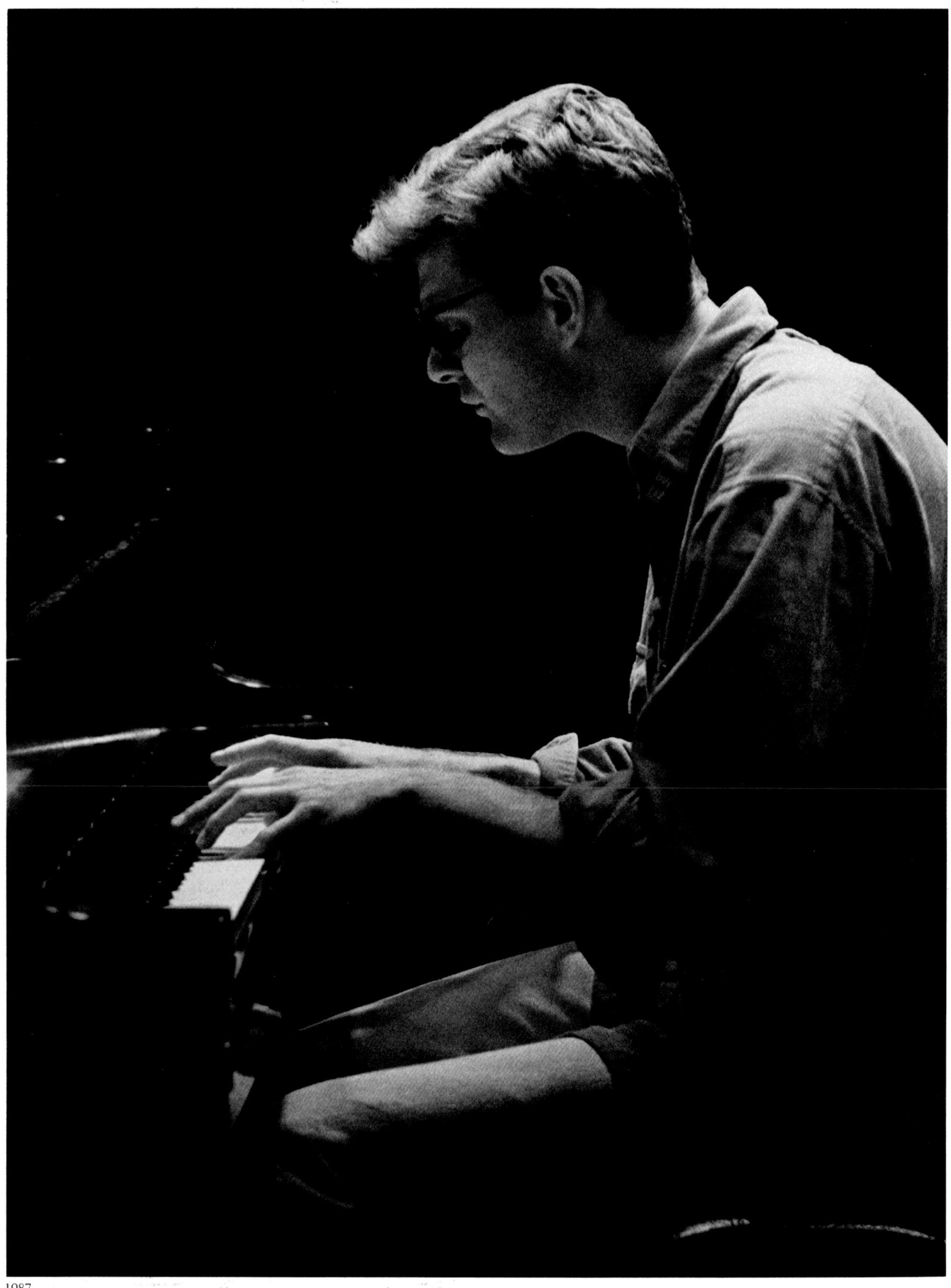

1987

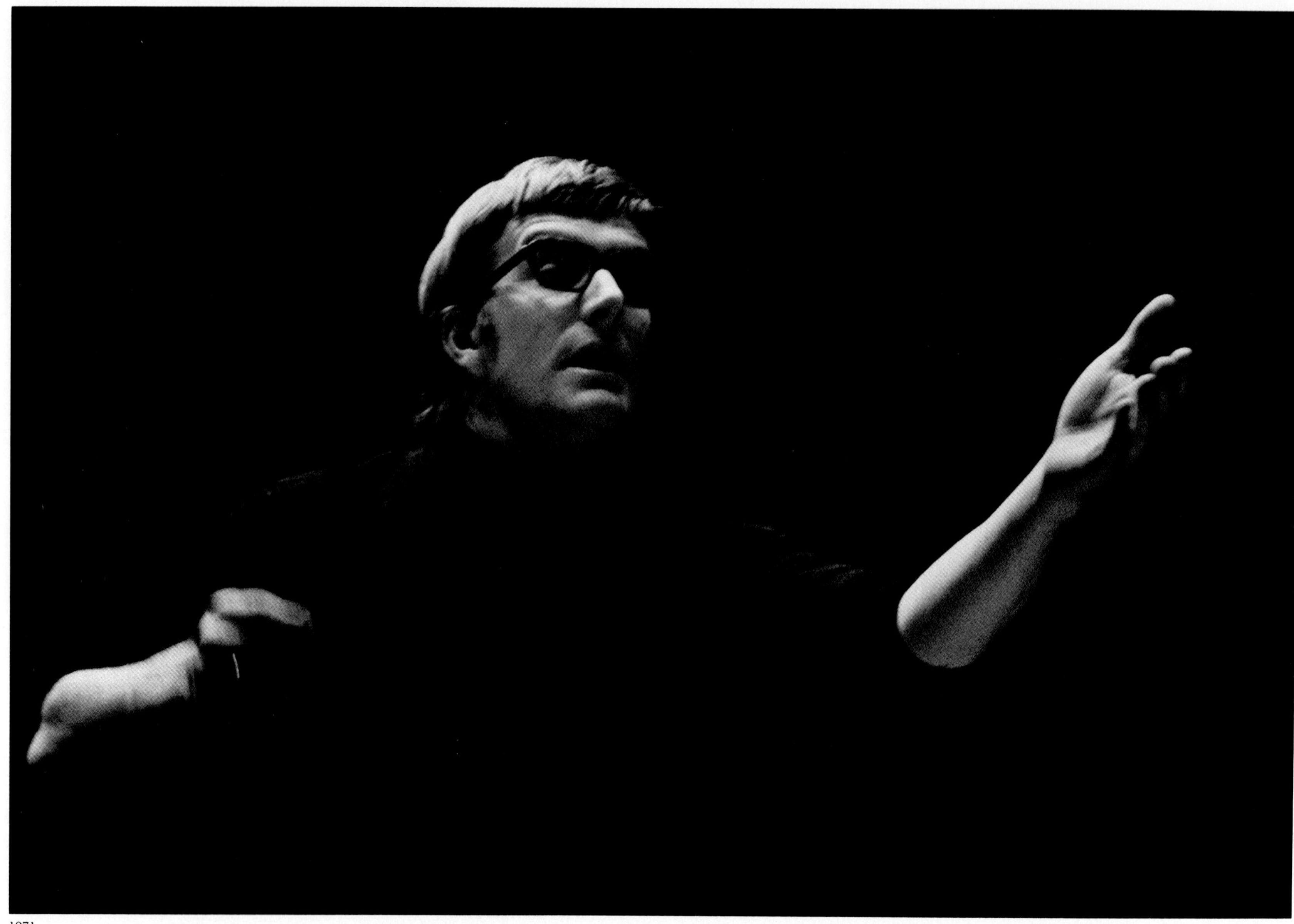

1971

Maxim Shostakovich studied the piano and gave the premiere of his father's second concerto when he was nineteen. He subsequently became a conductor, and from 1971 to 1981 was music director of the U.S.S.R. State Radio Orchestra. Shortly before his father died, Maxim promised that he would "bring the blood of Shostakovich to freedom," which he did in 1981, defecting with his son Dmitri (the composer's grandson and lookalike, also a pianist) while the two were on a tour with the Soviet orchestra in West Germany. In celebration of his freedom, Shostakovich accepted the invitation of his father's friend and fellow countryman, Mstislav Rostropovich, to conduct the National Symphony on the West Lawn of the U.S. Capitol on Memorial Day, 1981. He subsequently appeared with a number of other American orchestras as a guest conductor, and was named music director of the New Orleans Philharmonic.

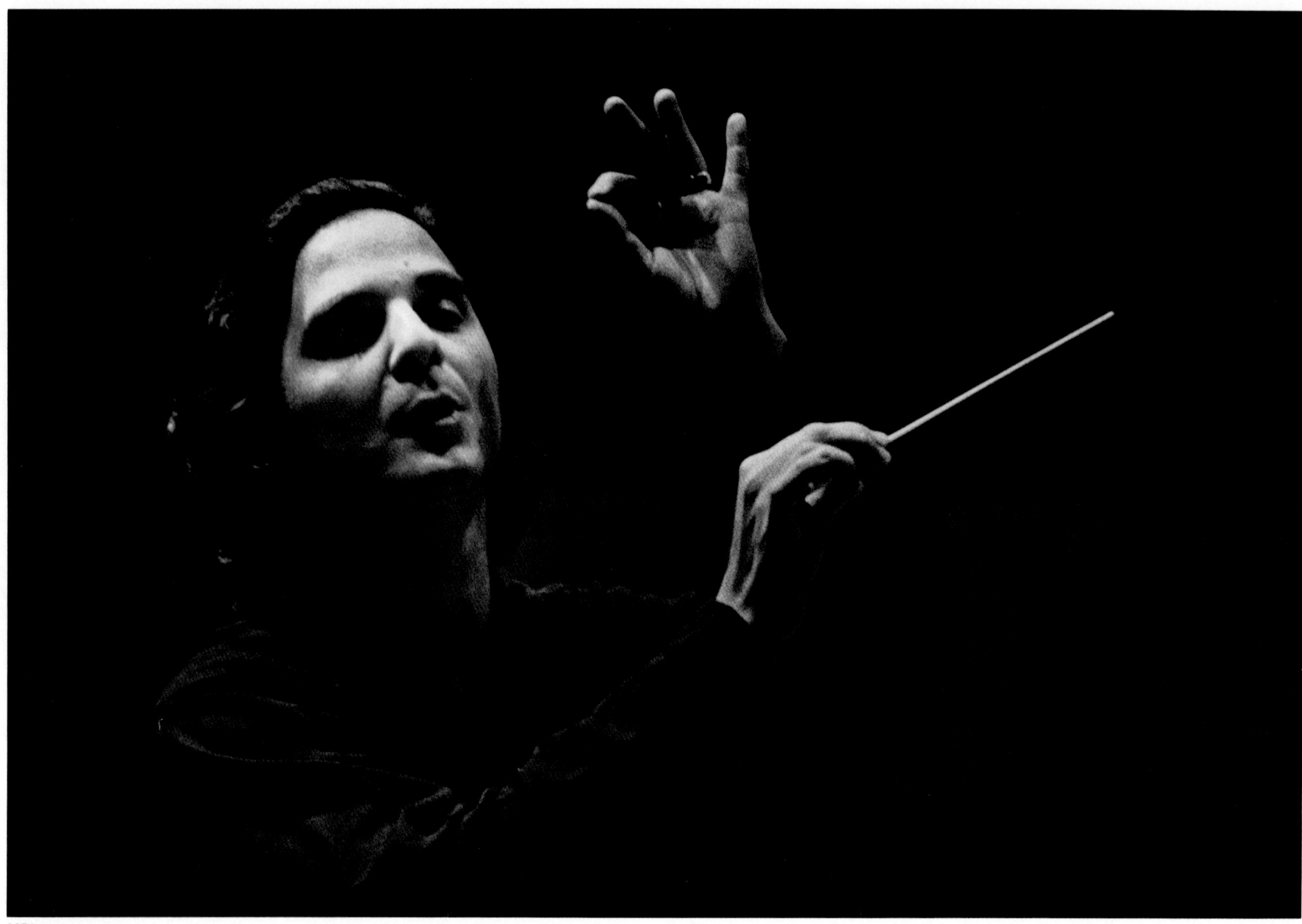

1976

The articulate and enterprising resident conductor of the National Symphony from 1973 to 1977, Murry Sidlin has subsequently served as the music director of the New Haven Symphony and Long Beach Symphony. A sensitive interpreter and shrewd musical diplomat, he has developed new approaches to programming and audience education, and done much to encourage the talents of younger colleagues.

GIUSEPPE SINOPOLI

When a wind player became ill at a concert he was conducting, the Venetian-born Sinopoli—who received his degree in medicine at the University of Padua and interned in surgery and psychiatry before devoting himself to the baton—stopped the performance, stepped off the podium, and attended to the player. One of the more controversial figures in the world of music today, Sinopoli is steeped in the arcana of serialism and psychoanalytic theory (both of which are of Viennese origin, interestingly enough) and approaches music with a rarefied and highly disciplined intellectualism that, on occasion, produces striking results. As a composer he is highly regarded in certain *avant-garde* circles; he has a good deal of chamber music and several orchestral works to his credit. Although he lacks many of the basic technical skills of an accomplished conductor, he has been able to achieve reasonably good results on record by working exclusively with world-class ensembles. In 1983 he was named principal conductor of the Philharmonia Orchestra of London.

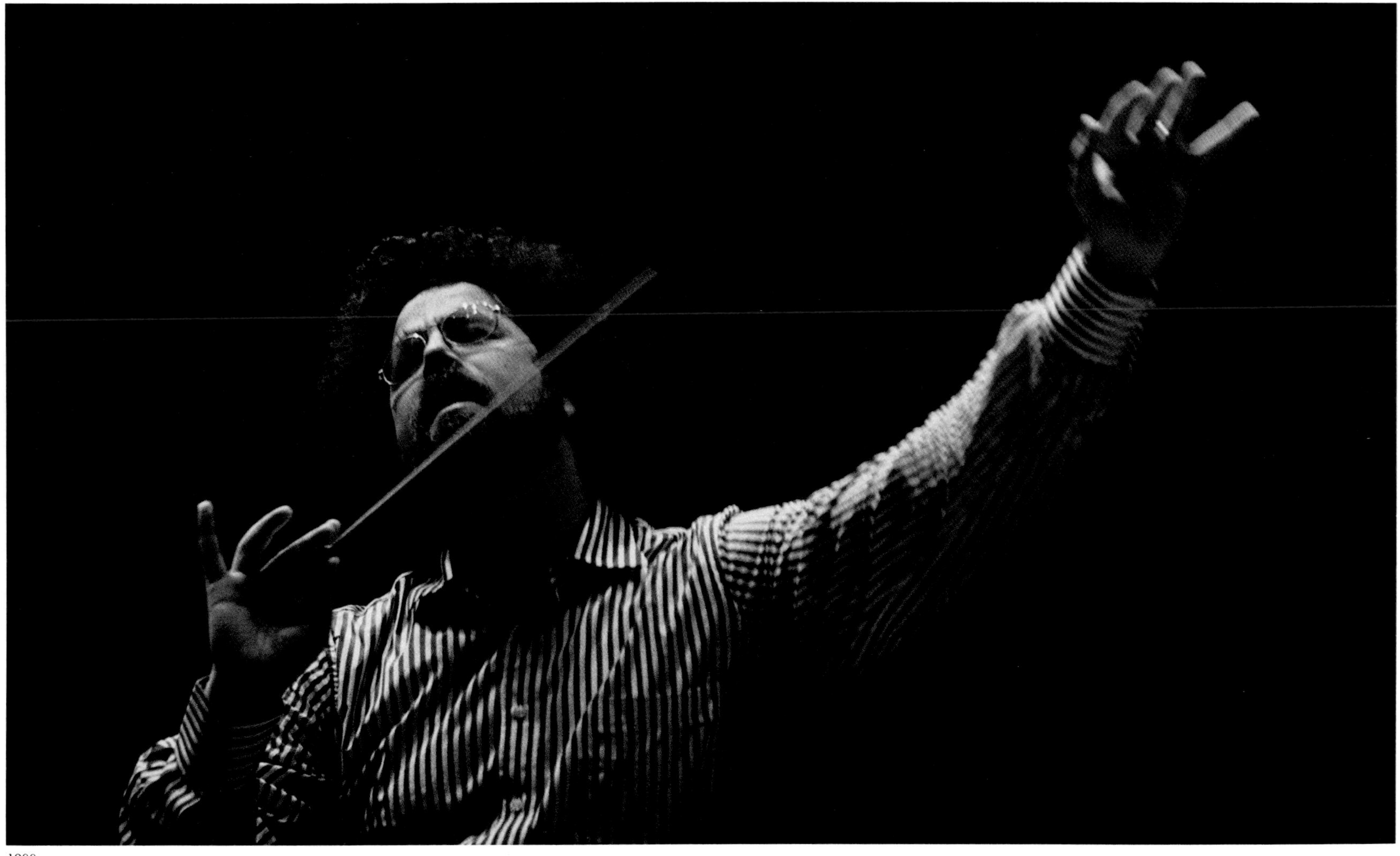

Stanislaw Skrowaczewski

The son of a brain surgeon, Skrowaczewski denies that he was a child prodigy, but it is hard to think of any other phrase to describe someone who wrote his first orchestral score when he was eight and who had it performed by the Lwow Philharmonic the very same year. Long associated with the Minnesota Orchestra, where he served as music director for nineteen years, he was appointed principal conductor and musical advisor to the Hallé Orchestra of Manchester, England, in 1983, and has conducted every major orchestra in the Americas, Europe, Israel, and Japan.

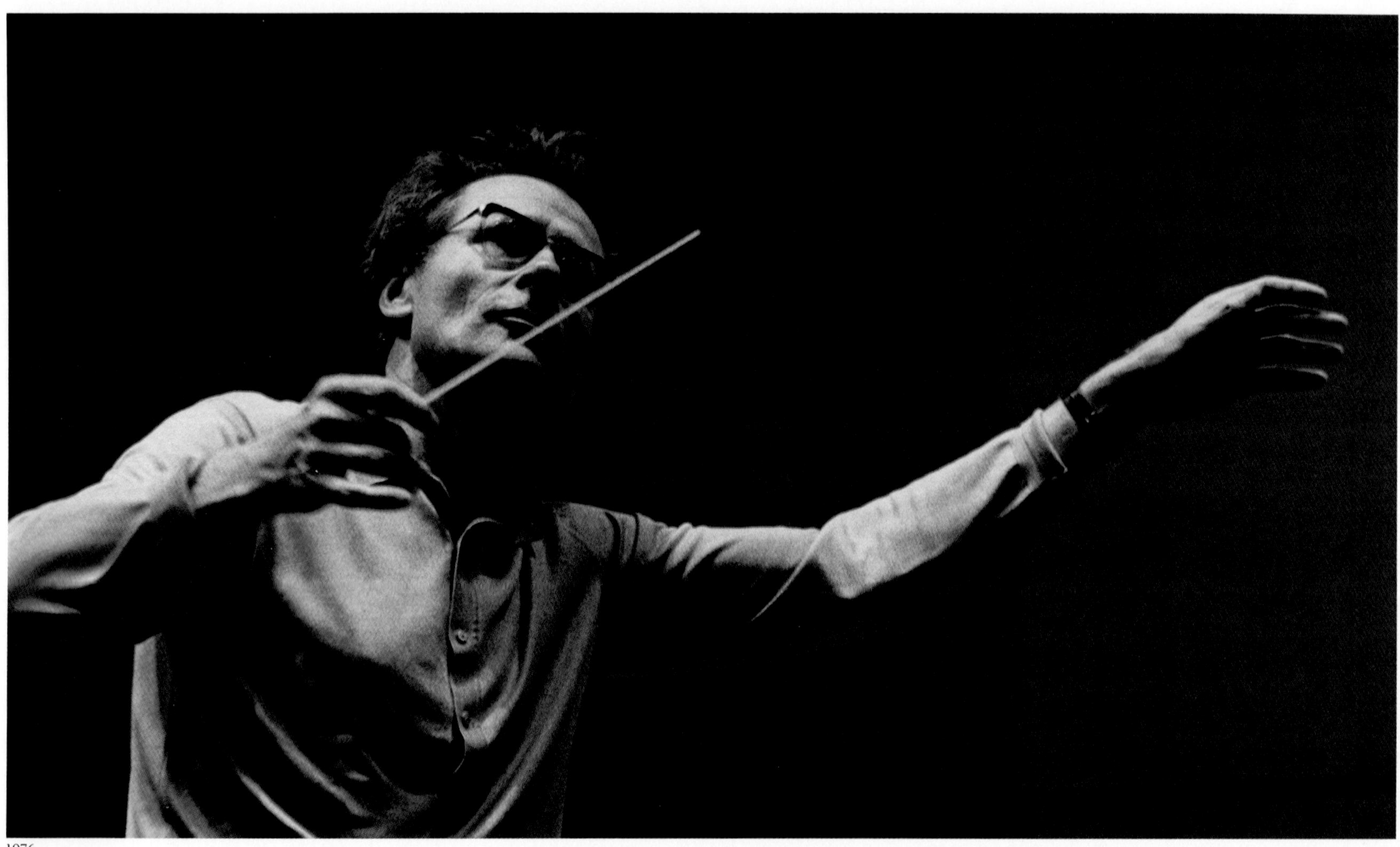

1976

WILLIAM STECK

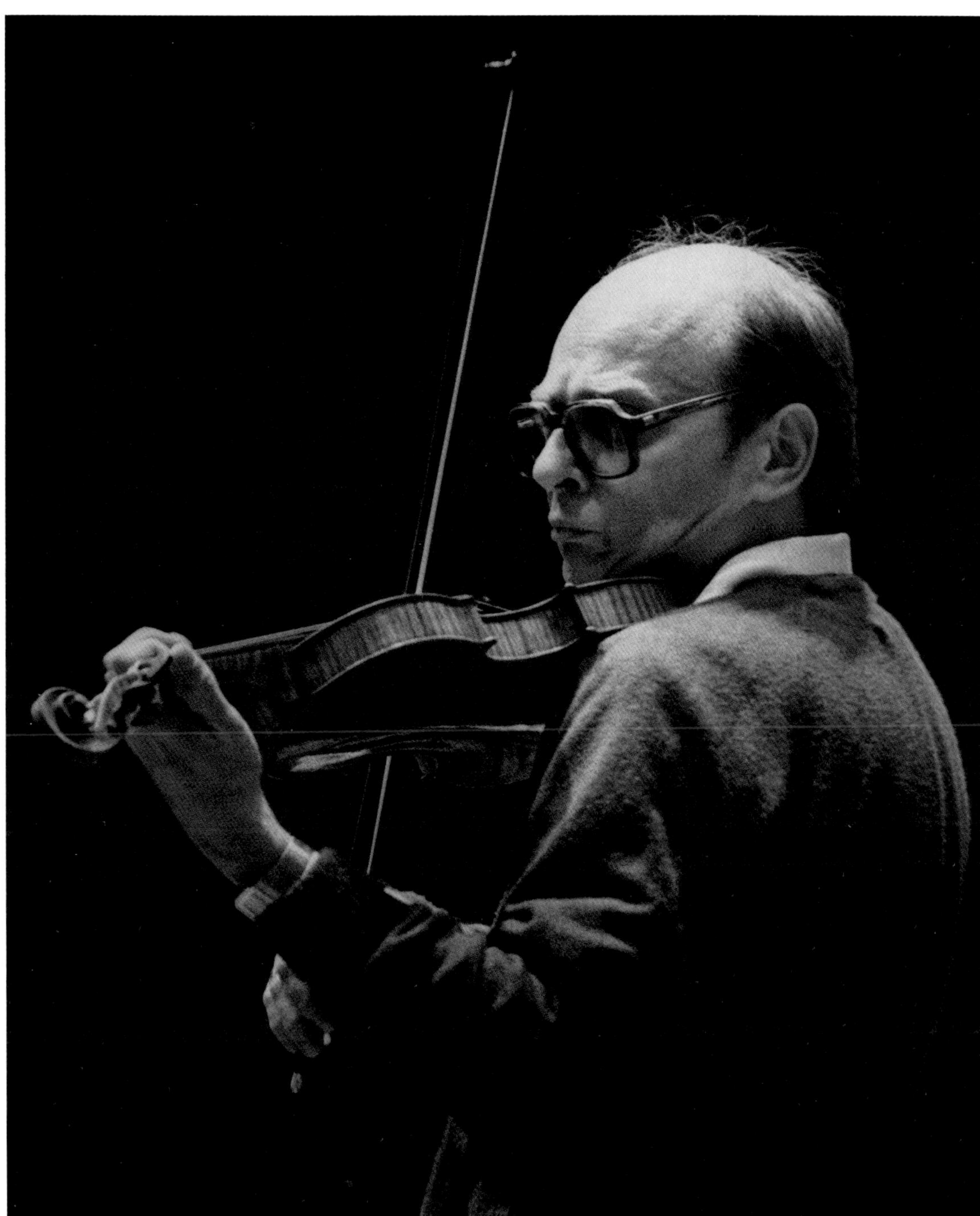

A concertmaster must be more than a confident solo player—he or she must be a leader who can help an orchestra's string sections play with unanimity, and a collaborator (sometimes even a teacher) who can help conductors and other soloists to achieve the musical results they seek. Skill, intuition, authority, and calm are required, along with uncommon reserves of energy. William Steck, concertmaster of the National Symphony since 1982, has it all.

ISAAC STERN

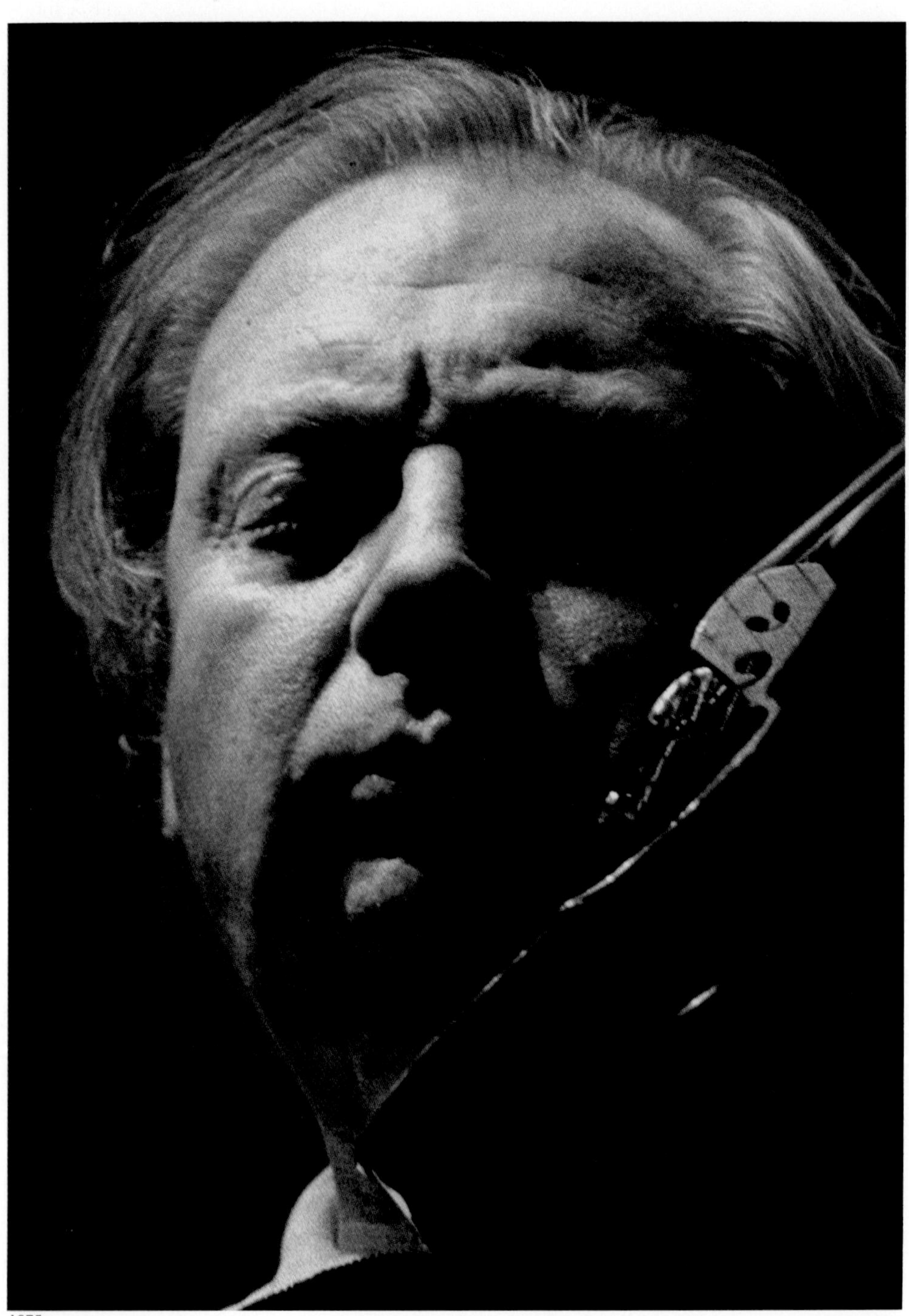

1975

Isaac Stern is the most influential musician in America today. He not only saved Carnegie Hall from the wrecker's ball in 1960, and spearheaded its reconstruction in 1986, but he was, and on occasion still can be, one of the supreme masters of the violin. He has collaborated with virtually every important American conductor of the post-war era, has commissioned and premiered major works by Penderecki, Rochberg, Dutilleux, and Davies, among others, and has recorded the literature from Vivaldi to Stravinsky. He has played a decisive role in the nurturing and development of younger talent, master-minding the careers of several musicians whose achievements may someday even surpass his own.

LEOPOLD STOKOWSKI

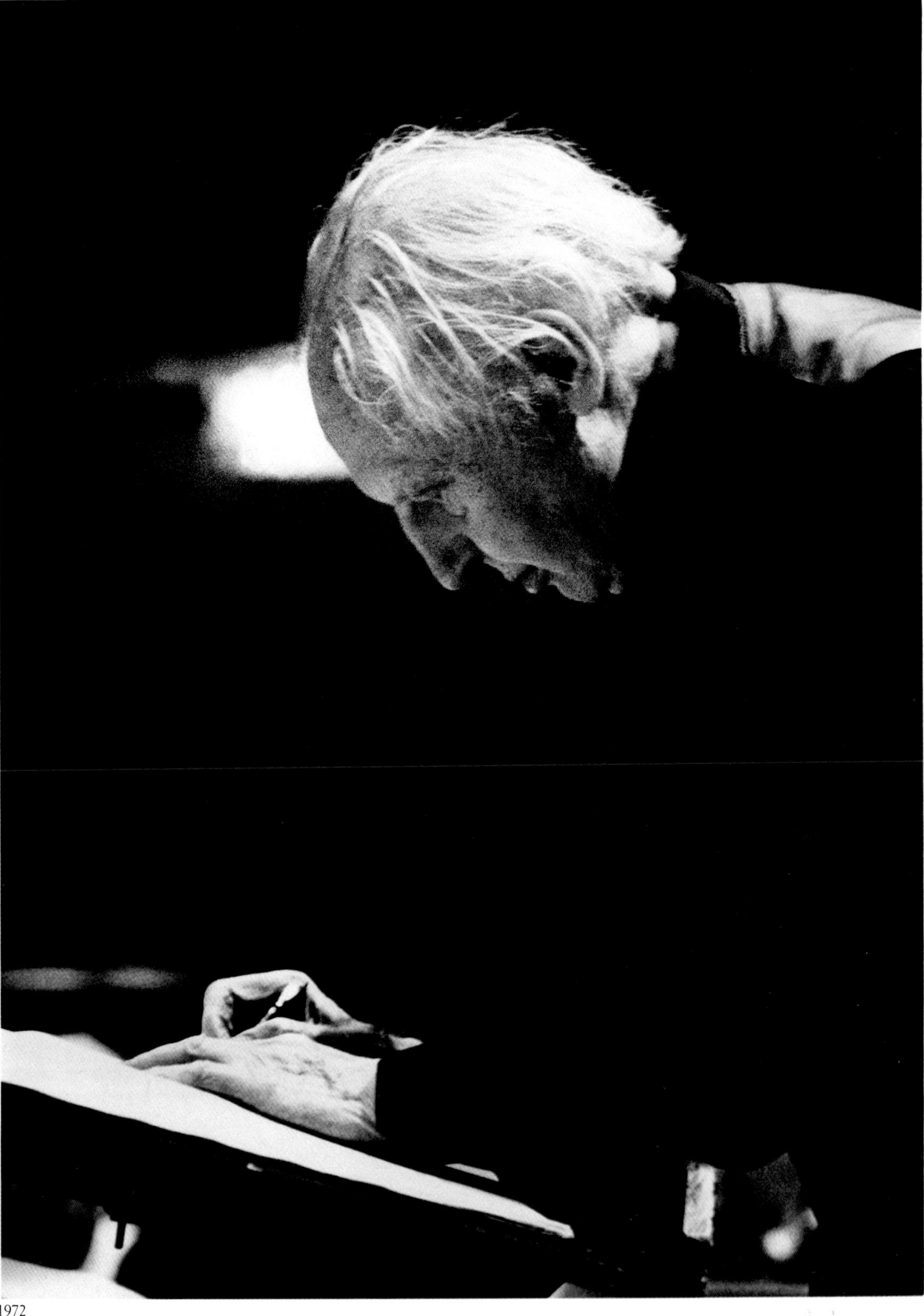

The greatest magician the podium has known, Stokowski more often than not created music in his own image. But during his years at the helm of the Philadelphia Orchestra (1912–1938) he fashioned it into the world's foremost symphonic ensemble, leading premieres of some of the century's most important works and cultivating a virtuosity and beauty of tone that were unsurpassed then and remain among the supreme examples of the conductor's art. Stokie was capable of making any orchestra he faced into a vehicle for his extraordinarily coloristic interpretations. He continued to be active on the podium and in front of the microphone into his nineties.

1972

HENRYK SZERYNG

There were two Henryk Szeryngs—the serious, profound musician, humble before the great works of the violin literature, and the dignified, at times somewhat arrogant artist who preferred to be thought of, and addressed as, the ambassador of his adopted country of Mexico. Yet the two were really one, and no matter where he went, Szeryng functioned as an ambassador for music, one whose elegance, impeccable taste and patrician manner compelled respect.

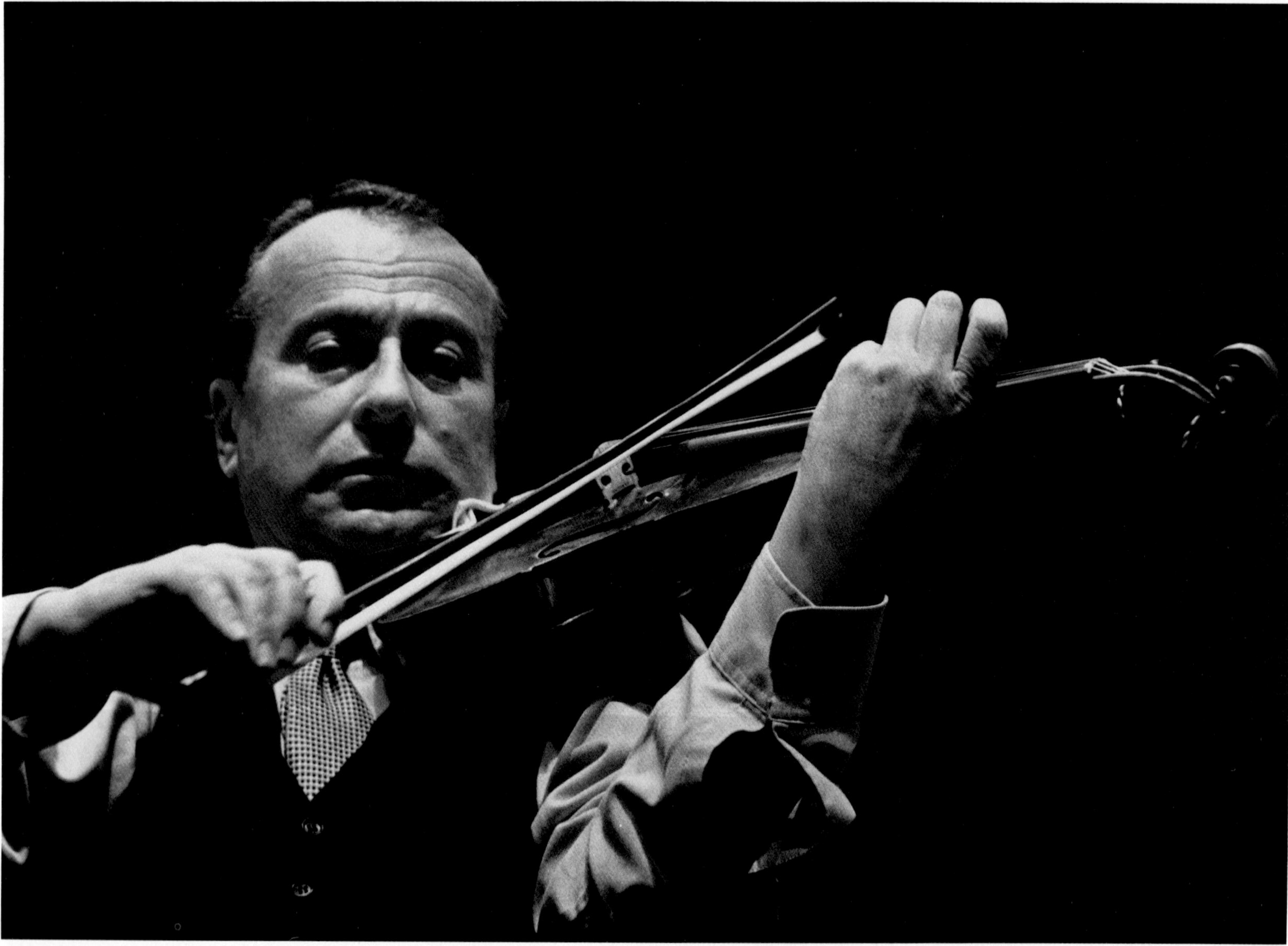

1975

EDOUARD VAN REMOORTEL

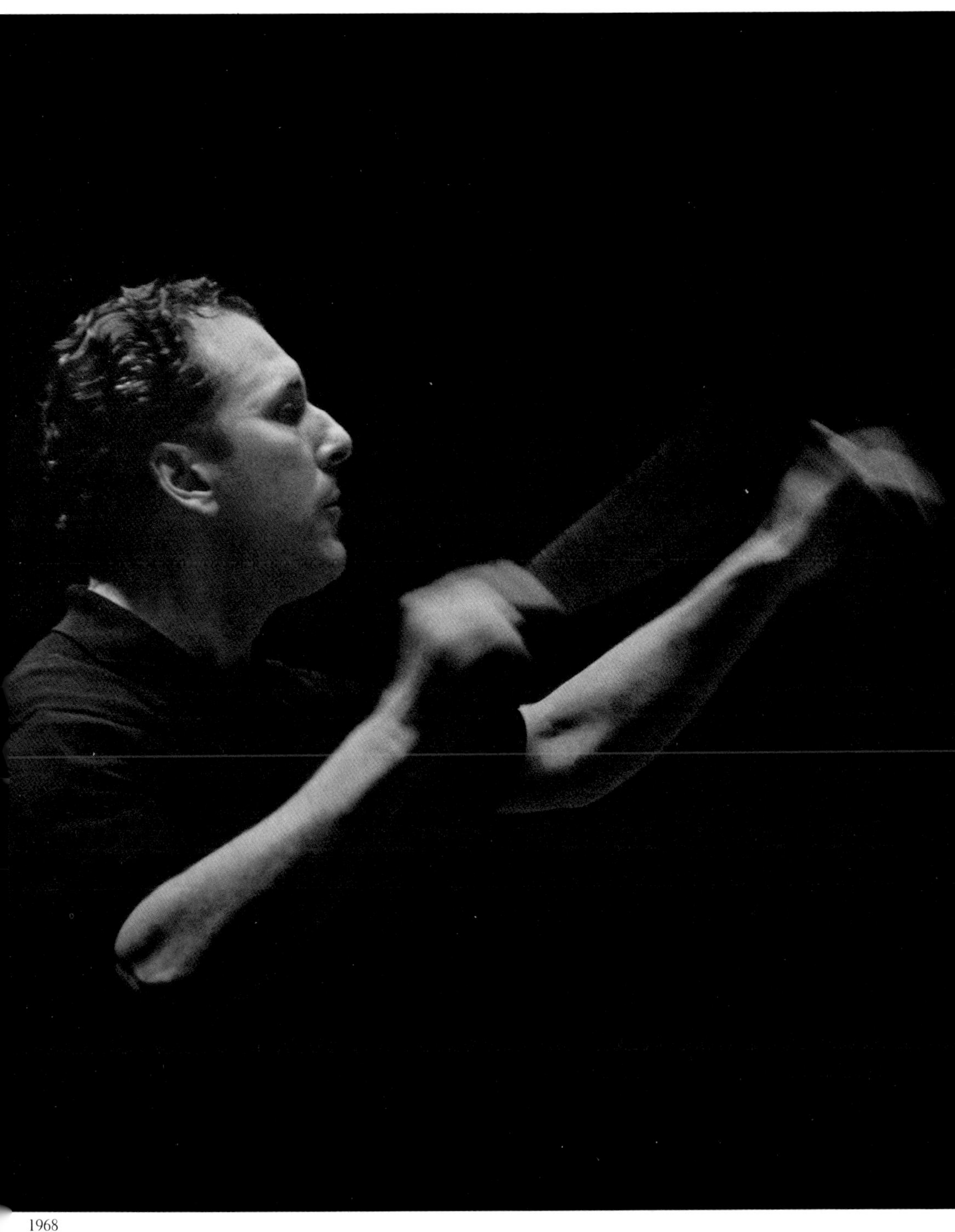

1968

He was the music director of the St. Louis
Symphony Orchestra from 1958 to 1962,
having served prior to that as principal
conductor of the Belgian National Orchestra.
In 1965, he became artistic consultant to
the Monte Carlo Opera Orchestra. He died
in 1977—two weeks short of his fifty-first
birthday.

Galina Vishnevskaya

The leading Russian soprano of her generation, Galina Vishnevskaya joined the Bolshoi Theater in 1952 and quickly rose to prominence in starring roles there. Her schedule, when her government allowed, also included dates in the major musical capitals of the West. She has been as impressive in recital—where her regular accompanist is her husband, Mstislav Rostropovich—as on the concert and opera stage, but it is as a diva that she is most widely known. Her portrayals of leading ladies in operas by Tchaikovsky, Mussorgsky, and Shostakovich have been especially vivid, one might even say definitive, and she has performed numerous roles with great distinction in operas by Verdi and Puccini as well. The solo soprano part in Benjamin Britten's *War Requiem* was written for her, as were a number of that composer's songs. In 1974, she left the Soviet Union with Rostropovich and their daughters Elena and Olga. Since then, she has been active as performer, stage director, and author—her memoirs, entitled *Galina*, are among the most compelling books written by any musician of modern times.

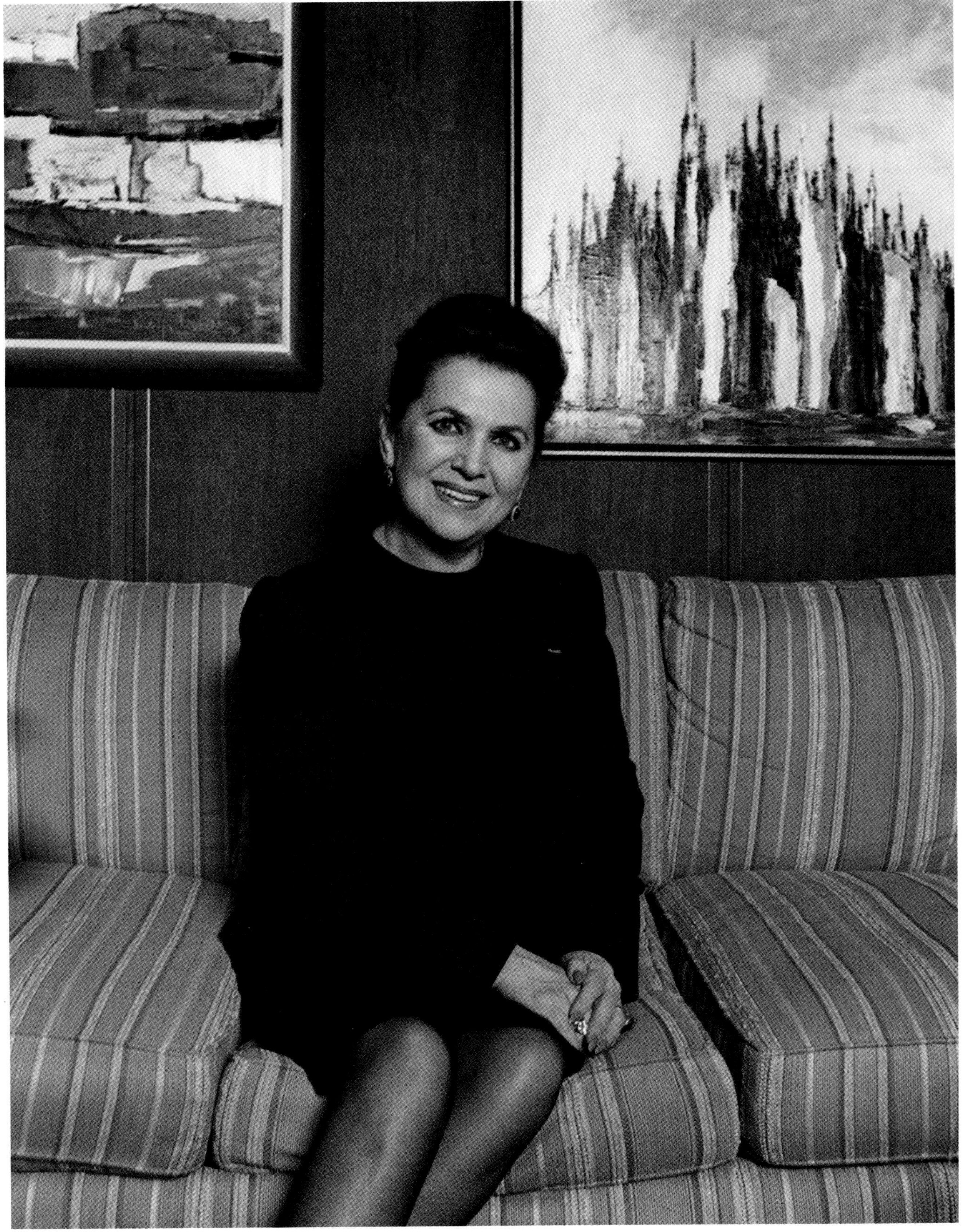

1988

ILSE VON ALPENHEIM

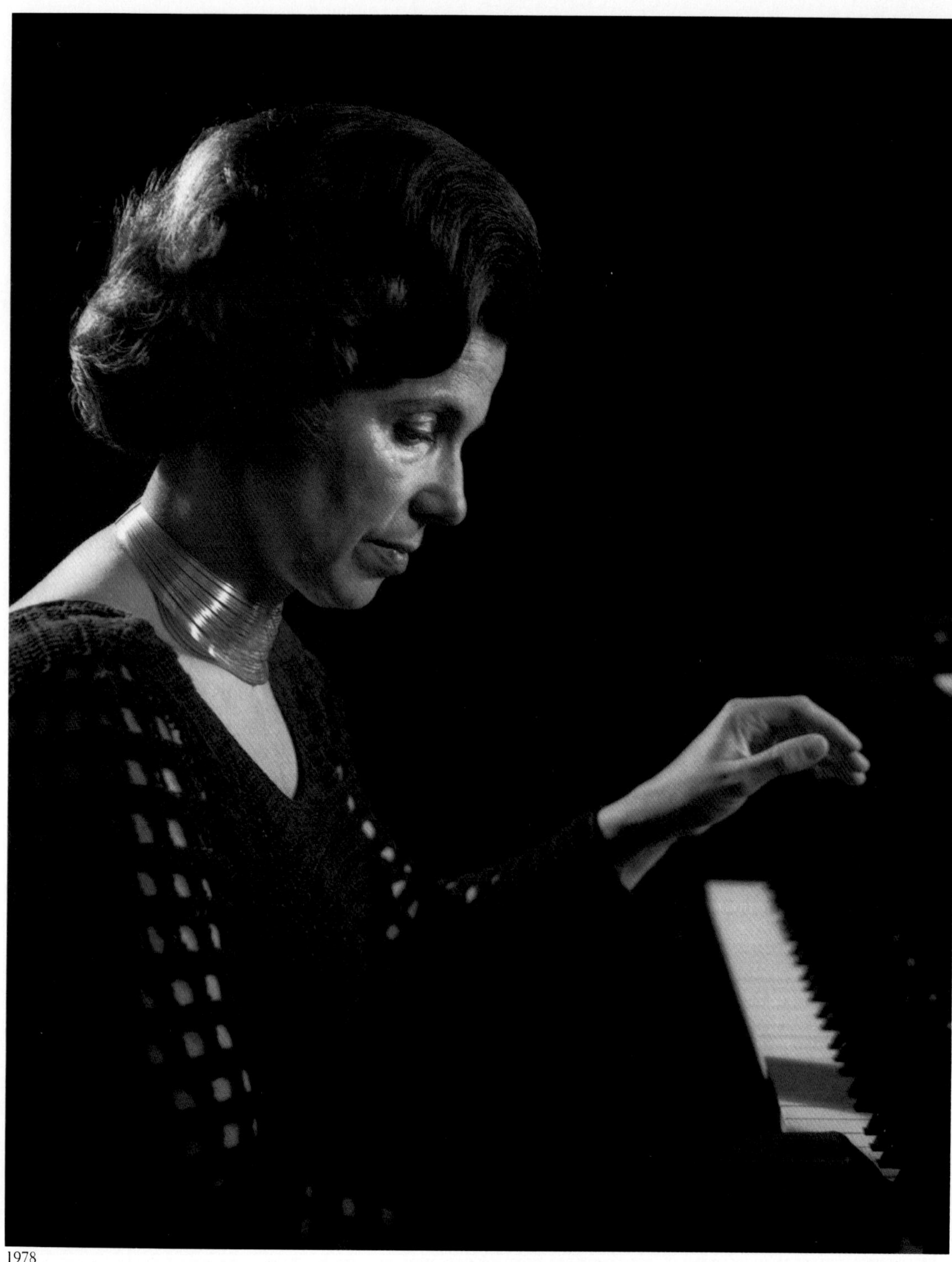

Ilse von Alphenheim has had a distinguished career as a pianist specializing in music of the Classical period. She frequently performs with Antal Dorati, her husband, on the podium.

1978

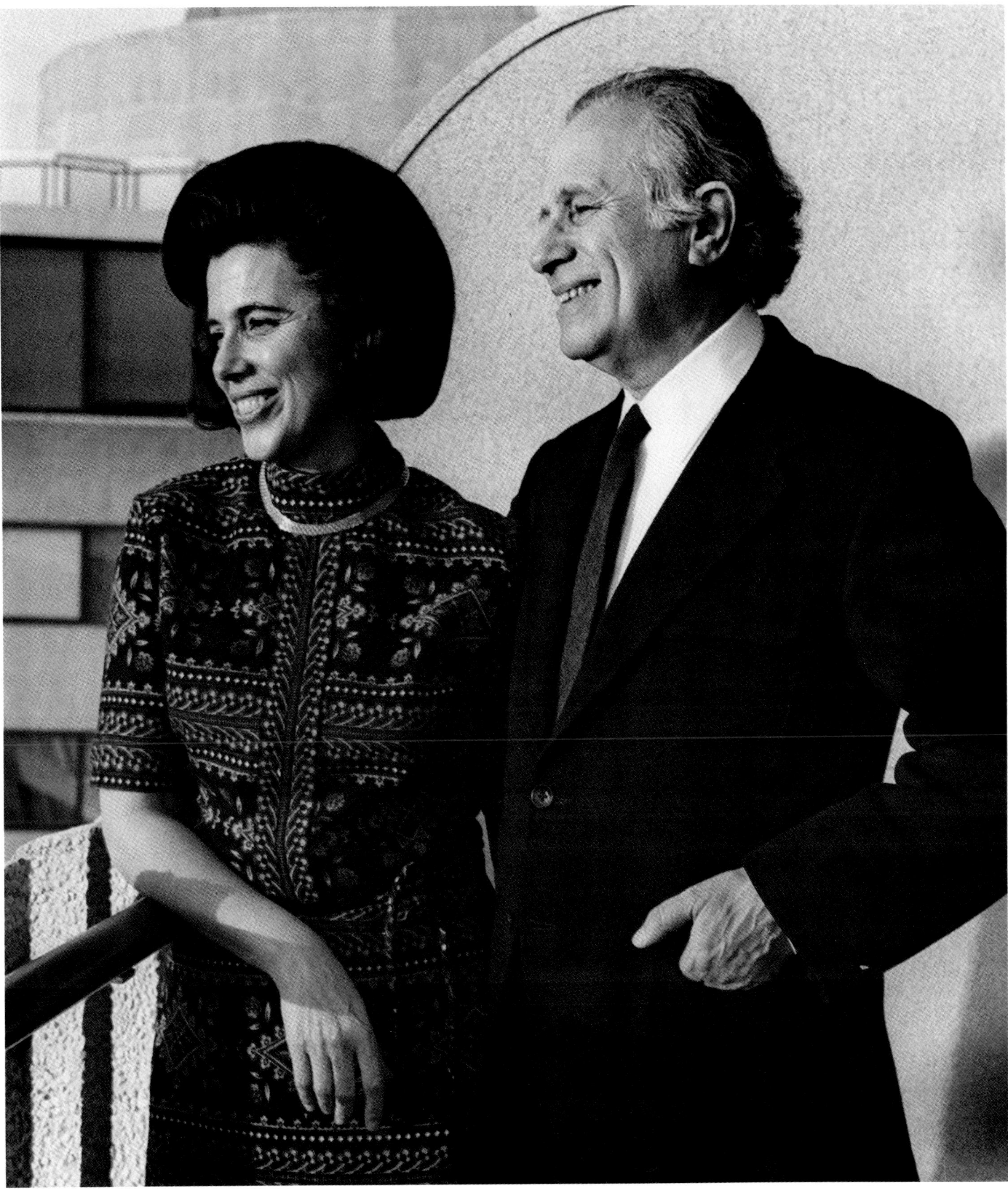

ALFRED WALLENSTEIN

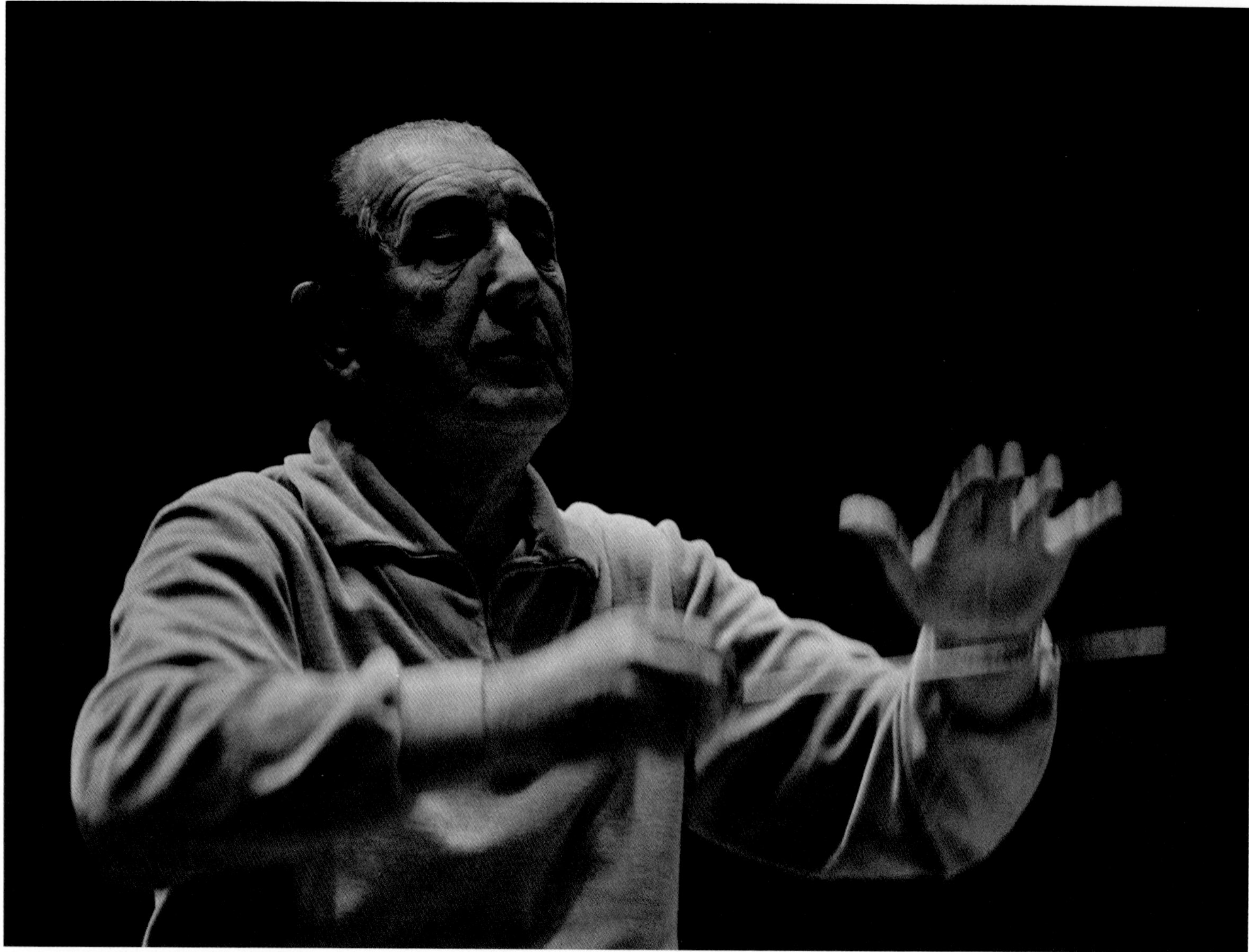

1967

He was born in Chicago at the turn of the century and grew up in Los Angeles, at a time when that city was little more than orange groves. The young Alfred Wallenstein was a prodigious cellist; at the age of 18, he joined the San Francisco Symphony, and in his early twenties began a seven-year stint with the Chicago Symphony. In 1929, Toscanini engaged him as principal cellist of the New York Philharmonic, a post he held until Toscanini's departure from that orchestra in 1936. It was Toscanini who encouraged Wallenstein to try his hand at conducting, and he rapidly developed into a maestro of major stature. He was named principal conductor of the Los Angeles Philharmonic in 1943 and remained with the orchestra until 1956, thereafter devoting himself to guest conducting and teaching at Juilliard. A knowledgeable and self-effacing musician—the kind other musicians invariably hold in high regard—he was much sought after as an accompanist in the concerto repertory.

ANDRÉ WATTS

Brilliant, a mesmerizing technician, a passionate, at times poetic interpreter of the great Romantics, an articulate, curious, self-critical, and thrilling performer, André Watts has been a favorite with audiences for two decades.

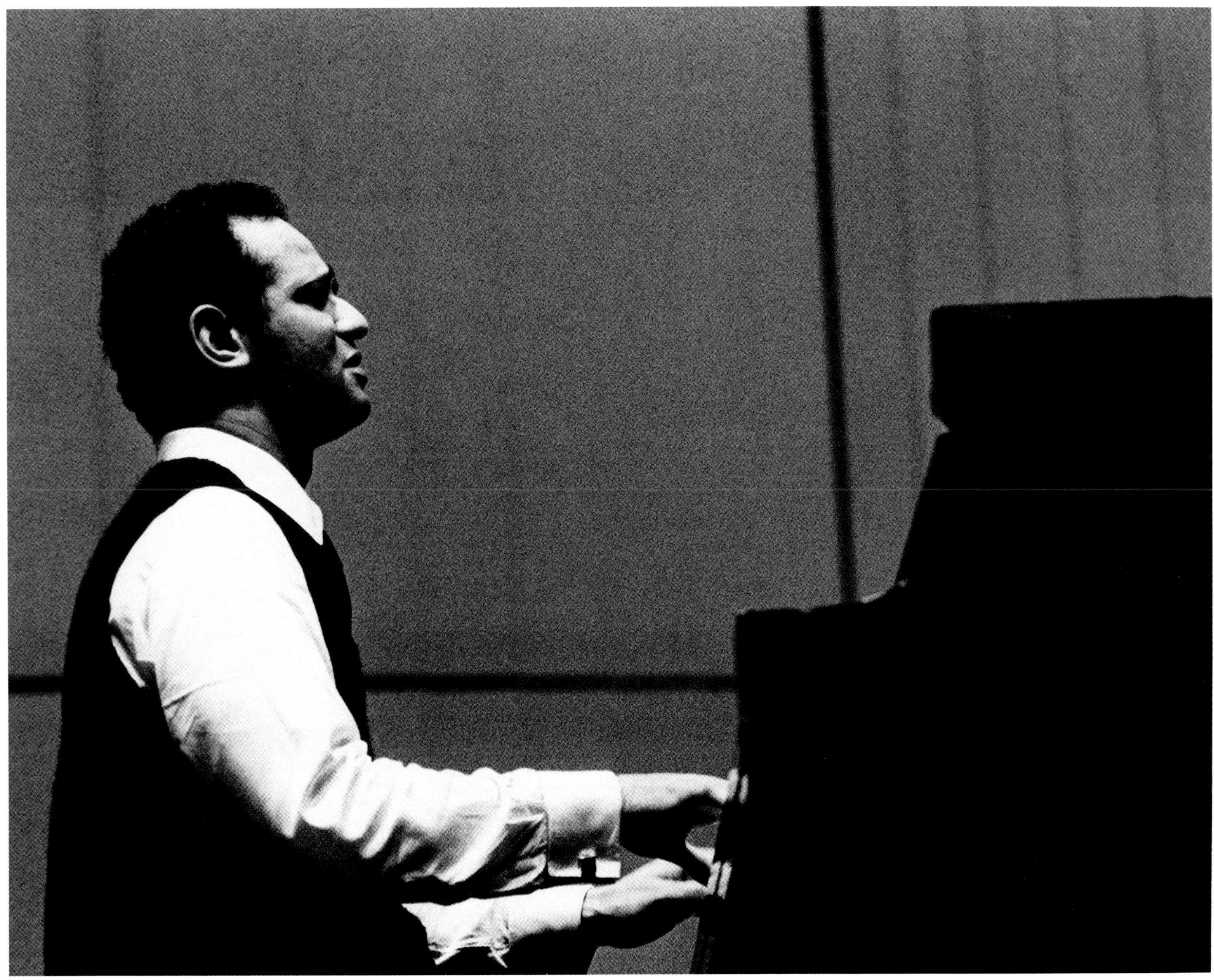

HUGH WOLFF

Immensely talented, this pianist-composer turned conductor has been moving up in the music world since he was a teenager. Born, like colleague Lorin Maazel, in Neuilly-sur-Seine, he had already won several prizes as a composer by the time he matriculated at Harvard. He was appointed assistant conductor of the National Symphony Orchestra in 1979, associate conductor in 1982, and became the music director of the New Jersey Symphony in 1986. In 1987, Wolff became the principal conductor of the St. Paul Chamber Orchestra. His repertory is large, and his efficient rehearsal technique and ability to master the most complex scores have won him the admiration of every orchestra he has faced.

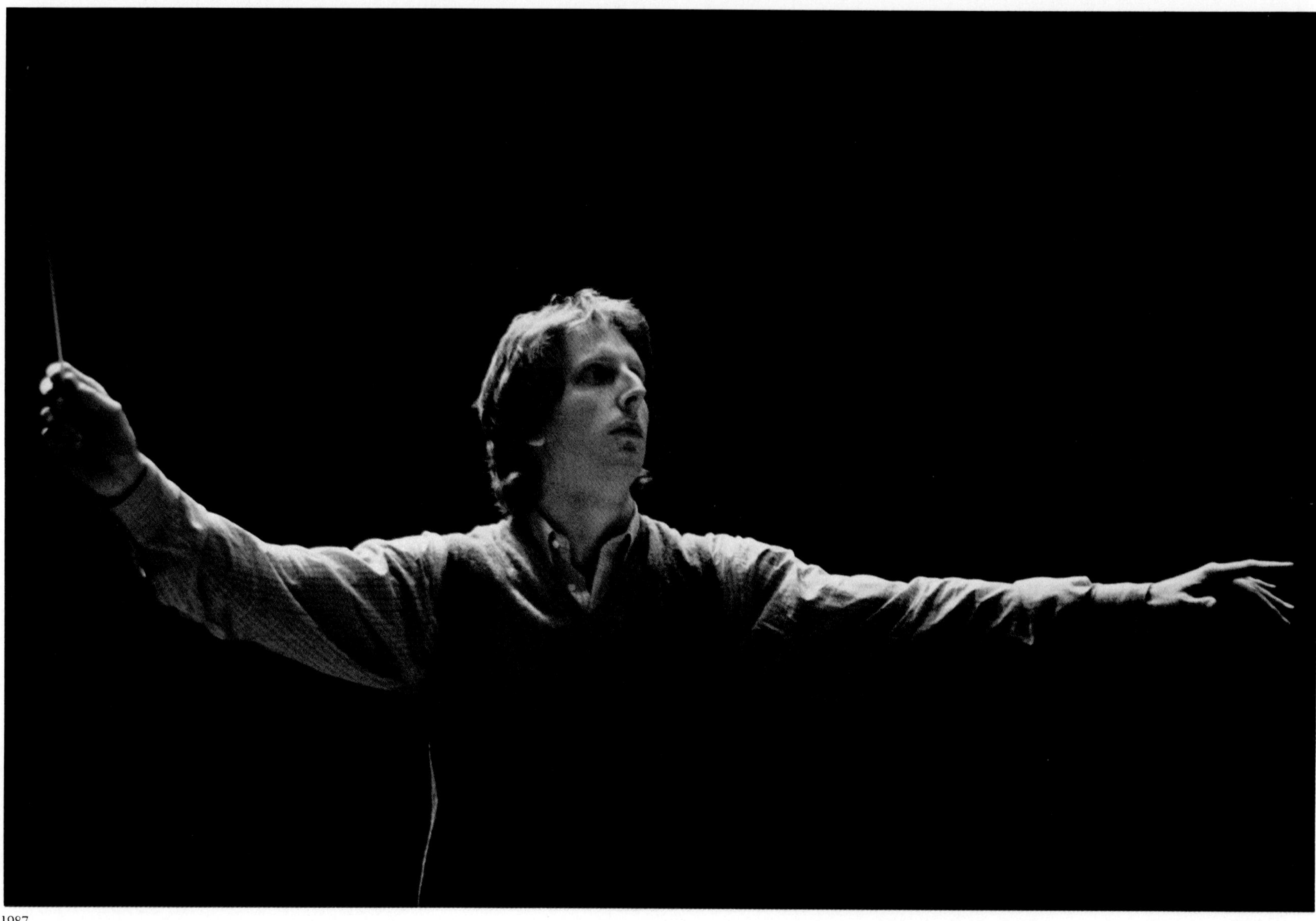

1987

NICANOR ZABALETA

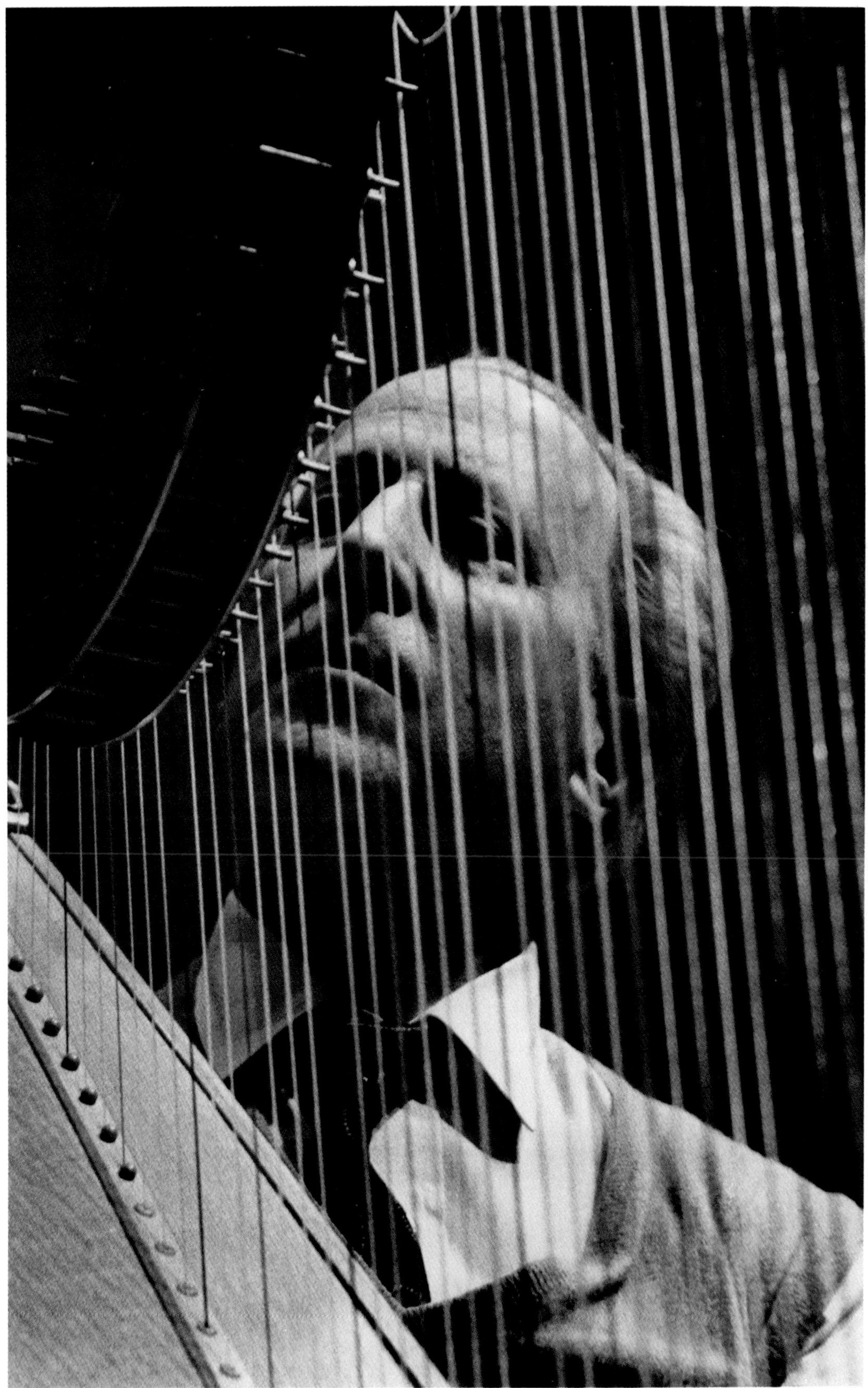

He is among the handful of truly distinguished harpists this century has produced. In his long career as a performer and recording artist he has done much to broaden the instrument's repertory while maintaining the highest musical standards.

1972

Pinchas Zukerman

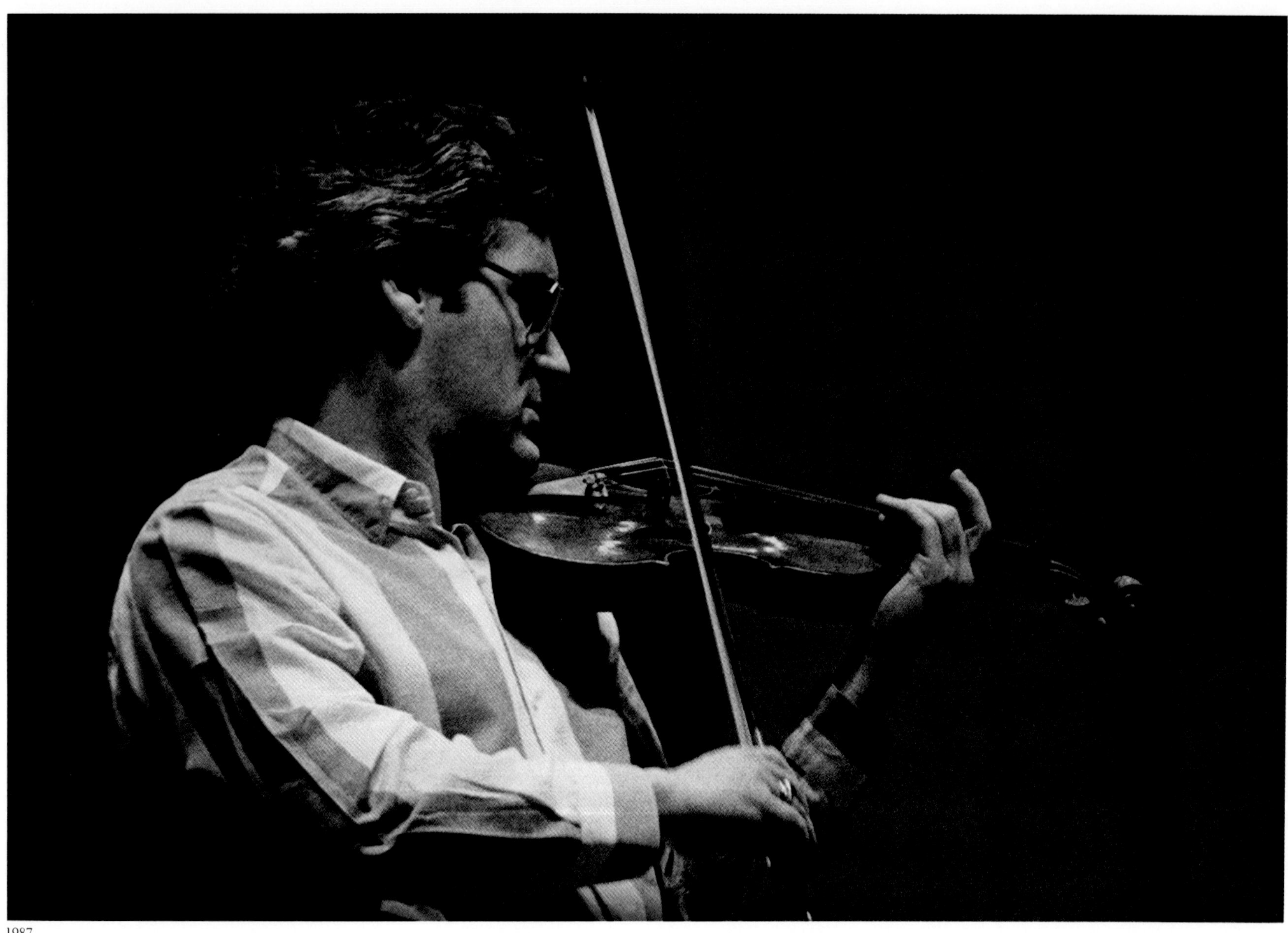

1987

Born in Tel Aviv a few months after the founding of the state of Israel, he came to America as a teenager to study with Ivan Galamian at Juilliard. A victory at the Leventritt Competition in 1967 made him an international celebrity and propelled him into a career in music's fast lane; more than twenty years later, he shows no signs of slowing down. As brilliant a violist as he is a violinist, he is best known for his intelligent and virtuosic interpretations of the concerto literature. He is also a superb chamber musician, and he loves to partner other brilliant musicians—such as violinist Itzakh Perlman and recorder virtuoso Michala Petri—in duets. From 1980 to 1987 he was music director of the St. Paul Chamber Orchestra.

With the challenge of literally thousands of notes to play each week, why does the professional string player take on the challenge of another demanding art form? Because only the conductor and soloist walk away with true feelings of accomplishment in a professional orchestra, most musicians continually search for artistic satisfaction. Many musicians turn to recitals, chamber music, and teaching.

I have found this inner fulfillment in teaching the viola, and in my photography. I know the feelings that go with developing a youngster into a mature artist, and there are really no words to adequately describe its deep satisfaction.

For me, photography is also very personally satisfying. I believe that these candid photographs best convey the depth, warmth, and life of the subjects. Photography is an art of awareness in life. The key to successful photography lies in a sensitive eye, knowledge of your equipment, and disciplined habits and techniques in the dark room. At its best, the camera is an instrument that stills emotion, records instantly the joy and sorrow of life around us, if we only pause long enough to see it.

In these few paragraphs I would like to share my feelings about a few of the artists that appear in this collection.

In the summer of 1955, I—like hundreds of other anxious young musicians—rang the door bell of the apartment of Leopold Stokowski for an audition. Fortunately, my audition was successful, and I spent the next three years in the Houston Symphony Orchestra working with him and learning from him. This man helped to add the depth and maturity of emotion that was eventually meaningful to me, not only in music, but also in photography and every other facet of my life. I soaked up the brilliance of this man as one soaks up the sun on a clear day, and his spell was overpowering.

Stokowski had his critics. But for myself—fresh from the conservatory, green in years and experience, and suddenly plunged into the overwhelming world of Leopold Stokowski—this giant of a man made an indelible impression.

Years later, however, and years apart from this master, I entertained the thought that perhaps my young and impressionable thoughts and feelings about him were inflated. When I worked again with him in Washington and renewed our acquaintance, I discovered the truth of my earlier impressions.

The maestro, now age 90, seemed to my eyes smaller, bent, and feeble, as he made his way slowly to the podium. He climbed the steps of the podium carefully. The orchestra fell silent, he straightened his back and as he raised his exquisitely expressive hands, it was as if suddenly the music made him young and he became again the exuberant legend I remembered. The resulting sound was electrifying. The aura of his inspiration once again confirmed his greatness.

The maestro is shown on stage at intermission during that set of rehearsals in 1972.

Unfortunately, music history will not be able to evaluate the immense talent of Mesru Mehmedov. He was one of thirty-five people killed when a Bulgarian Airlines plane crashed in Zurich, Switzerland, on the night of January 18, 1971.

The thirty-five-year-old musician was returning to his native Bulgaria to take up the directorship of the Sofia Philharmonic Orchestra when this tragedy occurred. Mesru had definite ideas and was extremely well-schooled in the art of conducting a symphony orchestra. He was a person of firm convictions on how a work should sound and how it should be performed. His programs, conducting, and concerts were very exciting.

Yet Mesru was very humble and sincere. I remember one amusing episode that occurred on his last visit to Washington. When I am shooting pictures I am usually loaded down with several camera bodies and lenses. Everything looks quite complicated to my fellow musicians. On this particular day, I was settling down to the rigors of rehearsing. Out strode Mesru to the podium with a look of concentration on his face. The orchestra grew quiet and the "A" sounded. We were prepared for his downbeat when he turned to the viola section and looked at me and said, "Mr. Scavelli, would you mind very much taking some pictures of me with my camera?" And out came his Kodak Instamatic. The musicians roared as I reached for his camera with a feeling of helplessness. I never knew how those photographs turned out, for this visit was the last time we saw our colleague Mesru Mehmedov alive. It is sad to note that musicians and music lovers will never know the true greatness that was within him.

A musician for whom fate has deemed great longevity is Yehudi Menuhin. After over seventy years (he was a child prodigy at the age of three) Mr. Menuhin is still youthful and enthusiastic. His career has been marked by his striving for only the highest standards.

Mr. Menuhin is a man of joy. His face expresses a complete absorption in his music. To converse with him you sense a deep commitment to his art, and yet a great humility. This sincerity of the man is felt by all who work with him and this quality easily comes through in photographs of him.

In recent years Mr. Menuhin has turned to writing, conducting, and teaching. Photographing this gifted figure is a task that I always enjoyed.

Another immortal musician is Artur Rubinstein.

My usual technique for taking photos is sitting in my section of the orchestra with my viola clamped between my knees during a ten-to-fifteen bar rest. It was during a fifteen-minute rehearsal break that I suddenly found myself all alone on the stage of Constitution Hall. The stage door opened and out strode Artur Rubinstein. He sat down at the piano that had been moved there for his part of the rehearsal. He welcomed me with a warm smile and greeting, and, seeing my camera, asked no questions. He began to play and I began to take pictures.

Later, when Rubinstein saw the finished photos, he was especially delighted with my favorite informal pose—so much so that he purchased a copy from me. I look back on this treasured experience with particular relish because all young musicians, myself included, have idols with whom they hope to perform once they become professionals. The name Artur Rubinstein is magic to the concert goer, but to the professional musician, the name Rubinstein needs no superlatives. His popularity, stamina, and vitality seemed to grow with his mounting years. Coincidentally, it so happened that this was his eighty-fourth birthday. It was always a grand occasion when he stepped onto the stage. On that day in January 1970, I had my grand occasion.

As a member of the National Symphony Orchestra, I had the privilege of working with, and photographing on many occasions, Antal Dorati during his tenure as conductor of the orchestra. He is a man of sharp contrasts, a man of great musical wealth, who can perform equally well works from any period. He is a musician's conductor. The maestro and his lovely wife, Ilse von Alpenheim, appear on these pages when I photographed them at their Watergate apartment on one of the many occasions when she performed with the orchestra.

Finally, there is Slava, Mstislav Rostropovich, great super-star of the cello and also current conductor of the National Symphony Orchestra. Bold, outgoing, friendly, and a great interpreter of the Russian composers, many of whom he knew personally, Slava enjoys life and this is reflected in his orchestral interpretations. It is also evidenced by his huge bear-hugs and kisses on both cheeks.

We shared a table and a bottle of wine in our home before a very special photo session, which yielded one of the photos that is printed here. The photographs of Slava encompass a twenty-year period and they illustrate his intensity, both as a cellist and conductor, and, of course, that great smile and personality.

Ramon L. Scavelli
1988